IT'S GOOD TO BE
THE KING

IT'S GOOD TO BE THE KING

THE KING

The Seriously Funny
Life of
Mel Brooks

James Robert Parish

John Wiley & Sons, Inc.

Published by John Wiley & Sons, Inc., Hoboken, New Jersey
Published simultaneously in Canada

For general information about our other products and services, please contact our Customer Care Department within the United States at (800) 762-2974, outside the United States at (317) 572-3993 or fax (317) 572-4002.

Wiley also publishes its books in a variety of electronic formats. Some content that appears in print may not be available in electronic books. For more information about Wiley products, visit our web site at www.wiley.com.

Library of Congress Cataloging-in-Publication Data:

Parish, James Robert.
   It's good to be the king : the seriously funny life of Mel Brooks / James Robert Parish.
     p. cm.
   Includes bibliographical references and index.
   ISBN 978-0-471-75267-7 (cloth)
   1. Brooks, Mel. 2. Comedians—United States—Biography. 3. Motion picture actors and actresses—United States—Biography. 4. Motion picture producers and directors—United States—Biography. I. Title.
   PN2287.B695P37   2007
   792.702'8092—dc22
   [B]   2006016533

Printed in the United States of America

10 9 8 7 6 5 4 3 2 1

For Mel Brooks fans everywhere

Contents

Acknowledgments

I wish to thank the following for their kind cooperation on this project: Academy of Dance on Film (Larry Billman), Patrick Agan, Bruce Bailey, Robert Bentley, Billy Rose Theater Collection of the New York Public Library at Lincoln Center, Ronald L. Bowers, Michael Buckley, Charles Callas, Catskills Association (Phil Brown), *Cinefex* magazine (Don Shay), John Cocchi, Stephen Cole, Bobby Cramer, Ernest Cunningham, Jacques D'Amboise, Joe Dante, Bernard F. Dick, Douglas Fairbanks Center for Motion Picture Study, Dream City Photo Lab (Jack Allen), Michael B. Druxman, Eleanor Knowles Dugan, Echo Book Shop, Rob Edelman, David Ehrenstein, Emorac, Inc. (Eric Monder), Filming Today Press (G. D. Hamann), Dave Finkle, Professor James Fisher, Sharon R. Fox, Dick Gautier, Alex Gildzen, Bruce Gold, Shecky Greene, Pierre Guinle, Ray Hagen, Harry Haun, Travis Michael Holder, Lawrence Holofcener, Ron Husmann, Judy Israel, JC Archives, Will Jordan, Matthew Kennedy, Allegra Kent, John Kern, Jeff Kisseloff, Sam Kisseloff, Tom Kleinschmidt, Richard W. Krevolin, Audrey E. Kupferberg, Shawn Levy, Ben Livingston, Alvin H. Marill, Lee Mattson, Rick McKay, Marty Meyers, Dr. Gerry Molyneaux, Museum of Television & Radio (Jane Klain), Charles Nelson, Stephen O'Brien, the late Richard O'Connor, Jay Ogletree, Kimberly O'Quinn, Albert L. Ortega, Patrick Pacheco, Photofest (Doug McKeown and Howard Mandelbaum), Michael R. Pitts, Jared Poppel, Seth Poppel, Bill Reed, Barry Rivadue, Jonathan Rosenthal, Brenda Scott Royce, Barry Saltzman, Brad Schreiber, Margie Schultz, the late Arleen Schwartz, Jonathan Schwartz, Joan Seaton, Nat Segaloff, Ted Sennett, J. D. Shapiro, Stephen M. Silverman, André Soares, Spyder, David Stenn, Steve Taravella, Allan Taylor (editorial consultant, copy editor, and indexer), Vincent Terrace, University of Southern California Cinema-Television Library (Ned Comstock), Lou Valentino, Dick Van Patten, Laura Wagner, Tom Waldman, Steven Whitney, Don Wigal, Max Wilk, and those additional sources who requested to remain anonymous.

With special thanks to my editor, Eric Nelson, and my agent, Stuart Bernstein.

Introduction

Yeah. I'm buoyant. I'm happy so I can respond to people in a very funny way. I prefer to be funny. Not hysterical. Hysterical only when there's a lot of people involved and then it is my bound duty to have them falling all over the floor laughing. Then I'm very funny. But comedy is a big risk. One clink. One sour note. And you're going to look bad. Comics are very brave people.

—Mel Brooks, 1978

Growing up in small-town America, I was thrilled when my family purchased its first television set. It was the late 1940s, and TV was still a fledgling commercial enterprise in the United States. I recall vividly one of the first programs I saw on the tiny 10-inch screen of our just-installed living room set. It was *The Admiral Broadway Revue*. For a youngster already fascinated with the magical world of entertainment (especially films), the variety and quality of live fare offered on this weekly TV program, and especially its successor, *Your Show of Shows*, was manna indeed.

Jumping ahead to the winter of 1962 in Philadelphia, it had become customary for me to put aside my college homework on Saturday afternoons to catch a matinee of the latest new play trying out in town. On this particular day I saw *All American*, a Broadway-bound musical starring Ray Bolger (the Scarecrow of MGM's *The Wizard of Oz*) and directed by the famous Joshua Logan. Whatever the show's flaws in its embryonic form, the lavish production—with its vivid costumes, slick turntable sets, and catchy score—left a strong impression on me for years to come.

A few years later, I was living and working in Manhattan and made a point of attending a new movie that had recently opened at a local art house theater. It featured Christopher Hewett, whom I had met during recent summers working as propmaster at the Cape Playhouse in Dennis, Massachusetts. I was curious to see him perform on the big screen. I watched the offbeat movie *The Producers* with fascination, and afterward

1

enthusiastically told friends about this outrageous comedy written by Mel Brooks, which costarred Zero Mostel and Gene Wilder. I soon purchased the sound track to *The Producers*, which contained not only the film's background music but dialogue interludes, as well as the highly contro- versial musical number "Springtime for Hitler" (which, according to the album's liner notes, had been written by Brooks himself).

Months later, when Brooks received an Academy Award in the Best Original Screenplay category for *The Producers'* script, I read several of the extensive articles published about this new Oscar recipient. Suddenly, I realized that Mel Brooks had been a key contributor to many wonderful projects. For TV, he had been a gag supplier for *The Admiral Broadway Revue* and a comedy writer for *Your Show of Shows* (and, later, *Caesar's Hour*). For the stage, he had authored the book of the musical *All Ameri- can*. (In addition, this same man had been featured on the legendary *2000 Year Old Man* recordings in the early 1960s and, thereafter, had cocre- ated a major TV hit with the satirical TV series *Get Smart*, 1965–1970.)

Thus, without knowing it, I had become hooked on Mel Brooks's tal- ent and zany persona—and remain so to this day.

• • •

Writing this book led me to examine the complex, lengthy, and cre- atively productive life of Mel Brooks—one filled with so many chaotic career and personal ups and downs. Here was a Jewish boy from a poor Brooklyn family who was tremendously driven to find his rightful place in life. Early on, he decided his means of achieving fame and creative/ financial success would be—had to be!—in the world of entertainment and, largely, in the field of comedy.

Because Mel was short of stature he always felt compelled to make "loud noises" one wacky way or another so that he would be a focus of attention—whether in his career or in his private life. Boisterous, zeal- ous, sometimes downright vulgar, and often overly opinionated, he would repeatedly prove over the decades to be a man of many dimensions and seeming contradictions. (How can a man greatly admire Dostoyevsky and Tolstoy and still delight in making a campfire farting scene the highlight of one of his classic movies, 1974's *Blazing Saddles*?)

As Mel Brooks has demonstrated over the years, he can speak out on a subject with authority and passion and, at the same time, with a dash of deflecting coarseness. "How do you explain comedy?" he once rhetorically asked a *New York Times* reporter. "How do you explain Chopin? I hear a Chopin prelude and I faint. I *swoon*. How can a human being with hair in his nose just like me create those gorgeous silver melodies?" On other occasions, however, Brooks can be extremely articulate, sensible, straightforward, and even elegant—as when he addresses the art of making people laugh: "You can't cheat an audience. You promise them comedy, you have to give them that magic carpet that'll lift them up over their own problems into giggles, laughs, and belly-laughs."

As to the genesis of his particular brand of "crude" humor (which may seem somewhat tame by today's "standards"), Brooks says with tremendous vehemence and seriousness, "My comedy comes from the feeling that, as a Jew, and as a person, you don't fit into the mainstream of American society. It comes from the realization that even though you're better and smarter, you'll never belong." Mel's ethnic background is a powerful factor in who and what he became, and why, in so many of his artistic works over many decades, he set out to ridicule history's greatest persecutor of the Jewish people—Adolf Hitler. As recently as 2001, Mel, the veteran creative force, told news correspondent Mike Wallace on TV's *60 Minutes*, "Yes, I am a Jew. I *am* a Jew. What about it? What's so wrong? What's the matter with being a Jew? I think there's a lot of that way deep down beneath all the quick Jewish jokes that I do."

• • •

If Mel Brooks the astute and talented artist can easily slip into Brooks the buffoon both in front of and behind the film and TV cameras and confuse some of the public as to which is the *real* Mel Brooks, he has similarly confounded the public about his private life. When, in the early 1960s, it was rumored that comedian/comedy writer Mel was dating the dazzling Broadway luminary Anne Bancroft, the running theory was that it must be a wild joke. After all, what would a vivacious and beautiful acting genius like Bancroft (who made such an indelible impression on the stage in *Two for the Seesaw* and *The Miracle Worker*) see in the daft Mel Brooks, an ex-Catskills performer and TV writer? When the "disparate" couple actually wed in the summer of 1964, the public took odds on how long this seemingly ridiculously mismatched pair would (or could) maintain their "absurd" marriage. As he did so often in his event-crowded, roller-coaster life, Mel proved the scoffers wrong. He and Bancroft, who became parents of a son, Max, enjoyed one of the longest-lasting and, to all accounts, happiest unions in show business history—a lengthy personal partnership that only ended with Anne's death from cancer in mid-2005.

· · ·

Looking back on his impressive, award-winning show business career— which has included stints as a Catskills summer resort entertainer; a TV comedy writer and sitcom creator and director; a Broadway musical comedy book author; a radio commercial writer and performer; a comedy record star; a TV talk show favorite; a film producer, director, scripter, and actor; a music video performer; and, more recently, a playwright and songwriter of a megahit Broadway show—Brooks once acknowledged, "If you want something, you have to do your homework, you have to take the trouble and make the necessary sacrifices. It's never easy."

Many times Brooks miraculously pulled a creative iron out of the fire in the midst of failure and climbed back into the highly competitive show business race once again. His ups and downs are partly the result of one of the most fascinating aspects of this irrepressible, complicated, often bedeviled, and frequently disorganized talent: placed into the standard role of sole writer, director, or comic, he often failed. His greatest professional success came when he went far out on a limb, beyond the limits where he could reasonably be expected to succeed, in transforming himself into a director, in suddenly becoming a composer, and even in playing the figurative Romeo to Anne Bancroft's intimidating Juliet. But in almost every case, he was only as good as the person holding onto the limb he went out on. In *Young Frankenstein*, for instance, the limb was not only the original film but the solid structure that Gene Wilder brought to the original story treatment and the screenplay, for which Mel got the lion's share of credit.

In examining his career, it is impossible not to admire his ability to adapt, cooperate, create, and excel under tremendous pressure. In fact, it's the way he seems to have done his best work.

1

Out of the Ashes of Despair

The difference [between a director and an auteur] is that a director who is working for a living simply does the job, which may not be akin to his philosophy, but it is not inconsistent to have the same man being both. The word is "hunger." If you are hungry and nobody will buy your original idea, you might get lucky, direct a Kellogg's cornflakes commercial and take home a few boxes.

—Mel Brooks, 1971

In the early 1970s, Mel Brooks had reason to find himself in an ironic position as far as his career was concerned. He had already won Academy Awards and Emmys, and had hit radio commercials and three successful comedy albums (such as *The 2000 Year Old Man*). He was a veteran of the writing teams for two of the most cherished series of American television's golden age: *Your Show of Shows* and *Caesar's Hour*. Brooks's recent association with the highly successful sitcom *Get Smart* had enhanced his visibility with the public and given him additional industry credibility. Although his movie *The Twelve Chairs* (1970) had failed to make any tangible impact at the box office, *The Producers* (1968) was well on its way to becoming a cult favorite.

Yet Brooks was now unable to get *any* new show business projects off the ground and into production. How many times, he must have wondered, did he have to crash through the establishment's barriers before he gained solid acceptance from his peers and the public? How long could he continue to subject himself to the ordeal of starting over—yet again?

For a time, Mel wanted to produce a film version of *She Stoops to Conquer*. He had seen an off-Broadway production of the Restoration-era comedy and hoped to interest Albert Finney in starring in the vehicle, which would be shot in England. (In Brooks's excitement over this potential screen venture, he forgot his recent oath to stick to mainstream projects that could be box-office winners.) However, as it turned out, the period piece did not appeal to Finney or to film studio executives. Brooks had to abandon that idea. This new rejection reinforced to Mel just how much Hollywood had turned a cold shoulder toward him as a movie-maker. Meanwhile, there was brief talk of Mel and Gene Wilder joining the cast of an upcoming MGM comedy, *Every Little Crook and Nanny*. However, when that feature film was shot, others claimed the suggested roles.

While Brooks was vainly searching for a filmmaking deal, he forced himself to keep busy in other aspects of show business, which, at least, would help keep his name alive in the industry. In this mode, Mel took assorted TV gigs, ranging from appearing on Dick Cavett's talk show to being a guest on the game show *Jeopardy!* Brooks also provided the voice of the Blond-Haired Cartoon Man on the PBS-TV animated children's series *The Electric Company*. In the winter of 1973, producer Max Lieb-man theatrically released the film *10 from Your Show of Shows* (a compi-lation of restored kinescopes from the beloved TV series), and Brooks and other regulars from that program received renewed media attention and were frequently interviewed. Meanwhile, when Professor Richard Brown taught his filmmakers course at the New York University's School of Continuing Education in Manhattan, Brooks was among the guest speakers, along with such others as Cliff Robertson, Shirley MacLaine, Eli Wallach, and Anne Jackson. When Marlo Thomas packaged her star-studded ABC special *Free to Be . . . You & Me* (1974), an animated chil-dren's musical, Brooks provided the voice of a baby boy.

But no matter how Mel tried to gloss over the facts, such activities were largely busywork, and he continued to brood over his inability to step back into the ranks of film directors.

Brooks's luck finally began to change for the better in 1973 when he had an auspicious accidental encounter with talent agent David Begel-man on the streets of Manhattan. Later, when Begelman, now his talent representative, first brought the *Tex X* project to Mel's attention, Brooks almost said no to shaping the treatment into a screenplay for Warner

Bros. He argued that it went against his belief that he should only develop his own ideas. Then he came to think better of the timely offer. At the very least, it would get him back to Hollywood and provide a decent paycheck. With a mixture of resignation and a what-the-hell attitude, Mel agreed to give the venture a shot. After all, what did he have to lose at this professional low point?

In setting to work on the *Tex X* screenplay, Brooks heeded his earlier pledge to surround himself with cowriters whenever he next wrote a script. Besides hiring Andrew Bergman—the original author of the screen treatment—Mel brought aboard the writing team of Norman Steinberg and Alan Uger, two men he already knew. Brooks also wanted to have an authentic black voice on the unorthodox project. Efforts to hire the bright, outspoken comedian Dick Gregory failed. Next, Brooks turned to Richard Pryor, a controversial stand-up comic who had already appeared in several film and TV projects. The maverick Pryor agreed to join the young writing squad.

Over the next several months, Mel and his crew labored over their task of creating a wild and wacky comedy that defied conventions and shattered current standards of political correctness. Their rule of thumb was "Go for broke." Putting a tempting spin on the emerging scenario, Brooks told the media, "It won't be a 'black' movie but more of a juxtaposition of hypocrisy, greed, flat-out fun and clichés that I've been watching since I was 3 years old. . . . The point is, we're trying to use every Western cliché in the book—in the hope that we'll kill them off in the process."

Mel explained further, "I decided that this would be a surrealist epic. It was time to take two eyes, the way Picasso had done it, and put them on one side of the nose, because the official movie portrait of the West was simply a lie. For nine months, we worked together like maniacs. We went all the way—especially Richard Pryor, who was very brave and very far-out and very catalytic. I figured my career was finished anyway, so I wrote berserk, heartfelt stuff about white corruption and racism and Bible-thumping bigotry. We used dirty language on the screen for the first time, and to me the whole thing was like a big psychoanalytic session. It just got everything out of me—all of my furor, my frenzy, my insanity, my love of life and hatred of death."

To Mel's amazement, the studio was impressed with the finished screenplay—despite its blatant irreverence—and ordered the writing team

to revise a few story-line points and to shorten the lengthy script. Once
that was accomplished, the project (now called *Black Bart*) would go
onto the active production schedule at Warner Bros. By now, Mel had
chanced bringing his wife, Anne Bancroft, and their infant child to Los
Angeles, where they moved into a new residence. (Their home was at
1718 Rising Glen Road, in the hills just above West Hollywood. The spacious house boasted huge glass walls overlooking a swimming pool, 12-
foot-high iron gates, and a long entrance driveway. The sizable living room
easily accommodated a billiard table and massive overstuffed couches.)

Brooks informed the studio that he wanted to cast Richard Pryor in
the pivotal role of the film's black sheriff. However, according to Mel,
the studio balked at this choice. Supposedly, the executives claimed that
Pryor lacked "sufficient" acting experience. Brooks was forced to look
elsewhere for his lead. Among other possibilities, he considered James
Earl Jones, but Jones did not work out. Finally, Brooks auditioned Cleavon
Little, a handsome stage/film/TV actor who brought a sly, disarming tone
to his screen test. Little was hired for the picture. With that accomplished, Mel sent the *Black Bart* script to veteran actor Dan Dailey, hoping he would play the alcoholic Waco Kid. The former hoofer was not
certain if he was right for a Western. He hedged about accepting a key
role in this antiestablishment picture, and eventually said no. In this
same period, Brooks pursued TV talk show host/comedian Johnny Carson, hoping to convince the conservative Carson to take the assignment.
However, Johnny had little faith in his own acting abilities or that this
wild screen project would be successful at the box office, and thus refused Mel's offer. With time running out to cast the crucial part, Brooks
contacted Academy Award winner Gig Young. The latter, who had a
well-known drinking problem, was in need of work and agreed to play
the role of the lawman's scruffy pal.

When Mel tested actresses for the offbeat role of Lili Von Shtupp (a
burlesque of Marlene Dietrich's screen persona in *Destry Rides Again*),
he was thrilled when Madeline Kahn came to his attention. She was a
striking new stage and film personality who possessed an operatic voice
and a fetching figure, and had a unique way with comedic scenes. Madeline had already made a stir in Hollywood with her scene-stealing performance in the Barbra Streisand comedy *What's Up, Doc?* and there
was good industry buzz about her performance in Peter Bogdanovich's
upcoming release, *Paper Moon*. Kahn recalled of her audition with Brooks,

"It lasted hours. I felt like I was at the Mayo Clinic. For a funny man, he's very serious."

Ex–professional football player Alex Karras was contracted to make his screen debut as Mongo, a powerfully built dunce, while comedic performer Harvey Korman (famous for his ensemble work on Carol Burnett's TV comedy/variety series) was assigned the role of the pompous, corrupt politician Hedley Lamarr. The buoyant Dom DeLuise was cast as the effete film director Buddy Bizarre. (Within the wacky plot, Bizarre is helming a musical on the studio lot where the surreal Western is unfolding.) For genre authenticity, veteran cowboy performer Slim Pickens was added to the cast as Lamarr's bigoted stooge. Because Brooks had so enjoyed emoting in *The Twelve Chairs*, he gave himself two contrasting roles in his mock Western: a Yiddish-speaking Indian chief and the greedy, buffoonish, lewd governor William J. LePetomane. (Mel also made a quickie appearance in the picture as an extra in a lineup of bad men, and Anne Bancroft agreed to be an uncredited extra in a church sequence.)

Filming on the movie—whose title soon was changed to *Blazing Saddles*—got under way in January 1973. One of the first scenes to be shot took place at a jailhouse, where the imprisoned Waco Kid is spotted in an upside-down position. While shooting this footage, Mel noticed that the colead, Gig Young, seemed especially into his performance as the drunk. In fact, Young was even foaming at the mouth. Initially, Brooks thought this was merely Method acting on Young's part. But soon it became clear that the actor was going through a severe withdrawal attack. He began to convulse, and then passed out. Gig had to be removed from the set by ambulance. Suddenly, at the start of his "comeback" project, Mel was without an essential lead.

Reeling from the disaster at hand, Brooks scrambled to locate a phone on the soundstage and placed an urgent call to Gene Wilder back in New York City. A panicked Mel explained the horrendous situation. Within hours, the producers of Wilder's upcoming screen project, *The Little Prince*, had agreed to delay that film's shooting schedule so Gene could immediately substitute on *Blazing Saddles*. By the next morning, Gene was on the *Blazing Saddles* set, ready to work.

Over a 10-week period, *Blazing Saddles* was shot at the studio, on various Tinseltown locations, and at a park in Agua Dulce, California, about 35 miles northeast of the Burbank movie lot. On this go-for-broke shoot, Brooks proved to be far more relaxed than he had been during his past two ventures. He was surrounded not only by his writing team, but by familiar faces from past Brooks films: producer Michael Hertzberg, choreographer Alan Johnson, and composer/conductor John Morris. (The latter also orchestrated Mel's songs for this film, including the satiric title number sung over the opening credits by Frankie Laine and Lili Von Shtupp's showstopping saloon piece, "I'm Tired.")

Again, Brooks was heavily involved in supervising the film's editing process. (During this several-month stretch of polishing his project, Mel and Carl Reiner recorded their fourth 2000 Year Old Man album, *Carl Reiner & Mel Brooks: 2000 and Thirteen*, on the studio lot.) Meanwhile, there was a minor flap with the Screenwriters Guild regarding *Blazing Saddles*. Somehow, Richard Pryor's name had been left off the film's official writing credits. Pryor was ready to let it go, but the guild insisted Pryor's name be added to the picture's credits.

Finally, it came time to screen the film for a few key Warner Bros. executives. The picture began unspooling, and none of Mel's outrageousness seemed to get a rise out of the studio decision makers. The extremely mild response from the conservative executives stunned Brooks. He was all set to cancel a large screening scheduled for that evening, but Hertzberg urged him to go through with the showing, and, in fact, to invite a lot more of the studio's secretaries and blue-collar workers to the event.

Brooks described what went on at this key screening: "So 8 P.M. comes and two hundred and forty people are jammed into this room. Some of them have already heard the film is a stinker, because of the afternoon disaster. So they're very quiet and polite. Frankie Laine sings the title song, with the whip cracks. Laughs begin—good laughs. We go to the railroad section. The cruel overseer says to the black workers, 'Let's have a good old nigger work song.' Everybody gets a little chilled. Then the black guys start to sing 'I get no kick from champagne.' And that audience was like a Chagall painting. People left their chairs and floated upside down, and the laughter never stopped. It was big from that moment to the last frame of the last reel."

When word of the tremendous audience response to *Blazing Saddles* reached the studio bigwigs, they swiftly reversed their plan to throw this irreverent comedy to the wind. They ordered further test screenings and previews, and each time the audience reaction was highly positive. According to Mel, "After those screenings of *Blazing Saddles*, I was cornered by the head of Warners. 'Mel,' he said, 'it's fine. OK they love it. But we can't have the farting scene.' So I made a little note and I said 'Fine. It's out.' And he says we can't have derogatory references to blacks. 'OK,' I say. 'That's out too.' Then he says, 'The animal rights people will come down on us if we have the horse being punched.' 'OK, OK,' I say, 'it's out, out, out.' The minute he left I tore up the notebook and never cut a thing. It's what I always tell young film-makers. Say yes, yes, yes to every damn fool thing the producers ask, then ignore it all. No one ever notices."

In so blithely defying the studio boss, Brooks also relied on the fact—which the executive had overlooked—that on all of Mel's movies he had demanded and received control of the picture's final cut. Most of all, Brooks had been determined from the start not to excise one bit of the movie's controversial farting scene. For him it represented everything his unconventional movie was about. "In every cowboy picture, the cowboys sit around the campfire and eat 140,000 beans, and you never hear a burp, let alone a bloozer. For 75 years these big, hairy brutes have been smashing their fists into each other's faces and blasting each other full of holes with six-guns, but in all that time, not one has had the courage to produce a fart. I think that's funny." For the irrepressible (and sometimes raunchy) Mel Brooks, keeping in the farting scene—which set a new standard in Hollywood for how vulgar a Hollywood mainstream comedy could be—was a do-or-die point of honor.

Brooks explained how he actually filmed this pivotal campfire sequence: "They didn't make a sound. I said, 'Lift, turn, cross your legs. Do the normal gestures you would do to let a fart escape.' Then afterwards, the sound editors got their friends together and they put soap under their armpits. Wet soap. And they slapped at it and made air pockets, and they did the noises that way. I came in to do some with my voice—a few high ones that they couldn't do from under their arms. Y'know, bvrrrrrrvt. But nobody put an actual fart on the soundtrack." Mel observed of this gross scene, "It's a funny thing about audiences. Every single human being I know abhorred that scene, myself included. But collectively we loved it. What could be lower low comedy than a bunch of cowboys breaking wind around the campfire? But it worked. People were ready for it. It was a broad, brave truth that had always been on the back of everyone's tongue when they were watching straight Westerns."

With its R rating, the 93-minute *Blazing Saddles* had a special promotional preview at Los Angeles's Pickwick Drive-in Theater on February 6, 1974. The guests of honor included 100 horses and their friends.
Robyn Helton (who played Miss Stein in the movie) was the hostess of
the unique event. The next day *Blazing Saddles* went into release, promoted with the advertising slogan "Never give a saga an even break."

Vincent Canby (of the *New York Times*) allowed that the Western
spoof was "Funny in the way . . . a rude burp in church can be." The
Wall Street Journal labeled the proceedings "an undisciplined mess."
On the other hand, Roger Ebert (of the *Chicago Sun-Times*) reported,
"There are some people who can literally get away with anything—say
anything, do anything—and people will let them. Other people
attempt a mildly dirty joke and bring total silence down on a party. Mel
Brooks is not only a member of the first group, he is its lifetime president. At its best, his comedy operates in areas so far removed from taste
that (to coin his own expression) it rises below vulgarity. . . . *Blazing
Saddles* is like that. It's a crazed grab bag of a movie that does everything to keep us laughing except hit us over the head with a rubber
chicken. Mostly, it succeeds. It's an audience picture; it doesn't have a
lot of classy polish and its structure is a total mess. But of course! What
does that matter while Alex Karras is knocking a horse cold with a right
cross to the jaw?"

In actuality, Ebert was exactly on target with his response to *Blazing
Saddles*. Most moviegoers of the time were entranced by this madly
unorthodox feature with its array of crude jokes, meandering plotline,
and caustic comments on a wide range of topics (racial discrimination,
homosexuality, the old West, and political hypocrisy). Following in the
tradition of his favorite screen comedians—the Ritz Brothers and the
Marx Brothers—Mel ensured that the antic *Blazing Saddles* was chock-
full of slapstick, puns, non sequiturs, and, most of all, outrageous verbal
and visual set pieces.

In its initial 1974 theatrical release, the atypical picture (which cost
about $2.6 million to make) earned domestic film rentals of some $25
million, and tallied approximately $15 million more in reissue in the next
few years. (This did not take into account pay and broadcast TV rights,
foreign distribution, or home entertainment editions of the runaway hit.)
Within short order, *Blazing Saddles* became the second-highest-earning

Hollywood screen comedy of all time, outdistanced to that date only by 1970's *M*A*S*H*.

With this megahit, the nonconformist Mel Brooks, at long last, had crashed the gates of the Hollywood establishment, and he intended to stay there.

2

Born into the Spotlight

I was adored. I was always in the air, hurled up and kissed and thrown in the air again. Until I was six my feet didn't touch the ground. "Look at those eyes! That nose! Those lips! That tooth! Get that child away from me quick, I'll eat him!"

—Mel Brooks, 1976

Like so many other comedians of his era, Mel Brooks became famous on TV, but before that he had success getting laughs in the Catskills, and even before that, hamming it up on the streets of Brooklyn.

By the early 20th century, many sections of Brooklyn were fast becoming overcrowded, as tenements and two-family houses—along with a massive array of stores—replaced the once-predominant single-family homes. This was especially true of Brownsville, located on the eastern edge of Brooklyn. In this ghettolike district, a great many Jewish immigrants, fleeing the latest onslaughts of pogroms in eastern Europe, had settled into overcrowded dwellings, competing for meager living quarters with the expanding African American population of the area. At best, Brownsville (which became known as the "Jerusalem of America") was a densely filled slum with oppressive tenement dwellings, sweatshops, ever-present pushcarts with vendors noisily hawking their myriad wares, and over 70 synagogues, generally lacking paved streets or a proper sewage system. By 1926, it was estimated, a good 75% of Brownsville's 400,000 or more dwellers were Jewish, a large number of these refugees having fled harsh living conditions in oppressive Russia and Poland.

One such Jewish family eking out a paltry living in Brownsville in the 1920s was the Kaminskys. Both Kate (née Brookman) and Maximilian Kaminsky were first-generation Americans. She had been born in Kiev (the capital of the Ukraine) and came to the United States when she was three years old. Kitty (as Kate was nicknamed) was raised in her family's tiny apartment on Henry Street on the Lower East Side. While her mother spoke the Yiddish of the old country, little Kitty was taught English in grade school. Because the girl's instructors were mostly Irish, the youngster learned English with an Irish-immigrant accent. As Mel Brooks has recalled, "My mother, as a matter of fact, said, 'erl' and 'berl.' . . . My mother actually did say, 'turlet.' She never did say toilet. She said, 'turlet,' like the Irish do."

When Kitty, a petite redhead who was less than five feet tall, was around 14 or 15, she became enamored of a neighborhood boy. He was Edward Israel Iskowitz, an enthusiastic, bright adolescent with big, saucerlike eyes and a buoyant personality. At the time, he was preoccupied with trying to become a show business performer, and the romance with Kitty never developed into anything serious on his part. Later, as Eddie Cantor, he performed very successfully in vaudeville, on the Broadway stage, in films, and on radio and TV. He would become an icon for Kitty's lastborn child. Kitty's heart was not broken over Edward, as she was more attracted to another young man, Max Kaminsky, whom she found even cuter than go-getter Iskowitz.

Max's parents, Shlaimie (later Samuel) and Basha Kaminsky, grew up in Grodno, Russia. In the late 19th century, they emigrated to the United States with their young boy, Max, and settled in Manhattan's Jewish ghetto on the Lower East Side. Back in Russia Samuel had peddled sewing equipment for a living. In the new country, the enterprising Samuel soon became a herring merchant. To ensure that he made good deals with the Norwegian fishermen, he focused on learning their language rather than on mastering English. Soon, Samuel became one of the herring barons of the Lower East Side. Back then they had herring barons, and Mr. Kaminsky was one of them.

By the mid-1910s, Kitty and Max, a process server, had married and were living in Brownsville, often struggling to make ends meet. Their firstborn, Irving, came in 1916, followed a few years later by Leonard, and then Bernard, born in 1922. On June 27, 1926, Brooklyn and the surrounding areas were suffering a sweltering heat wave. The oppressive weather had induced a crowd of over 500,000 to jam the beaches and boardwalks of Coney Island. However, Kitty Kaminsky was confined to her sweltering, overcrowded apartment, because she was expecting her fourth child any time. The next day, Thursday, Kitty went into labor. As was customary in her blue-collar neighborhood, she gave birth to the new baby at home. The family's kitchen table was used for the delivery of their latest offspring, Melvin.

The next two years were comparatively happy times in the Kaminsky household. Relatives, friends, and neighbors were constantly coming by the flat to see Kitty, Max, and their quartet of children, especially darling little Melvin, who quickly became the apple of everyone's eyes. This tiny bundle of energy and joy was constantly "oohed" and "aahed" over, whether by his parents and siblings or by visitors. The precocious infant had an instinctive ability to respond to the constant affection lavished on him, basking in the bright spotlight of people's interest. (Brooks has reminisced of this joyous time, "I was the baby in the family, so I just assumed I was adorable. Everybody threw me up in the air, punched my feet and told me I was terrific.") Being the pampered center of attention quickly became an important aspect of Melvin's life. This strong need to be coddled became an ingrained craving that never left Melvin, even as he grew older. It prompted the boy to do whatever came to his mind to keep people's focus on him, no matter how coy, outrageous, or humorous.

•   •   •

For the Kaminskys, the future seemed bright with promise. Even in the harsh slums of Brownsville, the general optimism of the Roaring Twenties made its positive mark. Max was doing quite well in his job as process server for the court system. An outgoing, congenial soul, he was often assigned special tasks, such as serving legal notices upon rather famous individuals.

He soon became known as the "process server to the stars." Better or worse than being a herring baron? Hard to say.

However, life for the Kaminskys took a sudden turn for the worse during 1928. Max became seriously ill, with what was eventually diagnosed as tuberculosis of the kidney. At the time there was no known cure for the debilitating illness and he soon became bedridden. Many grueling weeks thereafter, on January 14, 1929, the 34-year-old head of the household succumbed to the then-fatal ailment.

• • •

Everything changed for the Kaminskys in the wake of Max's death.

As Mel Brooks's longtime friend, the acclaimed novelist Joseph Heller, observed years later, "There's a side of Mel that will never be fulfilled, no matter how hard he drives himself, and it all goes back to his father's death."

Soon after Max's passing, Kitty and the four boys moved from Brownsville to a dreary tenement in the Williamsburg area of Brooklyn. Relatives, especially Max's parents (who lived a subway ride away on Seventy-sixth Street in Bensonhurst), helped to subsidize the grieving widow and her brood until they could get back on their feet financially.

Samuel Kaminsky was especially generous in supplying his daughter-in-law and his grandchildren with a seemingly endless supply of herring and, sometimes, with much-needed cash. Kitty's less well-off parents and her sister's family also contributed funds.

At first, with Melvin and his next oldest brother, Bernard, too young to be left with either relatives or friends, Kitty could not accept full-time work outside the home. (Making matters worse, the jobs open to women in this period were severely limited, with options even narrower for Jewish women, who had to cope with anti-Semitism.) In desperation, the determined Mrs. Kaminsky found a part-time job in Brooklyn's (sweatshop) garment district. Because the pay was so low, she carted home additional work to do in the afternoon and late into the night. Seated at the kitchen table for hours on end, Kitty was a whirlwind of constant activity as she sewed bathing suit sashes with ornamental rhinestones, accomplishing the tedious, detailed work without benefit of proper lighting. Of this difficult period, Brooks remembers, "One night I woke up, I was four years old and on the table was a mountain of diamonds. I said, 'Ma, we're rich!' She said, 'No, they're rhinestones.'"

Since Kitty was paid by the piece for her toil, she moved at an impressive speed, anxious to earn as much as she could at this wearying handwork both at the factory and at home. Despite her seemingly nonstop labor, which went on six days a week, the resilient little woman always managed to nurture her sons, making sure they were fed, their clothes mended, and the cramped apartment kept spotlessly clean. Mrs. Kaminsky also made time to devote special attention to her beloved "Melb'n" (as Kitty always pronounced Melvin's name). Her youngest child, in particular, gave her life great meaning, and she pampered him as much as the family's adverse financial conditions allowed. Melvin's older brothers spoiled him, too, with the two eldest acting as surrogate fathers to the pampered tyke. (As Brooks assessed in retrospect, "I was the baby and I always expected to be the king of France because I was treated like the king of France. I'm still waiting for my crown.")

This lavishing of affection compensated greatly for the persistent grief the youngest Kaminsky felt over the loss of his father. Reflecting back many years later on his father's death, Brooks, then a moviemaker, acknowledged, "I can't tell you what sadness, what pain it is to me never to have known my own father. . . . All I know is what they've told me. He was lively, peppy, sang well. Isn't it sad that that's all a son should know about his father? If only I could look at him, touch his face, see if he had eyebrows! Maybe in having the male characters in my movies find each other, I'm expressing the longing I feel to find my father and be close to him."

Unlike other individuals in similar circumstances, Melvin never felt overwhelmed by his doting, extremely overprotective mama. Years later, he insisted, "I could not mount a successful attack against my mother. In psychoanalysis, you can always find something bad about your mother. . . . I could not. All I could say is, 'She was swell.'" In fact, according to Brooks, since he spent so much quality time as a child in the company of his devoted, spunky, and optimistic mother (who also happened to be a terrific cook), "She really was responsible for the growth of my imagination."

• • •

By the start of the 1930s, the Great Depression had enveloped the United States. Kitty and the oldest Kaminsky boys were working part- or full-time at the Rosenthal and Slotnick knitting mills in Brooklyn, barely scraping together enough funds to keep the family going.

Meanwhile, Melvin continued to be especially bright in intuitively guessing how to prompt a laugh from his mother, brothers, or whoever else was around. He would provide a funny gesture or cutely crinkle his nose and, immediately, he had his audience in the palm of his hand.

Melvin began the first grade at the local public school, where he quickly discovered that (1) he did not enjoy being confined in the stuffy classroom, (2) he was not overly thrilled by any aspect of the educational process, and (3) he missed being in settings in which he was the center of attention. Despite such drawbacks, attending school did expand his circle of pals. Said Brooks, "There was always a gang of kids, and we were always playing one game or another. At Jewish holidays, we'd send hazelnuts spinning after walnuts, and if you hit the walnut, you got it, you owned it. We played all these wonderful games: we filled the tops of bottle caps with either orange peel or banana skin to give them weight, and used them as checkers. We didn't have enough money to play pennies against the wall."

However, not everything was halcyon for little Melvin. There were bumpy moments along the way. For example, one evening when he was out and about in the neighborhood, there was great excitement. A distraught woman had jumped off the top of a building not far from where the Kaminskys lived. When curiosity got the better of Melvin and he went to investigate, he peeked through the growing crowd and spotted a bloody corpse covered by a sheet. As the body was being loaded into an ambulance, the boy happened to notice the dead woman's shoes. His heart nearly stopped beating because the footwear very closely resembled the exact type worn by his mother. Engulfed by a mounting panic, the child raced home. His fears only increased when he let himself into the apartment to find that it was still empty.

Overcome with apprehension and fears of a new parental loss, he sat for hours waiting—and hoping against slim hope—to hear the telltale footsteps on the stairs that would alert him that his dreadful conclusion was miraculously unfounded. Time crept slowly by. Eventually, a key turned in the lock and in walked an unsuspecting Kitty. She was greeted by a highly distraught Melvin. After she comforted the still-shaking child, she explained soothingly that she had been asked to work overtime at her job. No matter how much she calmed and reassured him then or later, those torturous hours waiting for his "dead" mother were some of the worst Melvin Kaminsky had ever experienced.

• • •

As the continued efforts of the Kaminskys brought more money into the household, the family moved from a $16-a-month rear apartment (which faced the bleak, clothesline-laced backyard) at 365 South 3rd Street to a front unit (which cost $2 to $3 more per month). In their new tenement quarters, a fifth-floor walkup that boasted two bedrooms, Mrs. Kaminsky had one bedroom, and her four boys shared a single bed in the other. Looking back, Brooks found virtue in this close proximity with his beloved siblings. ("We slept across the mattress. I loved it because I loved my brothers and I loved all the action, and I loved being warm. You know, being poor was good! It was a good thing for me.")

One evening, several women from the building, including Kitty, were congregated on the front stoop chatting about the day's events. Meanwhile, up in the Kaminsky apartment, young Melvin—then about five years old—had the sudden, urgent need to urinate. Unfortunately, his brother Bernie was then using the apartment's only bathroom and he had locked the door. Whatever Bernie was doing in there, he was not responding to his brother's increasingly frantic knocks and pleas to let him in to use the toilet.

The next likely option for the panicked Melvin was to use the sink to pee in. However, it was full of dishes that Mrs. Kaminsky planned to wash after her stoop-side socializing. Desperate to solve his pressing problem, Melvin found his own solution. He rushed over to the open window facing the street and relieved himself. Downstairs, the housewives scattered from the unexpected precipitation. Already some of the rained-upon ladies were insisting loudly that the drenching had come from the Kaminskys' window.

Little Melvin could hear the racket below and ran to hide under the bedroom covers. He knew his angry mother soon would be galloping up the stairs to investigate. As Kitty charged into the apartment, Bernie was just exiting the bathroom. Unaware of what all the commotion was about, he innocently greeted his mom with a cheery hello. She responded with heavy slaps, the sounds punctuated by the surprised boy imploring, "What did I do?" (Years later, Brooks confessed that he could not recall if he ever had explained to his brother why, on that long-ago evening, he had received the sudden, inexplicable pummeling from his furious mother.)

3

The King of the Street Corner

To be Jewish, Brooklyn-born, fatherless, impoverished, and below average stature—no more classic recipe could be imagined for an American comedian. Or, one might suppose, for an American suicide.

—Mel Brooks, 1978

Unlike his three older brothers, who were always diligent students, Melvin Kaminsky did not settle down to his studies as he progressed through his first few years in the public school system. He felt confined and restless in the classrooms at P.S. 19. "I wasn't an avid reader, I was always an avid talker and doer," the reluctant student disclosed later in life, explaining that he found it hard to "sit still."

Instead, Melvin lived for the hours after classes, when he was free to hang out with his friends and play in the nearby streets. However, unlike his brothers Lenny and Bernie, who were especially adept at stickball, the youngest Kaminsky was not agile at this sport, or at punchball (a variation of baseball that did not require a bat), or even at the ghetto version of football (where the inventive, impoverished youngsters compressed a few brown bags together with string to make their ball). The one neighborhood game in which Melvin excelled—at least, until his interest wore thin—was ringalevio (a form of hide-and-seek played by teams). The diminutive Melvin was very quick on his feet, and this nimbleness led to his becoming, briefly, a local champion in 1932, when he was six years old.

He really shone, though, with the gift of gab. Melvin had a highly imaginative mind, which inspired his funny, quirky observations. He honed these skills in the all-important neighborhood meeting spot for children—the street corner. There, buoyed by the congenial company of his peers, he made snappy observations about individuals who passed by, including cute girls, or did amusing reconstructions of events that were the current talk of the town.

To be quick on your comedic feet was the core requirement, and he was the quickest.

Assessing his status as the "king of the corner shtick," he later said, "The corner was tough. You had to score on the corner—no bullshit routines no slick laminated crap. . . . And you really had to be good on your feet. . . . Real stories of tragedy we screamed at. The story had to be real and it had to be funny. Somebody getting hurt was wonderful."

Best of all, Kaminsky's capacity to express his unique outlook on life in an amusing, nonsensical fashion gave him what he craved most—attention.

His conscious preoccupation with a dread of dying began when Melvin was about nine years old. His pal Arnold casually announced that they were both going to die one day in the future. Taken aback by this blunt observation, the panicked Kaminsky responded, "You're obviously not right, you can't be right. We're not going to die, because why were we born? It wouldn't make any sense." His friend countered with, "What about your [maternal] grandfather? He died. And what about fish?" Melvin refused to be convinced. He reasoned that his granddad had been very elderly and, as to fish, they "had nothing to do with us." That ended the disagreeable topic of discussion for the time being. However, it was just the start of morbid ruminations on Kaminsky's part. ("That was the first time I knew I was going to die.") This excessive preoccupation with his own mortality would escalate over the coming years. He began to worry that he likely would die at the same young age (34) as his father *unless* he watched his health very carefully—and even then the fates would probably still win out and snatch him prematurely from life on Earth.

Melvin's constant focus on the state of his physical well-being as it pertained to his mortality led him to take an avid interest not only in his own health but also that of everyone around him. "I always thought it was great to be able to make people feel better. It was a little like being

God. So I started to take charge when anybody got hurt playing ball. 'Get the Mercurochrome. Put a Band-Aid on. Quick! Flappy fainted. Bring an egg cream!'" In later life, it would impel the celebrity to become a devoted reader of medical journals and dictionaries and a man always ready to provide free consultations (and follow-up discussions) regarding any acquaintance's latest health problem.

• • •

Melvin the kibitzer and jokester soon learned that, like any sensible performer, he needed constantly to freshen his material or risk losing his audience. He became more adventurous in his verbal jests, in his array of imitations of Williamsburg characters, and in his brave stunts. He might have been short of stature with an inborn dislike of heights, but Kaminsky knew the crowd constantly expected—and demanded—bigger and better feats from him. If that meant walking perilously on a fence, or deftly swinging from a fire escape, then so be it. The approval of his mates more than compensated for the fear such exploits engendered within him.

This esteem from the local kids also served another useful purpose for Melvin. His reputation as an impressive purveyor of gags, verbal thrusts and barbs, and daring deeds led those in his social circle to feel duty-bound to protect him from the neighborhood's older boys (Jews or Gentiles) who might find it amusing to pick on, or beat up, that puny Melvin with the funny-looking face. Sometimes Melvin was able to ward off abuse from his adversaries on his own—with a few jokes, quips, and lots of bravado. As Melvin later articulated, "If your enemy is laughing, how can he bludgeon you to death?"

If restrictive school life had been a bore before, now that he was nine years old and his teachers were doling out odious homework, he felt compelled to retaliate. When called upon by instructors to recite information he should have absorbed from his daily homework assignments, he deflected their stern gaze by answering with a quip or a brief routine executed at his desk. (Once when asked to hold forth on Christopher Columbus, the boy responded with, "Columbus Cleaning and Pressing, Fifth and Hooper." Another time when directed by his teacher to read a class composition assignment aloud, he suddenly turned into a whirling dervish. He flailed his arms dramatically as he announced in his high-pitched youngster's voice, "My Day at Camp," and launched into his theatrical recitation.)

Such increasingly smart-alecky shenanigans in the classroom made the other youngsters laugh at Melvin's audacity. It gave him newfound respect of sorts with his mates for being a rebel against the academic Establishment. However, in the 1930s, when mild corporal punishment was an accepted method of dealing with student misbehavior, Kaminsky received a healthy share of physical rebukes. Decades later, he'd recall such reprimands from his teachers with a tinge of pride (and, perhaps, a bit of exaggeration). "The class would laugh and I'd get hit. But by then I'd be laughing so hard I couldn't stop. Slapped, grabbed by the hair, dragged to the principal's office, couldn't stop laughing. Hit by the principal, kicked down the stairs, bleeding in the gutter, couldn't stop laughing."

• • •

During these early formative years, Melvin found himself falling in love with the movies, an entertainment art form that had largely switched from silents to talkies in the years just after Kaminsky's birth in 1926. As a tyke, Melvin had joined family members on occasional excursions to Coney Island: "We'd go there, and we'd get a frankfurter, a root beer and a boiled-to-death ear of corn at Feldman's, which was before Nathan's Famous Hot Dogs. In the back, they had a silent movie theater [where the admission was free or next-to-nothing if one bought food up front]. The screen was just a white sheet. They had this flickering machine. That was the first time I saw this angel with a white face and these beautiful eyes. I knew this was something special. It was the first time I saw [comedian Buster] Keaton. He wore a flat pancake of a hat, and I just couldn't believe the man's grace."

For Melvin, watching these silent pictures was love at first sight. This special enjoyment expanded over the next years: "I never cared about religion, but I prayed to silent movies. It was my contact with things soulful. I'd go there as often as I could. I'd sneak in, actually and watch the movie without buying the frankfurter or the knish."

By the time the boy was five, he was joining friends for a visit to the Marcy Theater, a small Williamsburg cinema where they showed talkies. He paid the small admission price with pennies his doting mother scraped together for him. One of his most memorable outings was seeing *Frankenstein*, the horror film starring Boris Karloff. It was first released in late 1931 and, thereafter, was a popular item in reruns, especially for children's matinees.

The James Whale–directed feature made a stunning impression on the future filmmaker. "I had a recurring dream that he [i.e., Frankenstein's monster] was climbing up my fire escape. Now, I never really analyzed why Boris Karloff, or why the monster, would pick 365 South Third Street in the Williamsburg area of Brooklyn to climb that particular tenement fire escape. Or why he would stop at apartment 5-B and try to get into my bedroom. I never figured that out. But I knew for sure he was after me. . . . And that's one of the reasons I made *Young Frankenstein* [1974], I said, I don't want this dream anymore. I want him to be a friendly guy. I want to exorcise this dybbuk, this devil, from my system."

Despite his alarming dream, Melvin, being a prankster who exerted his imagination to uncover the funny side of most everything in life, was able to translate the nightmare-inducing experience of *Frankenstein* into his own brand of comedy. At the time, one of his closest school chums was Eugene Cohen. Kaminsky could launch his loyal pal into hysterics just by singing the Irving Berlin song "Puttin' on the Ritz" in the manner of Boris Karloff. "It got so bad that . . . [Eugene] couldn't hear that song near a window, because he might roll out and fall to his death. I would start to sing and he would collapse. He would have to be dragged to the principal's office by his feet, with his head banging on the step, still laughing."

• • •

Besides moviegoing, Melvin had another entertainment passion. It was the radio, which brought free, wonderfully varied diversions right into one's own home. One of his mother's—and his grandparents'—favorite shows was *The Yiddish Philosopher*. On this offering, the program's lead player made all sorts of pronouncements on a variety of topics—much in the manner of Melvin's own grandfather Samuel Kaminsky. (Said Brooks, "It was a way of talking that certain Jews his age had. He offered an expert opinion on any subject, as if he was [the great German philosopher Arthur] Schopenhauer.")

A particularly popular radio entry with Melvin—especially after he learned about his mother's girlhood connection to the star—was Eddie

Cantor's weekly comedy program. "It was very important to me," the budding entertainer noted years later. "Very influential on my work. Along with his timing was his particular delivery. He took his time, didn't rush. There was nobody like Eddie Cantor, that's why he was great." According to Melvin, listening week after week to *The Eddie Cantor Show* taught him a useful gambit that would come in handy decades later when he was directing film and TV projects where he needed to mesh the cast into a harmonious troupe. "The sketches were fast and furious—and Cantor was great at supporting the other guy in the sketch. He had a special genius for starring his featured players—and then supporting them. You might think the other guy was getting the laugh, but it was Cantor who was making it all work for me."

• • •

Of all Melvin's relatives he was most encouraged by his mother's brother, Joe. Like Kitty Kaminsky, Joe was very short of stature (scarcely five feet tall). As such, when he was at work driving a taxi he had to sit on a pile of phone books so he could see over the steering wheel, and he had to rely on specially constructed gas and clutch pedals for his feet to reach them.

Through his cabbie work in and about Brooklyn, the congenial Uncle Joe was acquainted with a wide variety of doormen and concierges in the borough. These were the men who often got tickets to Broadway shows for the tenants in their fancy buildings. One Friday in 1935, Joe rushed over to the Kaminskys' apartment with exciting news for his youngest nephew. He had done a favor for one of these doormen and, in appreciation, he had been handed two tickets for a Saturday matinee of Cole Porter's *Anything Goes*. Joe announced that the next day he would take Melvin into Manhattan to see the hit show, which had debuted in November 1934. The two of them went to the Alvin Theater the next afternoon, and there from the balcony they watched and listened to Ethel Merman, William Gaxton, and the other cast members as they performed the musical comedy, which boasted such numbers as "I Get a Kick Out of You," "You're the Top," and "Blow, Gabriel, Blow." It was the youngster's first encounter with a live professional stage show.

This exciting theater outing was a monumental experience for young Melvin. "I had goose bumps. I almost fainted. . . . And oh, the glory of the sound that came from that orchestra pit, led by the brass section, those blaring trumpets and thrilling trombones reaching for the moon." According to Brooks, "When the final curtain fell, I leaped to my feet and cheered my 9-year-old head off; way up there at the top of the balcony, I figured that I was as close to heaven as I'd ever get." As the entertainer vividly recounted years later, "I began weeping, just couldn't contain myself. I said, 'When I get big, this is what I'm gonna do. I'm gonna write for the theater. The real world stinks. This is the world I want to live in, the world of imagination.'" This decision prompted Mel to conclude that night as he lay awake, too excited to fall asleep, "Being a Broadway songwriter, I decided, would be even better than playing shortstop for the Brooklyn Dodgers, which up until then had been my most fantastic dream."

• • •

Like many other adventurous youths of the time, Melvin went through a phase in which he snitched a few penny candies from the corner candy store. Everyone else seemed to do it, and he thought little about the possible consequences of his delinquency. Later, he and a pal or two developed the habit of hanging out at the local five-and-dime, where a short Filipino man was often present to demonstrate his virtuosity on a yo-yo and induce onlookers to buy the product. Kaminsky and company saw this as a golden occasional opportunity to fill their pockets with yo-yos when the demonstrator's back was turned. Such petty thievery was undertaken several times without anyone's seemingly noticing.

One day, Melvin and an accomplice returned to the scene of their repeated crime. Suddenly, stealing yo-yos no longer held its once magical allure. As Kaminsky and his pal wandered up and down the aisles of the store's game section, Melvin's eyes fastened on a toy gun. Stealthily checking to see that the coast was clear, he maneuvered the toy weapon into his jacket pocket. Kaminsky and his accomplice began making their escape from the store. Suddenly, a voice said, "Halt!" The boys nervously turned around and found themselves staring into the piercing eyes of the irate store manager. He demanded the return of the stolen toy, promising dire consequences thereafter. Although his frightened friend stood thunderstruck, Melvin sprang into inspired action. Pulling the fake pistol from his pocket, he pointed the "weapon" in the direction of his accuser.

Mimicking the manner of cinema gangsters (such as James Cagney and Edward G. Robinson) whom he'd seen many times on the screen, Kaminsky snarled, "Stand back or I'll plug ya!" His astonished captor recoiled in apparent shock, and Melvin and his confederate used this opportunity to flee the store.

On another occasion, Melvin and his favorite cohort, Eugene Cohen, snuck into the RKO Republic Theater on Keap Street, about a quarter of a mile from where the Kaminskys lived on South Third. In short order, the errant boys were apprehended by eagle-eyed ushers and escorted unceremoniously to the manager's office. At first the young wrongdoers thought the situation was terribly funny. However, the manager quickly changed their mood when he announced ominously, "You have your choice. I could call the police or give you a beating." While Cohen shouted, "The police," Kaminsky simultaneously loudly opted for the beating. (Melvin feared having this misdeed go on his record and disgracing his family's name.) Taken aback by the offenders' conflicting choices of punishment, the manager decided to let the boisterous miscreants go, warning them never to do such a thing again.

4

Hello and Good-bye to Brighton Beach

When I was a kid, I was very confused by what the Jew was in the outer world. I knew what he was in Williamsburg. He was a runner and a rat and scared as hell. But Jews in the outside world I heard different, conflicting things about. First of all I heard they were the communists, overthrowing all the governments in the world. When I was in high school, I thought a Jew's job in life was to throw over every government. The other thing I heard was the Jews were capitalists and had all the gold and the banks and that the Jews' job was to kill all the socialists and the radicals. So I never really figured out what the Jewish mission was. Should I kill the capitalists and take all their money? No, I'd be killing Jews. Should I stamp out the radicals so that we could keep our money? No, I'd be killing Jews. Very confusing.

—Mel Brooks, 1975

Not too long after Melvin's bar mitzvah in mid-1939, the family relocated to Brighton Beach, an area adjacent to Coney Island made famous in Neil Simon's 1980s' Broadway play *Brighton Beach Memoirs*, which was later made into a movie. The Kaminskys' new community was approximately 15 miles away from Williamsburg, but it felt to the adolescent as if he was very much a stranger in a strange land. He missed his old pals and the familiar landmarks in which he had grown up.

The immediate advantages of the move were that the Kaminsky clan now lived much closer to the ocean and its cooling breezes. Then too,

residing in Brighton Beach placed Melvin in far closer proximity to his
beloved Coney Island and all the wonders that its boardwalks, amusement park, food stands, and beach held for him.

It was while living in Brighton Beach that Melvin matriculated at
Abraham Lincoln High School. There the smart-mouthed young man
made a new set of friends. One of them was Mickey Rich, who lived
down the street from the Kaminskys. One afternoon Melvin and another
recently acquired pal, Billy, stopped by the Riches' home. In the course
of the visit, Melvin noticed a set of drums in one of the rooms. Mickey,
the son of veteran vaudevillians, explained that the instruments belonged
to his older brother, Bernard. With Melvin's love of music, it was not
long before he—uninvited—began tinkering with a snare drum. He liked
the attention-getting sounds it made. As he tinkered with the instrument,
Mickey's older brother happened to come home. Bernard stood in the
doorway listening to the visitor's attempt at percussion playing. "Not
good. But not too bad," he judged.

Looking first at Bernard and then at the drum set, which bore the
logo "A.S. B.R.," Melvin quickly figured out who this drummer was. He
was the talented Buddy Rich, who was then employed in the band of one
of Melvin's musical favorites (Artie Shaw), and who would soon be joining Tommy Dorsey's famous group. (Rich was also billed, for some time,
as the greatest drummer in the world.) Melvin expressed his great enthusiasm for Shaw's band, and, in particular, for Buddy's remarkable percussion work. One thing led to another, and soon the good-natured Buddy
suggested that Melvin drop by on weekends and, if Rich was not on the
road with Shaw's band, he would give him drumming lessons.

Melvin was ecstatic at this fortuitous turn of events. Over the next
several months, whenever he learned that Buddy was home, he would
come by the Riches' for a free drumming session. With the boy's innate
sense of rhythm, he was soon mastering the basic licks. (He was elated to
realize that with his enthusiastic, loud drum playing he now had an
option for holding people's attention other than just his patter of jokes
and stories.) Weeks later, Buddy kindly arranged with Artie Shaw for
Melvin to attend some of the band's recording sessions in Manhattan.
Kaminsky would sit very quietly in the studio watching, listening, and
thrilling at his brush with musical greats. It was another memorable event
in his life to date. (Several years later when Melvin, now established in the

entertainment field, encountered Artie Shaw, he talked enthusiastically and reverently with the band leader of those long-ago halcyon days.)

Being a very practical soul, Mrs. Kaminsky did not share her beloved youngest son's enthusiasm for show business—let alone his growing penchant for drumming. (Eventually, Melvin wangled a set of drums for himself and his constant, noisy practicing nearly drove her to distraction.) To his mother, Mel's banging away was a lot of crazy, useless noise that would lead nowhere, certainly not provide her last-born with a useful career. Her three eldest boys had all proved to be diligent students, who, between their work at the knitting mills and in other jobs, still found the time and energy to complete high school. They even went on to college (albeit night classes). In fact, Irving would become a chemist, a fact that made Kitty Kaminsky very proud.

However, the self-willed Melvin was another story. He just could not, or would not, settle down in the classrooms, and his poor grades reflected his continued lack of interest in the curriculum. Even on those rare occasions when he applied himself to academics, he demonstrated that, unlike his siblings, he had no real aptitude for math. This failing soon ruled out Melvin's occasional thoughts of doing something "sensible" with his life, like becoming a chemist, or even something more exciting, such as a pilot.

•   •   •

Despite her family's improved living situation in less crowded, less run-down Brighton Beach, Kitty greatly missed the old neighborhood—especially her dear friends from the ghetto. So a year or so after they had left Williamsburg, the Kaminskys returned to their former Brooklyn neighborhood. Their new address was 111 Lee Avenue, a five-story brick building located a bit north of Hooper Street and less than three-quarters of a mile from their old residence on South 3rd Street.

By now, Kitty was fully convinced that something must be done—at once—to put Melvin on the right, practical path to ensure his future. Her decision was that the boy should go to the Harren High School of Aviation Trade, where he could, God willing, learn a practical craft as an airplane mechanic. When his older brother Irving heard of this, he put his foot down. He insisted that Melvin should and would go to regular high school like the rest of the Kaminsky boys had done and that, later, he would go on to college. Irving had a great belief in Melvin's intelligence, even if, so far, the undisciplined teenager had been a conspicuously poor student. Eventually, Mrs. Kaminsky acceded to Irving's demand.

So instead of going to a trade school, Melvin transferred to Brooklyn's Eastern District High School, which was situated several blocks from the Kaminskys' Lee Avenue apartment. However, old habits stuck with Melvin in his new environment: he remained an unrepentant poor student and a dedicated classroom clown. He just would not (or could not) take academics seriously, and most of his teachers concluded that this persistent troublemaker did not have a bright future. One exception was Mr. Rubenstein, his French teacher. Although Melvin was failing the language class, the instructor was impressed by his "impeccable accent" and thought that, with application, Kaminsky could actually make something of himself. (Many years later, the world-famous comedian and filmmaker would characterize this classroom mentor as "my first fan.")

If Melvin, now 14, did not have a reputation as a scholar in high school, he had further cemented his standing on neighborhood street corners in front of the local drug store or candy shop. According to his Eastern District classmate Mark Nelson, Melvin "was always on. Mel really commanded an audience. He mesmerized all the boys. But it was only the boys, the girls never paid him much attention. . . . He always had a great wit. He was funny in his way and I in mine and we'd always try and outwit each other. . . . We'd hang out at the candy store on Lott Street. Sometimes we'd talk about the girls we never could date. . . . We tried making time with women—but we both struck out."

5

Swimming in the Borscht Belt

In the Catskills, Jews could become Americanized while preserving much of their Jewishness. The resort area was the vacationland and workplace of Jews, mostly from Eastern Europe, starting at the turn of the twentieth century. . . . Jews could have a proper vacation like regular Americans, but they could do it in Yiddish if they wished, and with kosher food, varying degrees of religious observance, and a vibrant Jewish culture of humor, theater, and song. Jewish-American humor grew up in the Catskills, where any Jewish comedian worth a laugh got his or her start.

—Phil Brown, *In the Catskills* (2002)

E ven at the height of the 1930s Great Depression, many Jews from the New York City area still found the requisite funds to make their annual pilgrimage to the Catskills. To staff these institutions (particularly the more upscale operations), the Catskills lodgings relied on teenagers (preferably college students) who would work for next to no wages for the privilege of a summer in the mountains, where they received free room and board and could, one way or another, socialize with the patrons. Usually when such staff members left the Catskills in September, they were exhausted from a nonstop work routine that had seen them do double or triple duty (as cooks, waiters, maids, lifeguards, social hosts, and/or performers) to meet the exacting requirements of their bosses and the guests.

With so much demand for nightly entertainment (above and beyond bingo games, movie nights, and charade evenings), there was a great call

for talent of all kinds. Some of this was provided by amateurs comman-
deered from the establishment's workforce. Other performers were fledgling comedians, actors, and other types of entertainers, drawn from the
ranks of radio, nightclubs, and (the now dying) vaudeville. The better of
these performers were in such demand that they developed a strong following among Catskills guests who looked forward to seeing them perform during their mountain stay. To accommodate so many potential
audiences throughout the summer months, bookers developed a "Borscht
Belt Circuit" in which various acts played one-night engagements at a
string of venues in the greater area. If a bigger establishment booked a
particularly popular entertainer, word would soon get out, and guests
from surrounding hotels would walk, canoe, or drive over, hoping to see
the talent perform. (These interlopers often snuck into the entertainment
halls to get for free what the hotel's guests were paying for.)

Such was the situation in the early 1940s when young Melvin
Kaminsky first abandoned the summer heat of Brooklyn in exchange for
a stay in the legendary Jewish Catskills.

• • •

Melvin's escalating interest in the glamorous world of entertainment had
been fostered by his love of movies and radio, by attending the occasional
Broadway play, and by his playing the drums. In the early 1940s, all of
this prompted the teenager to apply for summer work of any sort in the
Catskills, hoping against hope to rub shoulders with amateur and professional entertainers and, in the process, learn more about his dream profession. Like many others starting out in this resort training ground,
Melvin's initial work duties cast him as a jack-of-all-trades. Part of the
time he was a lowly busboy, schlepping endless heavy loads of dishes
back and forth to the kitchen. Sometimes he filled in as a waiter, and
learned how difficult it was to cater to the many demands of the paying
clientele. At other times, he was in charge of renting out the hotel's row-
boats; acted as a pool boy, fetching towels and snacks for impatient guests;
or was tasked with keeping the poolside area clean. Eventually, such
humble duties led to his becoming a pool tummler.

A tummler was a modern counterpart to the medieval court jester,
one who entertained guests—no matter what it took—to ensure that
these highly critical paying customers remained content and preoccu-

pied throughout their stay at the resort. It was reasoned that if the tumm-ler kept patrons in a continuously jovial frame of mind, the coddled guests would be too distracted to contemplate what other entertainment amenities might be missing from the lodging's lineup, or just were not being offered to them.

Poolside, Melvin quickly developed several routines to amuse the guests. For example, he might announce suddenly to the sun-soaking clientele, "I'm a man of a 1,000 Faces." He would then start his dramatic countdown: "Face number one" (and he would make a crazy grimace that distorted his already unique face), "face number two" (and he would contort his face into another wacky expression) . . . This gambit would continue until either the guests grew bored or Melvin was worn to a fraz-zle from his do-or-die-trying routines. Years later, when he kidded about this amateurish act, he said that, typically, one elderly Jewish woman in the crowd would say at some point, "Enough already with the funny faces. . . . You know Melb'n, I think I liked face number 612 the best."

On other occasions, the novice laughmaker would come running out to the pool wearing a heavy overcoat (despite the sunny, hot weather). The short young man struggled to front-and-center lugging a big valise in each hand. Upon catching the crowd's momentary attention he would scamper onto the diving board and announce gravely, "I can't take it any-more. I'm going to kill myself." With that, the fully clothed prankster would leap into the swimming pool, where he quickly sank to the bot-tom, weighed down by his waterlogged clothing and the heavy suitcases he clutched. It was prearranged that the resort's lifeguard (often a tall, blond Gentile) would then jump in and rescue the drowning Kaminsky, who was by no means a swimmer of any sort. Once in a while the helper forgot or ignored his crucial part in the skit, and a half-drowned Melvin barely struggled to the surface of the pool and to eventual safety. The generally blasé onlookers thought all this was pretty funny, at least for a few fleeting seconds.

On a rare occasion, Kaminsky was conscripted into performing in the evening dramatics. (As was then the custom in the Catskills, he, like other employees, received no extra pay for such extra chores.) Usually, these makeshift productions would be bowdlerized versions of current Broad-way shows. One such time, the 14-year-old Melvin found himself playing an elderly district attorney in a tabloid version of *Uncle Harry*, a new thriller then on the New York stage. Kaminsky had been given a wig, a mustache, and makeup to make him look much older. He had only one line of dialogue to recite. Anxious to expand his moment in the limelight, he decided on his own to add a little stage business to his part. He chose to bring a glass of water with him onto the stage. When it came time to speak his few onstage words, stage fright got the best of him and he lost his grasp of the tumbler. It fell to the ground and broke into many pieces. The audience sat in stony silence.

Not letting matters go, the young amateur strode front and center and, taking the offensive, pulled off his wig and mustache. He yelled to the crowd, "Whaddaya want from me? I'm 14 years old." According to the culprit, "Everyone burst out laughing, but I took off with the owner running right after me. . . . The audience couldn't stop laughing. They never did finish the play, but probably no one ever forgot it either. I knew I had to go onstage after that."

The errant resort worker did not get sacked for his brazen stage speech because, as he explained years later, "What was good about the Catskills is, you never got fired. You had a chance to do a lot of different things, and you performed all the time. But you had to work your way up."

•   •   •

Surviving his ordeal under fire in the Catskills, Melvin hoped to work at more prominent venues in coming vacation seasons. Taking note of Melvin's ambition, his brother Lenny introduced him to Don Appell, a Brooklyn-based friend of one of the older Kaminsky boys. Appell (who went on to write the book for such Broadway shows as the 1961 musical *Milk and Honey*) was then a young actor who had performed in such stage offerings as Orson Welles's 1941 production of *Native Son*. Through Don's show business contacts in the Jewish Catskills, Melvin negotiated a summer job at Butler's Lodge in Ellenville, New York.

At this more prestigious site, Melvin was officially hired as a member of the house band. As the drummer, Kaminsky's chore during the routine was to punctuate the comic's punch lines with a rim shot. (As a result, he had great opportunities to observe the house comedian do his nightly business on stage and to learn more about the pacing needed to make a comic's routine resonate with the audience.)

One evening, an agitated Pincus Cantor, the veteran manager at Butler's Lodge, rushed backstage to speak to Melvin. The resort's staff comic suddenly had fallen ill. This dire situation required an instant solution. Cantor needed an immediate replacement and decided that the meshugge Kaminsky would make a good substitute. The manager—who had a heavy, old-world accent—told "Melbmnnn" (as he called Kaminsky), "We know you're cute and funny so jump on the stage and amuse the guests."

Always best under pressure, the surprised employee readily agreed to the task.

That pivotal night, Kaminsky struggled through the ordeal of his comedy debut on stage by repeating pretty much the same stale jokes and anecdotes that his predecessor had been using all season long to amuse the hotel's guests. Somehow, Melvin survived the highly stressful evening. Best of all, the audience had not booed him, which boosted his confidence tremendously. Thus, the next day, when the house comedian continued to be incapacitated, Pincus decreed that Kaminsky should go on again that night.

What could he use to fill his time more effectively on stage? All day the teenager pondered and worried about his creative options. However, he refused to fall back on tried and true routines.

As the time drew near for Melvin to step out on stage to entertain the crowd, he still had not resolved his creative dilemma, and his fretting had turned to desperation. His dread of failing both the audience and himself had pushed him into an adrenalin overdrive that left him in a cold sweat. Suddenly, Kaminsky hit upon a linchpin for his opening gambit with the hotel guests. Earlier that day, a Butler's Lodge chambermaid had, somehow, locked herself in a linen closet. Her repeated banging on the door failed to rouse anyone and the increasingly upset worker began screaming in Yiddish "Los mir aroys!" ("Let me out!") Her desperate cries for help soon led to her liberation, and her rescue plea became an instant catchphrase at Butler's.

So that night Kaminsky launched onto the stage with a mighty cry: "Los mir aroys!" The familiar phrase brought instant laughter and applause. Melvin was emboldened by his "success" and followed up with a series of ad-libbed, humorous observations on the latest goings-on at the resort establishment. The crowd gave the novice comic an enthusiastic send-off when he ended his stand-up act. Melvin was jubilant when he left the stage. This gig for a paying audience had given him far more of a rush than he had experienced when he did his chatter on a Brooklyn street corner for his peers.

Despite this well-received stage turn, Kaminsky vowed to himself that he would further hone his material on coming nights. (The house comic showed no signs of making a recovery anytime soon.) Much later, Melvin explained his instinctive compunction to improve the caliber of his act: "Look, I had to take chances or it wasn't fun being funny. And you know, there was a lot of great material lying around in the Catskills, waiting to be noticed."

In subsequent turns before the lodge's guests, Kaminsky did not always enjoy the same beginner's luck. Through trial and error he discovered that some of his latest wild, irreverent, and often desperate bits would never succeed with this tough crowd. It caused him to reach out in every direction to find something—anything!—that might appeal to the guests. Sometimes, drenched in sweat from fear of flopping, he'd grab at any straw to keep his act moving along. He might say, "And here's my impression of Thomas Jefferson." He'd then stand there in a stately pose, hoping it might catch the onlookers off guard and prompt a sympathetic chuckle. That would give him a moment's reprieve to think of something new to do to amuse the clientele.

As Melvin gained more self-assurance in his stand-up comedy performances during the course of the summer, he grew more bold and inventive in his onstage gambits. One evening, Kaminsky organized a brief blackout skit, using a female staff member as his assistant. He called the spot "S. and M." Melvin recounted, "The girl and I walked out from the wings and met in the center of the stage. I said, 'I am a masochist.' She said, 'I am a sadist.' I said, 'Hit me,' and she hit me, very hard right in the face. And I said, 'Wait a minute, wait a minute, hold it. I think I'm a sadist.' Blackout. That was the first sketch I ever wrote."

Despite the frequent occasions when Kaminsky's material failed to interest his audience, he never gave up the creative challenge of entertaining them, somehow. Occasionally, after the young man had completed his energetic gig and was walking among the guests, he might hear one of the little old women shout out, "Melb'n, we love you, but you stink!" (Another time, he allowed of his haphazard apprenticeship as a comedian, "But I wasn't a big hit, not at first. The Jews in the rear [of the] room, the Jewish ladies with blue hair, would call me over and say, 'Melvin, we enjoyed certain parts of your show, but a trade would be better for you. Anything with your hands would be good. Aviation mechanics are very well paid.'") Even such negative responses did not greatly discourage him. He smiled at the naysayers and determined to do better at the next performance.

Performing a two-hour show every night, week after week should have been exhausting, even to the overenergized Melvin. However, that was not the case. Years later, by which time he had gone on to international success, he described this grueling summer schedule: "We thought nothing of it. We thought that's the way it is in show business. After that, the big time was a cream puff. One show a week on television, one picture a year in the movies. Are you kidding? I've spent the last 20 years catching up on my sleep."

The summer over, Melvin returned to Brooklyn and to his family and friends and life at Eastern District High School. By now he'd stockpiled plenty of stories to tell his Brooklyn cronies about his Catskills adventures. As he reflected on his many successes (why think of the moments of misfire?), he told himself that he could never go back to "just" being a drummer. His heart and soul now belonged to the world of comedy, where his wit, personality, and physical being could all be a vital part of his self-created act.

6

Off to War

Even when I went into the Army I should have had a nervous break-down, because you are not the baby of the family in the U.S. Army. When D-Day happened they just took us all out and sent us overseas. So now I was a combat engineer and I wasn't trained for that kinda thing. It was very scary and there were mortar shells. It was a lotta noise, you know.

—Mel Brooks, 1977

N ow in his mid-to-late teens, Kaminsky's constant goal was to score with the girls. However, with his less-than-average height and his unconventional looks, "crazy" Melvin met with little success, despite being a quasi-experienced laughmaker in front of resort audiences.

By now, he had already adopted a more American-sounding name for professional purposes. He called himself Melvin Brooks. Variously, the future celebrity has said that he made the name change because he decided Melvin Kaminsky would not fit easily on a personalized set of drums or on a marquee. Another time he suggested that he altered his name so he would not be confused with the celebrated cornet player Max Kaminsky.

In actuality, Melvin was following the tradition of many entertainers who had abandoned their ethnic-sounding original names in favor of a moniker that sounded more American and less Jewish. Thus, he joined the ranks of Benjamin Kubelsky, Emanuel Goldenberg, Milton Berlinger, Joseph Abramowitz, and David Kaminski, who, respectively, transformed themselves into Jack Benny, Edward G. Robinson, Milton Berle, Joey

Adams, and Danny Kaye. Melvin's altered name came from his mother's surname of Brookman, which he shortened/adapted into Brooks. (Later, Melvin would further simplify his moniker by shortening his first name to the less formal Mel.)

As Melvin grew comfortable with his show business alter ego, he wove his stage name into a rhyme that he used as a performance opener. He hoped the ditty would ingratiate him with audiences even before he launched into his comedy act, which now included his crooning songs (especially those of Al Jolson and Eddie Cantor) that would be familiar to audiences in the Catskills. The verses began with:

> Here I am, I'm Melvin Brooks
> I've come to stop the show.
> Just a ham who's minus looks
> But in your heart I'll grow.

The next refrain set forth what his audience could expect from his solo act:

> I'll tell you gags, I'll sing you songs,
> Just happy little snappy songs that roll along.
> Out of my mind
> Won't you be kind?
> And please love Melvin Brooks.

Typically, Melvin ended his beseeching introduction on one knee, sporting a big toothy smile, with his arms spread wide in the tradition of the great Jolson. Young and still naïve, Brooks was so enthralled with this "showstopping" routine that it did not dawn on him for a long time that this gambit was quite derivative and threadbare.

• • •

In the spring of 1944, 17-year-old Melvin Kaminsky graduated from Eastern District High School. In the class yearbook, Melvin's school activities were listed beneath his photo: "Class Day Committee, Senior Council, Dean's Assistant, Fencing Team." A few of these extracurricular activities seemed unlikely for this particular student. However, Kaminsky's stated ambition in life was more true to the actual Melvin: facetious, comical, but with an oversized belief in his potential for the future. He gave as his career goal: "To be President of the U.S."

•   •   •

After graduating, he enlisted in the army (as part of the Army Reserve Specialized Training Program) and was dispatched to the Virginia Military Institute (founded in 1939) in Lexington, Virginia. He and other new recruits were put through basic training, which included such arcane activities as riding and learning to use a saber. "They had us ride horses and cut down flags on bamboo poles. . . . I was trained to become a Confederate officer."

Being stationed in the South was an education in and of itself for Melvin. For the Brooklynite, living in this dissimilar world was "oh so different from living on the asphalt and cement all my life."

One part of the army regimen that really appealed to Melvin were those occasional evenings when he and his fellow trainees were allowed to attend the cotillions at the nearby Washington and Lee School. At these dances, the unskilled Casanova experienced the best and worst of times: "I met the flowers of Virginia there. The most beautiful girls. Southern belles. It was one of the best times of my life, but I was just this Jew from New York and not so good-looking." With further self-deprecation, he added, "I think it was right there and then that I decided I had to go into show business. That's the only way I'd ever get these girls to notice me."

While Melvin was going through military training in Virginia, the Allied armies had undertaken the D-Day offensive (June 6, 1944) in German-occupied France. This successful campaign against the Axis forces was an early sign that an Allied victory in Europe was both inevitable and not that far in the future. Meanwhile, Kaminsky was assigned to complete his basic training at Fort Sill in Oklahoma. By the time he had finished this phase of his military preparation, the Allies had driven the Nazi regime from Paris. The final assault against the Third Reich on German turf was imminent.

During basic training, Kaminsky lost his remaining baby fat and shed any naïveté he may have had about all Caucasian men being equal in the U.S. Army. (In this war, African Americans were largely segregated into their own units.) Melvin repeatedly encountered overt anti-Semitism. It made him furious and prompted some reckless reactions on his part. One day when yet another soldier slung anti-Jewish slurs in Kaminsky's direction, he could take it no longer. He angrily marched over to the bigot, asked him to remove his helmet (after all, he didn't want to destroy government-issue gear), and then used his mess kit to whack the offending G.I. over the head. Kaminsky felt he had made his point, and he shrugged off the punishment he received for his action.

• • •

In early 1945, Melvin and many others at Fort Sill were sent by troop train to the East Coast. There, they boarded a troop ship, which zigzagged its way across the Atlantic Ocean and docked in Le Havre, France. Next, the soldiers were loaded into trucks and dispatched to the front lines, passing through countless bombed-out French villages, the roadways lined with the corpses of recent victims. Melvin and his fellow troops headed into Belgium, where they encountered "little actual shooting," but according to Melvin, "there was plenty of mortar and artillery fire, and it was very noisy, and I thought that I would not want to be in the war very long, because of the noise. The earth was very hard when I was there, and I could not dig a V-shaped foxhole, as I wanted to, and stay down at the bottom of the V for the rest of the war. All these hot fragments of shrapnel and stuff were flying around, and I did not want to die, so it was awful. I remember hiding under a desk in a kindergarten while there were air battles going on above us, and bombs rattling."

At one point in the ongoing campaign, Melvin was assigned to be a forward observer/radio operator. "We'd figure out our position and tell the artillery, you know, to knock out a German post somewhere. And the minute we broadcast, we had to high-tail it out of there, because 10 seconds later, the road would be strafed with 88 shells. I mean, they would zero in, and they were amazingly accurate." However, Kaminsky was soon transferred from this task because he "couldn't learn the artillery argot. You're supposed to give them map coordinates. . . . But I'd say, 'No, no! You're missing it! You're going over, dummy! You're not even near! Aim for the big tree by the church. Say, listen, did the chow come up yet?' Very unmilitary. I didn't last long as a forward observer."

In actuality, Kaminsky had been trained to be a combat engineer as part of the 1104 Engineer Combat Battalion of the 78th Division. (Said Melvin, "I was a Combat Engineer. Isn't that ridiculous? The two things I hate most in the world are combat and engineering. I was a little kid from Brooklyn, getting his hair combed every morning by my mother, and suddenly I am doing 40-mile hikes, and being expected to eat grass and trees.")

On the battlefront his chief task was to help clear land mines so that advancing Allied troops and tanks could pass safely through the treacherous terrain. Melvin and his fellow soldiers were part of an Allied wave that pushed across the Rhine River at Remagen. Then they moved into Alsace-Lorraine on the German/French border. (Years later, Melvin made light of the dangerous situation by joking, "We would throw up bridges in advance of the infantry but mainly we would just throw up.") En route to victory, Kaminsky and his fellow soldiers experienced several skirmishes with the Germans, who, by now, were largely in flight. "I mean, we were fired on by a lot of kids and old men who were left in the villages. They were called werewolves, snipers."

Sooner or later—even in the midst of the chaos of war—it was inevitable that Melvin's zany personality would erupt in full force. At one juncture, when he and the others were playing cat-and-mouse with the German forces, the Nazis began blasting propaganda messages over powerful bullhorns, exhorting the Allied soldiers to surrender because they could not possibly win the war. The impulsive Kaminsky decided such nonsense deserved an appropriate retort. He scurried around and located a bullhorn of his own to offer the enemy a rendition of "Toot, Toot, Tootsie," in Al Jolson "Mammy" style. One can only imagine what the bewildered Germans thought of this foreign-language assault on their ears. This was not would-be crooner Kaminsky's only musical outing during World War II. One time back at base when he was assigned to odious latrine duty, he used the occasion to create a "melodious" diversion. He took Cole Porter's popular tune "Begin the Beguine" and converted it into the satirical number "When We Clean the Latrine."

Melvin's battlefield habit of making up and singing funny songs made perfect sense to him. It was his antidote to the terror of the wartime situation. "Some guy would say, 'We're gonna be killed; we'll never get out of this war,' and I'd say, 'Nobody dies—it's all made up.' Because otherwise we'd all get hysterical, and that kind of hysteria—it's not like sinking, it's like slowly taking on water, and that's the panic. Death is the enemy of everyone, and even though you hate Nazis, death is more of an enemy than a German soldier."

• • •

When the war concluded, Melvin found himself with an offer he could not refuse. It was based on his reputation for being his barracks' goofiest character, an unusual man who could find humor even in deadly chaos and who used his offbeat perceptions to amuse his fellow soldiers and keep up their morale. Kaminsky's major suggested, "Melvin, why not stay with us and travel around providing the boys with entertainment?" It did not take the soldier long to accept the appealing gig.

Not only was Melvin promoted to the rank of corporal, but he was issued a classic old Mercedes-Benz for his transportation. Rising to his elevated sense of self-importance, Kaminsky asked his commanding officer to assign him a soldier to be his chauffeur. While that request was vetoed, the major agreed to a compromise. Kaminsky was given a small allowance to hire a German civilian driver. Melvin detailed about his new job: "So I found a German fiddle player named Helga, who became my 'chauffeuse.' My official title was Noncom in Charge of Special Services, and I did shows for enlisted men and officers' clubs. Sometimes for a whole division, with tens of thousands of people out front. I told big, lousy jokes. Every time Bob Hope came by, I would write down all his jokes and use them. Nothing frightened me. I sang like Al Jolson. Everybody could do the low Jolson, but I did the high Jolson that nobody else could do—things like 'I love you as I loved you when you were sweet sixteen.' People said they appreciated that. My chauffeuse played the fiddle for them, and together we fiddled in the back seat of the Mercedes."

Melvin had a wonderful time in his new capacity. "I used to go to Frankfurt with my special pass and obtain certain rare cognacs and stick them in my car. There wasn't a nineteen-year-old soldier who got drunker than I did. Helga played Brahms' 'Lullaby' beautifully. I'd say, 'Pull over to the curb and play Brahms' Lullaby.'" But, alas, eventually, the pleasant period came to an end. Kaminsky was advised that his special services duties were being terminated and he would be shipped back to the United States to be processed back into civilian status. Kaminsky hated to have his recent good times end and claims to have countered, "No, no—let me die in the back of the Mercedes with Helga." Nonetheless, he was ordered back to the States.

• • •

As Melvin prepared to return home, he reviewed his relatively brief participation in World War II. "They always say 'War is hell.' War isn't hell. War is loud. Much too noisy. All those shells and bombs going off all around you. Never mind death, a man could lose his hearing. So I used to put Camels in my ears. When I was discharged, the doctor looked in my ears. They wouldn't let me out of the army because my ears were so brown. I had all this Camel juice inside my inner tubes. I might be the first man to die of emphysema of the inner ear."

As Melvin observed repeatedly in the coming years, "I'm grateful to the army. Grateful to Hitler too. *The Producers* made me the first Jew in history to make a buck out of Hitler."

7

Becoming Mel Brooks

After I got out [of the military], I had three choices. I could go to college and hang out a shingle and make $10,000 a year. Another thing for a Jew to do would be to become a salesman. . . . And [the third choice was] show business. But you got to understand something: Jews don't do comedy in winter. In summer, all right.

—Mel Brooks, 1975

L ike many returning soldiers, Melvin wanted desperately to get on with his life. He realized quickly that relatives and friends on the home front could never understand the horrors of war he had experienced and seen on the battlefields of Europe. The angst and anger he felt at the Axis atrocities he had witnessed or heard about burned deep within the teenaged Kaminsky. Sometimes, it led him to erupt suddenly into fits of fury or unveiled disgust with the world. On other occasions, he lapsed into moods of total hopelessness over the inhumanity of man to his fellow human beings.

Brooks vowed that no matter what, he would never ignore his Jewish heritage (despite his lack of religiousness). Moreover, he swore to himself that he would never allow others to overlook or ignore his pride in being a Jew. (In the coming years, Mel often referred to himself in interviews and conversations as "your humble Jew." As recently as 2001, he vehemently told 60 Minutes interviewer Mike Wallace, "Yes, I am a Jew. I *am* a Jew. What about it? What's so wrong? What's the matter with being a Jew? I think there's a lot of that way deep down beneath all the quick Jewish jokes that I do.")

• • •

Once a civilian, Melvin Kaminsky strove to find his way back to some form of "normalcy." Because all of his brothers had attended Brooklyn College, he felt he owed it to his mother and them to follow suit. He used the G.I. Bill of Rights to enroll. However, over a 10-month period, the ex-soldier scarcely attended classes, and, eventually, he dropped out. Sometimes, to earn spending money, Melvin worked at the Abilene Blouse and Dress Company. At another point, he was employed in a clerical position at the post office. However, his heart remained tied to show business, and he made a few forays back to the Catskills as a tummler.

Then, in late 1946, Melvin Brooks, as he now called himself to one and all, found work with Benjamin Kutcher. The latter was a seedy theater impresario who operated from a rundown office on Manhattan's West 48th Street that boasted a grimy bay window that looked out onto the street. "For about six months, I did everything for him. I ran errands for him. I put placards in barber shop windows. He was a kind of circuit producer for many little towns around New York, like Red Bank, New Jersey. Wherever there was a little theater, he would book some old play—Alan Dinehart's *Separate Rooms*, something like that—he didn't care what it was about. If it had two sets, he wouldn't make money. If it had more than five characters, he wouldn't make money. He always wanted a hit, and he never had one. Never.

"He wore a charcoal-gray thick alpaca coat in the summer and the winter and a Broadway producer's hat all the time—a homburg—and he screwed a lot of little old ladies out of a lot of cash. I loved him. He'd say, 'Melvin, I'm going to be busy for an hour.' That meant he was going to screw a little old lady out of some cash. They'd give him checks made out to Cash and say, 'What's the name of the play?' He'd say, 'Cash.' They'd say, 'That's a funny name for a play,' and he'd say, 'So is *The Iceman Cometh*.'"

If this sleazy show business figure sounds familiar, it should. The colorful theatrical figure became the basis for Max Bialystock, the grotesque character around whom Mel Brooks shaped his breakthrough 1968 film, *The Producers*.

• • •

In the late spring of 1947, through his multitudinous chores with his fourth-rate producer boss, Mel learned of an upcoming summer job opening. It was with a new theater group in Red Bank, on the north shore of New Jersey. Brooks decided to drop everything for the chance to be on stage—or at least to work backstage—with this low-budget troupe, which was based in the auditorium of the local high school. The biggest attraction of this flimsy enterprise was that it was an Equity company. This meant Mel would be mingling with real theater professionals. As it turned out, the venture was operating on a truly meager budget. If the cast/crew—which included comedian/impressionist Will Jordan—each took home more than $6 a week after kicking back most of their modest official salary to the crafty producer, they were lucky indeed.

By now, at the ripe age of 21, World War II veteran Brooks had become increasingly cynical about life. Part of his temperament was overshadowed by a sense of inferiority. Emotionally, Mel was still frozen in adolescence, and seemed unable—or unwilling—to break out of that mode and move on to "normal" maturity. At times, he thought himself a real loser. On the other hand, on those occasions when his ego and confidence were riding high, he felt superior to everyone about him.

One day, the preening director of the Red Bank theater, Percy Montague, chastised Mel repeatedly in front of the company for having dared to commit some minor infraction. Brooks bristled with anger at the injustice of it all—and especially resented the public humiliation. He promptly shifted into an arrogant mode. The previously quiet underling caught the fatuous director off guard when he announced with great bombast, "I will not be the scapegoat!" To emphasize his firm position on the matter, Mel burst into a tirade filled with enough big words and erudite references to convince everyone in earshot that he was not a man to be taken lightly. For this show business neophyte, being taken seriously—even if his frequent bizarre behavior precluded receiving any high degree of respect from associates—was of paramount importance.

By midsummer, management had had enough of the pretentious Percy Montague, and he was given his marching papers. Shortly thereafter, the man in charge of the company announced he was quitting the failing operation. He offered the troupe the option of following suit or, if they so wished, finishing out the season themselves. Mel and his two roommates rose to the occasion. John Roney added production responsibilities to his acting duties, while performer Will Jordan took on some of the managerial tasks. With the post of company director still vacant, Brooks—always at his best when stretched the thinnest—volunteered for that daunting assignment.

To everyone's surprise—including his own—Mel blossomed in his position of authority. Although he was inexperienced in the demands of stage directing, he had an instinctive flair for knowing when the cast needed to be guided in one direction or another and how to convey his instructions to his coworkers. Amazingly, the season at Red Bank continued onward with relatively few hitches.

• • •

When the summer ended and the troupe departed Red Bank, Mel returned to the city. His absorbing New Jersey theater experience had enticed him into thinking big and trying his hand at acting on the Broadway stage. Summoning up his chutzpah, Mel personally made the rounds to the offices of various established Broadway producers. Typical of Brooks's brazen determination was his visit to the headquarters of Kermit Bloomgarden, one of the reigning New York theater impresarios. Mel strode cockily into the producer's office suite, surveyed the crowd (which included some well-known actors) seated in the waiting room, and swept over to the receptionist's desk. In his best stentorian voice, he announced, "Paul Muni is here and I have to go in three minutes." The inexperienced secretary jumped to attention and immediately summoned Bloomgarden to greet the visiting stage/film veteran. Kermit emerged into the waiting room, took one look at the young interloper, and said, "This boy is not Paul Muni." Cheeky Mel was not about to admit defeat. He explained (in a non sequitur), "Muni's name is Harold Gottwald. I am the real Paul Muni." Bloomgarden grasped Mel by the collar and said, "You've got a lot of moxie. I'm going to remember you." (Unfortunately or not, Brooks never did get his audition with the august Bloomgarden.)

If Mel could not obtain any actual theater assignments for himself, he at least could bask in the glory of his growing circle of show business comrades. In the process, he reasoned, he could, perhaps, pick up some professional tips and connections. One evening, with too much free time on his hands, Brooks trekked out to New Jersey to see one of his new pals perform in a cabaret. The entertainer was Philadelphian Ronny Graham, a talented entertainer in several guises (including actor, comedian, songwriter, and pianist). After the gig, the seven-years-older Graham, who would become a lifelong pal of Brooks's, offered to give Mel a ride back to Manhattan.

En route, the duo stopped at an all-night diner that catered to truck drivers. Brooks later recalled, "Ronny was still wearing his stage makeup and some pretty avant-garde clothes, and these big, hairy men all swiveled round and started to stare at us. Some of them even stood up. While we were eating, everything went very quiet. I was terrified. Suddenly, I turned on Ronny like a cobra and said, 'I want my ring back.' He said, 'What?' I said, 'You *spoke* to that man. Back at the club. Don't think I didn't see you speaking to him, because I did. *I want my ring back.*' And we both went into this berserk faggot row. Finally I picked up my cup of coffee and threw it in his face. Then I flounced out to the car with Ronny right behind me, wiping his eyes and screaming. Some of the truck drivers followed us out . . . [into] the parking lot. They just stood there, dumbstruck, with their hands on their hips, as we drove off, kissing and making up. I waved at them out of the window."

8

Hail Caesar!

Sid [Caesar] was a genius, a great comic actor—still is—the greatest mime who ever lived. Only he didn't impersonate celebrities; he did types. . . . Sid had this terrific angle in him; he was angry with the world—and so was I. Maybe I was angry because I was a Jew, because I was short, because my mother didn't buy me a bicycle, because it was tough to get ahead, because I wasn't God—who knows why. Anyway, if Sid and I hadn't felt so much alike, I would have been a comic ten years earlier. But he was such a great vehicle for my passion.

—Mel Brooks, 1975

Many media historians credit Milton Berle (1908–2002) as being America's "Mr. Television." He was the veteran comic who burst upon the fledgling television scene in 1948 with *Texaco Star Theater*. His weekly NBC-TV comedy/variety show quickly became a national craze and prompted many consumers to purchase their first television sets in order to see his Tuesday night funfest. The onetime child actor (who had been on Broadway, in silent films, and in vaudeville) had spent the 1930s and 1940s as a radio, film, and club personality best known for his amiable buffoonery. Berle relied largely on physical slapstick, snappy patter (rather than anecdotes), and an overbearing presence to capture audiences' attention. He transferred this forceful performance style directly to the small screen, where his fearless persona mesmerized and bowled over audiences. In his no-holds-barred fashion, he entertained home viewers with his vaudeville-style telecasts. However, he really did *not* create an art form tailored for the intimacy of the new mass medium. That honor belonged to Sid Caesar.

•   •   •

Mel first heard about this new, funny saxophonist named Sid Caesar from their mutual friend Don Appell. Later, news spread in the Jewish Catskills that Caesar (born in 1922 in Yonkers, New York) was the brightest and most engaging new talent since Danny Kaye had risen to fame in the mountain resorts area a few years earlier. Brooks—who was always vastly curious about the competition—decided to find out for himself whether this highly touted musician was as amusing as people claimed and, if so, what he might learn from his rival's technique. On a rare day off, Mel went over to the Avon Lodge to see Sid perform. In typical Brooks manner, he analyzed how he stacked up against the "competition." They both were Jewish and, in their families, each was of the first generation to be born in America. Similarly, Mel and Sid were both the youngest of several brothers and had a great respect for and attachment to their hardworking families. Like Mel the drummer, Sid the adept saxophonist had accidentally found himself gravitating from staff musician to house comic where his innate sense of rhythm stood him in good stead in giving his act its proper pacing.

However, as Mel observed, there were many marked differences between the two emerging talents. Mel was still learning the ins and outs of his comedic trade as a (pool) tummler, while the four-years-older Caesar was already developing a rich reputation as a solo laughmaker among the tough Catskills audiences. (Then too, Sid's talents as a sax player demonstrated that he was a far more serious and proficient musician than Mel was.)

On other levels, the sensitive Mel also felt inadequate in comparison to Sid. For one thing, Brooks was short (less than five feet five inches) and possessed a funny-looking face that included a very prominent nose that looked more ethnic than noble. In contrast, Caesar was tall (six feet, two inches) and brawny and had a handsome profile.

Most important, Mel appreciated that Sid had a remarkable, innate ability for comedy that was subtle, deep, and not derivative like much of Mel's performance material at the time. (For Mel to make such an admission to himself was rare. By now, the young man had developed a self-protective bravado regarding the quantity and quality of his own talents, all of which served to mask his insecurities about his actual abilities.)

Much later, with a few films and a stage revue under his belt, Sid and Max Liebman (a veteran revue producer with whom Caesar had worked during World War II) revamped several old Caesar routines and added fresh material, honing everything into a polished whole. Along with such supporting acts as Gale Robbins, Bill Shirley, and a chorus line of leggy Copa gal dancers, Caesar opened his nightclub stint on January 2, 1947. It generated excellent reviews and club business. During the popular run, Sid's old pal Don Appell dropped by the Copa to congratulate the show's star. Appell came backstage accompanied by another Catskills veteran, Mel Brooks. The hyperactive young man was quick to praise the reserved Sid and to remind him of their past meetings at Avon Lodge when Mel was still going by the name of Melvin Kaminsky.

Following Sid's solid run at the Copa, Caesar and Max Liebman packaged a revue that toured major clubs in the United States. By October 1947, and once again under Liebman's aegis, Sid was back in Manhattan. This time he was starring in a condensed stage revue at the cavernous Twentieth Century-Fox flagship movie palace, the magnificent Roxy Theater. There Caesar and his supporting acts performed several times daily between showings of the slightly risqué costume spectacle *Forever Amber*. Sid and company received far better critiques than did the 138-minute blockbuster and enjoyed a several-week engagement at the Roxy. During the much-hyped run, Caesar welcomed several visitors backstage at the Roxy between performances. Among them was Mel Brooks, fresh from his "triumph" at the struggling Red Bank, New Jersey, theater.

Brooks enthused to Caesar how much he enjoyed Sid's Roxy showcase, and the two began to chitchat amiably on many subjects. Since Sid was always a man of relatively few words in social situations, it was the loquacious, nervous Mel who usually did most of the talking in their increasingly frequent get-togethers. It developed into a ritual that Brooks, who was out of work, would regularly come backstage to kibitz with his successful new friend. It was an unspoken part of the dynamic between these two men that Caesar was the important figure and that Brooks, at least for now, was merely an amusing—often wacky—hanger-on. At the time, the lopsided relationship seemed to satisfy both individuals.

In early 1948, Sid opened on Broadway in a smart new musical revue, *Make Mine Manhattan*, which would run for a year. One day, backstage at the Broadhurst Theater, when Mel and Sid were conversing, Caesar informed Brooks that Max Liebman had been presented with the opportunity to produce a weekly television revue that would air simultaneously on both the NBC and Dumont networks. Liebman wanted to feature his protégé, Caesar, on the program. The taciturn Sid allowed that he was inclined to accept the offer, which, he felt, would provide a good opportunity to break into a new medium.

9

Smashing into the Ranks

Ever since I had worked in the Catskills, I had considered Mel [Brooks] to be sort of a groupie. . . . He loved comics and obviously wanted to be one himself. . . . He was funny and ingenious and he liked my type of humor, so he hung around me.

—Sid Caesar, 1982

To staff Sid Caesar's upcoming TV show, titled the *Admiral Broadway Revue*, Max Liebman immediately turned to talent already well known to him. To write the weekly skits, he hired Lucille Kallen and Mel Tolkin, who had been loyal staff writers (of skits and song numbers) for Max for several summer seasons at the Tamiment mountain resort in Pennsylvania. The bright, inventive Lucille was then in her late twenties and hailed from Los Angeles, while the erudite, serious Tolkin was slightly older and came from Russia via a long stopover in Canada. To perform the skits, Liebman signed not only his protégé Sid Caesar but also Mary McCarty (a brassy Broadway, club, and film talent). In addition, he hired the versatile, agile Imogene Coca. (She was a pixielike performer who boasted a tremendously expressive face, was extremely adept at pantomime and skit comedy, and was an accomplished dancer. This show business delight had been performing since childhood and had worked with Max in the late 1930s in *The Straw Hat Revue*.) Others slated to be part of the upcoming series included such on-the-rise performers as the stylish dancers Marge and Gower Champion.

Frantic preparations got under way to air the new hour-long show—live on NBC-TV and simulcast on the Dumont network—each week beginning Friday, January 28, 1949. With so many loose ends to tie together quickly to meet the debut deadline—let alone the need to map out plans for each succeeding show—Max Liebman was in a whirlwind of hectic activity to meet the show's diverse challenges. Despite all the pressures, Liebman was convinced that he was ideally suited to provide a first-class TV showcase that would please its sponsor, reviewers, and, most of all, home viewers.

During this tornado of preparation, Sid Caesar completed his run in *Make Mine Manhattan*. During the lengthy engagement, which finally closed on January 8, 1949, Mel Brooks and Max Liebman had their first encounter. It occurred one day when Liebman came by the Broadhurst Theater to chat with Sid. As had become Mel's habit, he was hanging around backstage, happy to be in Caesar's impressive orbit. Hardly had Sid said hello to his mentor, than he turned to his diminutive hanger-on and urged, "Do for Max what you just did for me." The anxious-to-please Brooks immediately heeded the command of his revered leader. (Besides, the cheeky Mel was always ready to "audition" at a moment's notice.) Brooks ran out onto the empty stage and, in his slightly raspy voice, launched into a full-force rendition of his trademark intro number, which he had employed repeatedly in the Catskills. He didn't miss a beat as he gave an especially hard sell to his rendition of "Here I am, I'm Melvin Brooks." He crooned—Al Jolson style—right through to his finish, fell down on one knee, smiled big, and ended his manic performance with his arms spread wide apart. Sid beamed as his zany pal intently "sold" the number. However, show business veteran Liebman was not impressed by this bizarre, clichéd solo turn.

A somewhat dismayed Liebman turned to Caesar and scoffed, "Who is this meshuggener?"

• • •

By January 1949, rehearsals were well under way for the fast-approaching opening show. So far, the eager Mel Brooks had been left out of the exciting action.

The fact that Mel had been ignored by Max Liebman, the kingpin of the program, remained only a minor stumbling block to the ambitious

Brooks. Brazenly, he decided to show up at rehearsals anyway and, some-how, make himself part of the proceedings. That was far easier said than done, even for the seemingly shameless Brooks. When Mel attempted to storm the International Theater, he was advised by burly security guards that he was *not* on the list of those authorized to be admitted to the inner sanctum. Pushy Mel then invoked repeatedly and insistently the name of his protector, Sid Caesar. A short time later, Sid's manager, Leo Pillot, turned up to see what all the ruckus was about. Pillot claimed not to know who this noisy young man was or what he might want with the show's busy star.

"I know Sid Caesar," Brooks persisted. "We talked about my writing a couple of jokes for him, and I'd like to see him." Unimpressed by the interloper's unrelenting plea, the annoyed manager gave the guards the order to "throw him out." Mel was assisted in making an unceremonious exit from the premises. Undeterred, he returned to breech the fortress again. Tenaciously, he repeated his reasons for wanting to go inside. Again the security men ejected him from the building. All told, accord-ing to Brooks, he was tossed out three times.

Whereas others, by this point, might have slunk away in abject em-barrassment, not so the obstinate Mel Brooks. He doggedly made a fresh assault on gaining admission to the building. This time he was even more agitated than before and began screaming, "I know Sid Caesar! . . . Sid! . . . Sid! . . . Sid!" Eventually, the growing din outside caught Cae-sar's attention and he left his rehearsal to investigate the source of the commotion. Discovering it was merely little Mel making all the racket, he quickly made provisions for Brooks to come inside. However, the inter-loper was instructed to remain quietly in the background, far away from the actual proceedings.

For the driven Mel, every small step forward was a victory of sorts. In his heart of hearts, the ambitious outsider knew it could not be long before everyone had to realize just how valuable he could be to making the *Admiral Broadway Revue* a big success.

On schedule, at eight that Friday night in late January 1949, the new TV program bowed live before an enthusiastic studio audience. The four clumsy, primitive TV cameras captured the proceedings in black and white for home audiences via the live broadcast to 24 stations and 17 other outlets by means of kinescope. (This was a predecessor to the taped filming of shows. In this crude process, a movie camera filmed the transmitted program as it aired live on a TV monitor. Thereafter, the kinescope could be aired by a television station at a later time and/or date.)

On the positive side, John Crosby (of the *New York Herald-Tribune*) enthused about the *Admiral Broadway Revue*, "For an hour's entertainment, I can't think of anything better in New York's expensive nightclubs." In its appraisal, *Time* magazine judged, "Its jokes and patter are brittle, rowdy, funny, and full of satirical references." *Billboard* magazine applauded, "Everybody concerned can take a long, deep and repeated bow."

The networks and the sponsor were pleased, and Max Liebman was jubilant. He bragged to a reporter for the *New York World-Telegram*: "Whereas it takes months and months to put on a two-hour revue on Broadway, we do an original one-hour show, with singing, dancing, and comedy—in one week. Theatre die-hards speak of the thrill of opening night. Hell, we have one every night."

In the next few weeks, *Admiral Broadway Revue* plowed onward, mixing both old and new skits, and fighting the clock to, somehow, be prepared to air live again on its next appointed Friday evening time slot. It was during the fourth week that Mel Brooks's dogged patience regarding this show business venture finally paid off.

One day in late February, Sid and company were rehearsing a skit, "The Professor and the Jungle Boy." Somehow, it was not coming together. During the dress rehearsal a few hours before the actual broadcast, the star, Liebman, and the writing staff (Mel Tolkin, Lucille Kallen, and, sometimes, Ray Carter) concluded that something was missing from the piece. No one could quite put his or her finger on what new funny ingredient needed to be introduced or which facet of the skit required quick reshaping. Finally, Caesar signaled one of his group to go find Brooks, who was sure to be nearby. Soon, Mel rushed onto the scene. He was full of his usual energy, and beamed a bright smile at being so summoned—so obviously wanted. He inquired solicitously what he could do to help out. Sid concisely recounted the stumbling block they were experiencing with the skit. That done, he ordered Mel, "Do something. Write!"

Brooks always operated best under extreme pressure—it made his creative juices flow. He swiftly suggested a few off-the-wall ideas that did not meet with much approval from the others. Then inspiration suddenly hit him. He proposed using a bizarre noise (which he called "the Cry of the Crazy Crow") to demonstrate how the boy in the troubled sketch ordered his morning meal back in the wilds. Sid was pleased, and, minutes later, the strange, harsh cawing sound was heard on air as part of the skit. It worked—the studio audience laughed.

Having proven himself so admirably under fire, Mel was no longer persona non grata with some of the staff, although Max Liebman continued to ignore this annoying pip-squeak. The official show writers tolerated Brooks as long as he didn't interfere with their skit-writing chores, which were often carried out in the building's hallways or in their cramped assigned quarters in the overcrowded theater facility: the jockstrap-strewn dressing room of the show's male dancers.

It was not too long before Caesar, who knew all too well what it was like to be poor and to live from hand to mouth, felt duty-bound to provide Brooks with some sort of actual weekly stipend. He asked Mel how much he wanted to remain on tap day in and day out to provide the *Admiral Broadway Revue* with comedic bits (i.e., shtick) as the occasion demanded it. Mel quickly shot back that $50 a week would be good. (This was the amount some of the others on the show's staff were then earning.)

Caesar countered, "That's unheard of. Let's make it forty."

Brooks insisted, "No, I need fifty."

Caesar suggested, "Tell you what I'm gonna do. I'll give you forty-five if Max [Liebman] gives you the other five." Sid consulted with Max, but Liebman, still vastly unimpressed with the unorthodox, unseasoned Mel, said, "No!" So Caesar, wanting to help Mel keep afloat and sensing that this go-getter had the fertile imagination to provide useful comedic ideas in the future, decided to pay Brooks $40 a week from his own wallet.

Time passed. Mel continued to contribute ideas to Sid for the weekly allotment of TV sketches. One of Brooks's specialties became a recurring skit called "Nonentities in the News." In this piece, utility cast member Tom Avera portrayed a reporter assigned to interview a series of strange characters played by Sid and other cast regulars.

By springtime, Mel had gained more confidence from his assorted contributions to *Admiral Broadway Revue* and boldly approached Caesar for a salary increase. Sid was inclined to say no but decided to see for himself where Mel was then living. (He wanted to judge in person if Brooks's claim that he was living in a hovel was merely a dramatic exaggeration.) The TV star traveled down to Broome Street in Greenwich

Village to check out Mel's basement residence. It required only a quick look for Sid to realize that his cohort was not living in a hovel but *beneath* a hovel. Caesar promptly bumped up Brooks's stipend to $50 a week.

With a solid response from home viewers, it was assumed that *Admiral Broadway Revue* would continue on beyond its first season. However, by May 1949, word came down from on high. The Admiral Corporation was not renewing its sponsorship of the hit program for another season. It made no sense to the staff, but they knew that in the world of show business, logic was often not the order of the business day. On June 3, 1949, *Admiral Broadway Revue* aired its 19th and final production. Only weeks later did Sid Caesar learn the actual cause of the puzzling cancellation. The head of the Admiral Corporation informed Caesar that because the *Admiral Broadway Revue* had been so surprisingly successful, there had been a huge, unexpected consumer demand for Admiral TV sets. It had required the company to suddenly expand its manufacturing facilities. As a result, they could not afford to do that and continue to sponsor the TV series. It was the first and one of the very few occurrences of a TV program being terminated because it was too popular and had done its job of selling the sponsor's products too well.

Once again, Brooks wondered where his next job would come from and how he could engineer a new industry assignment. He understood that recurring unemployment was part and parcel of the up-and-down life of show business. However, this hardly mollified his prideful belief that he was far too talented to be subjected to such typical nerve-wracking periods of professional idleness. When, he wondered, would everyone awaken to the fact that Mel Brooks would *never* abandon his goal of becoming famous in the world of entertainment? Why did they not realize that these obstacles in the way of his gaining success never could overwhelm his drive to prove to everyone (including himself) that he really was somebody and a talent to be reckoned with?

10

Your Show of Shows

I should have been impressed [being part of *Your Show of Shows*] but I
was a cocky kid. I was filled with hubris and marvelous ego. I thought
I was God's gift to writing . . . and I was.

—Mel Brooks, 1996

Within a short time after it was announced that *Admiral Broadway
Revue would be going off the air, Sylvester "Pat" Weaver met anew
with Max Liebman. The trendsetting television industry VIP had a fresh
offer to make the Broadway (and now TV) showman. Weaver confided to
Liebman that he envisioned an ambitious, fresh project for his network's
lineup. It was *NBC Saturday Night Revue,* a three-hour weekly offering
that would provide high-caliber entertainment so enticing that the public
would gladly stay home on Saturday evenings to watch the exciting new
show. Since Pat was such a fast-rising top executive at NBC, he was in a
solid position to carry out his elaborate vision.

After Weaver's discussions with Liebman (sometimes with Sid Caesar
present to provide feedback), it was decided that *NBC Saturday Night
Revue* would be the umbrella title for two offerings to be aired consecu-
tively: a 60-minute show broadcast live from Chicago from 8 P.M. to 9
P.M., starring the snappy stand-up comedian Jack Carter, followed by a
90-minute entry presented live from New York City from 9 P.M. to 10:30
P.M. *The Jack Carter Show*—the first hour of *NBC Saturday Night
Revue*—would utilize a vaudeville-style format of assorted acts, much like
Milton Berle did so successfully on his Tuesday night TV showcase on

the *Texaco Star Theater*. The next segment, *Your Show of Shows*, would be a revue-style presentation. Liebman would be in charge of the latter. The deal was soon put in place.

Max brought over to the new series much of the talent he had utilized on *Admiral Broadway Revue*. This included key performers Sid Caesar and Imogene Coca, as well as writers Lucille Kallen and Mel Tolkin, set designer Frederick Fox, choreographer/dance performer James Starbuck, conductor Charles Sanford, and several others. What really excited Max about the venture was that he would no longer be confined by a meager $15,000 weekly budget, but now would be allowed to expend up to $65,000 on each production during the 39-week season. To further demonstrate their faith in Liebman's capabilities, the network provided Liebman and his team with four floors of headquarters at the enormous City Center facility at 130 West 56th Street.

With the expanded time slot allotted him, Max, a culture maven, grandly envisioned presenting both the expected comedy skits as well as such added attractions as full-blown dance numbers (including ballet) and sophisticated segments that would feature classical music and opera. Besides the core group of performers, *Your Show of Shows* would contract name guest stars to host each week's presentation and to appear in sketches and/or musical numbers within the envisioned classy vehicle.

With its much-touted debut set for late February 1950, Max quickly added to the roster of show regulars. These included opera singers Marguerite Piazza and Robert Merrill, the dance team of Mata and Hari, the Billy Williams Quartet, the Hamilton Dancers, and handsome young vocalist Bill Hayes. Liebman decided that Sid Caesar and Imogene Coca, who had begun performing skits together on *Admiral Broadway Revue* partway through the season, would continue to be paired on *Your Show of Shows*, as well as handle solo spots that played to each of their particular artistic strengths.

Since the lineup of sketches within the 90-minute format would occupy less than half of the allotted time slot, the budget-conscious Liebman felt that his reliable writing team of Kallen and Tolkin could "easily" handle the weekly load of creating the needed sketch material and occasional new song offerings. Max continued to ignore the overeager Mel Brooks, who was waiting impatiently on the sidelines to learn about his possible status—if any—on *Your Show of Shows*. Actually, if Liebman had had his way, the bothersome young hanger-on would have been barred from the proceedings altogether. However, Caesar refused to let that happen. As the bigger of the top two stars of this major new TV project, he had more clout than before and exerted his power to protect Brooks's interest. Sid informed Max that for the time being, he would continue to pay his friend $50 weekly from his own checkbook. Liebman was anxious to focus on more pressing considerations and gruffly agreed to go along with Caesar's wishes in this trivial matter. However, Max warned his leading man that he would brook no interference from this undisciplined mascot—this *schlepper*. It was understood that Brooks would keep far away from Max unless his immediate presence was requested to help resolve a skit problem. When Brooks learned the news, he was relieved to be again "employed" in the business, but it certainly rankled him that Liebman continued to have so little regard for his talents. (In typical Mel Brooks style, he buried such hurt and insecurities beneath a compensatory bluster.)

When *NBC Saturday Night Revue* premiered on February 25, 1950, the critical response (at least for the *Your Show of Shows* segment) was even more favorable than that accorded previously to the *Admiral Broadway Revue*. Jack Gould (of the *New York Times*) enthused that the Manhattan-based portion of the evening was "really out of the top drawer, boasting variety in the true sense of the word and having an adult flavor throughout." *Variety* concurred that NBC had a winning Saturday night entry, especially with *Your Show of Shows*. The trade publication rated the premiere a "solid block of big-time entertainment and sales potentials." Sylvester Weaver was jubilant that his continued faith in the highly capable Max Liebman had paid off so richly.

•   •   •

During the first follow-up episodes of *Your Show of Shows*, the caliber of material and the production values continued to improve. And where was the overeager Mel Brooks during these crucial first weeks of the season as the program's staff worked furiously to iron out the wrinkles in each new weekly offering? Largely, the outsider was relegated to pacing the halls of the City Center production headquarters or waiting nervously out on the street hoping to join Sid and others when they emerged for a lunch break or to indulge in an occasional afternoon visit to a local steam bath.

Those times when Mel was summoned by King Caesar to provide last-minute skit shtick, he jubilantly jumped into action. This fireball of energy and bravado would spit out wild comedy premises, bits, and comedy lines to help Caesar and the other creative forces sail through an artistic impasse. Liebman aside, many of the *Your Show of Shows* team had come to admit that the tenacious Brooks actually was proving to be a useful creative backup. While he was certainly an odd, abrasive mix of chutzpah and thinly veiled insecurity, he also was a man who wore a cheery smile and sang/hummed upbeat songs. However, beneath this bluster lurked a growing reservoir of cynicism that verged on fatalism. (Because Brooks was so obsessed with the ongoing state of his health, many in the group thought him an overzealous hypochondriac.) This quirky little man hung on Sid's every word and was his taciturn boss's biggest champion (next to Caesar's ever-present factotum, the hulking Dave Caesar). But it was becoming obvious to some shrewd on-the-scene observers that Mel, the former Catskills tummler, had such a large ego that one day even the mighty Sid Caesar might not be able to control him.

By the time the seventh episode of *Your Show of Shows* aired in April 1950, Brooks had so often stormed the fortress that a weary Max Liebman finally conceded defeat and allowed Mel actual screen credit on the series. (This situation was prompted because Mel, on his own initiative, had submitted a full skit that was used on the latest show. In the routine, Caesar was cast as a colorful Russian actor who is a devotee of Method acting and demonstrates the process for onlookers. First he becomes a pinball careening wildly about a pinball machine, then he takes on both roles in a burlesque version of *Romeo and Juliet*.) Thus, that night's closing crawl of credits included a new listing, "Additional Dialogue by Mel Brooks."

Having won this pivotal battle with the strong-willed producer, the ambitious Brooks moved on to his next goal: becoming an actual salaried member of the team. He aggressively demanded—and soon won the concession—to be paid out of the show's production budget rather than receive the embarrassing handouts from Sid Caesar. With one foot now solidly in the door, Mel doggedly pursued his next objective: to be given screen credits as a *full* member of the writing squad. (As a bemused Caesar assessed his friend's ascension: "He was pushing his way into the writers' room through a combination of raw talent, inertia and sheer chutzpah.") By the 1951–1952 season, Brooks had achieved his latest goal.

The show's crawl was changed to state, "Written by Max Liebman, Sid Caesar, Lucille Kallen, Mel Tolkin and Mel Brooks."

• • •

Now that the relentless Brooks was actually a legitimate part of the show's writing team, it soon became a habit among the program's staff to refer to Mel Tolkin as "Big Mel" and to Brooks as "Little Mel." As Liebman increasingly devoted more of his focus to the program's segments of classical music, opera, and song-and-dance production numbers, it fell increasingly to the erudite Tolkin to take on the mantle of the series' head writer. Because Lucille Kallen was the sole woman in the writing group—and since this was in the era before feminism and sexual equality in the workplace—she was assigned to take notes at the writers' work sessions. (What bound her to that secretarial task was that, unlike the other writers, she could type.) Much more so than Imogene Coca, Sid made a point of attending these writers' meetings. Caesar not only had many viable suggestions to contribute, but he realized that it was the best way for him to have quality control over the skits in which he would perform. Sid did none of the actual script writing. Instead, after he introduced a possible premise to the others, his main input was to channel the flow of ensuing discussion.

The writing staff generally worked well together under the constant pressure, excited by the repeated challenge to outdo their past creative efforts. Each of these diverse talents had his or her particular strengths and weaknesses (especially Caesar, who was becoming intensely moody), but this writing squad was a well-oiled machine. Its members were in sharp contrast to the freewheeling Brooks.

"Little Mel" had great difficulty even showing up on time at the scheduled writers' meetings. By nature he worked best on the spur of the moment and found it very hard to adapt to the rigors of a structured work environment. He was further inhibited from being a compliant team player by being plagued with insomnia. No matter what he did (including changing his diet to adjust his blood sugar levels) he couldn't fall asleep until very late at night. By the time he had managed a few hours' rest, it was well past the time he should have been at the office. It forced him to race to get dressed for the workday and then scurry uptown to West 56th Street.

Mel's situation also was complicated by his suffering from extreme professional insecurity. There were many contributing factors to his plight. He was extremely sensitive to the fact that—unlike his confreres—he did not have a college education or formal experience as a comedy writer, and that he had had to blatantly push his way onto the writing staff (through the sponsorship of Caesar). Therefore, he felt at a great disadvantage to his peers. Others in a similar position might have compensated for such "failings" by bending over backward to follow the work schedule at the TV show and by being overly solicitous of their coworkers. But not the iconoclastic Brooks. Years of fighting the odds to stay afloat had left him pessimistic—even fatalistic—about the outcome of most every situation in his life.

With all of Brooks's emotional baggage he could not avoid being the odd person out among the writers of *Your Show of Shows*. He would arrive for the day's work hours late, offering absurd excuses for his tardiness. He did not deign to make an unobtrusive entrance but made his arrivals a perpetually noisy affair. He might stride into the room clasping his bagel, coffee, and newspaper, and sit on the arm of a chair (or even leap upon a table) and demand to know what the others had come up with during his absence. Other times he might make a more dramatic entrance by throwing open the office door. Next, he'd sprint in and slide across the floor as if he were stealing to third base, and yell some non sequitur.

Once "settled" down, Brooks was a hotbed of ideas, which he spewed forth. For every several unusable ones he tossed out, he typically came out with a gem that met with Caesar's instant approval. His specialty on *Your Show of Shows* soon came to be Sid's "Professor" skits, in which the star would appear as an eccentric expert from abroad who was being interviewed at the airport and would offer nonsensical responses to the reporter's queries.

To be sure, the other writers in the group were not always models of decorum. Lucille Kallen once described a typical work session: "To command attention, I'd have to stand on a desk and wave my red sweater, Sid boomed, Tolkin intoned, [Carl] Reiner [the show's recently installed second banana comic who had become a frequent attendee at the writers' conferences] trumpeted, and Brooks, well Mel imitated everything from a rabbinical student to the white whale of *Moby Dick* thrashing about on the floor with six harpoons sticking in his back. Let's say that gentility was never a noticeable part of our working lives."

The very professional Max Liebman deliberately allowed this circus-like atmosphere because he believed that informality sparked creativity and originality. By this he was following the golden rule of the veteran Hollywood movie producer Samuel Goldwyn, who observed once, "From a polite conference comes a polite movie." However, where Brooks was concerned, Liebman was less indulgent, especially since Mel so often pushed Max's tolerance to the limit with his hyper, often crude, and always disruptive behavior. When Liebman thought the bothersome upstart had gone too far and was becoming much too much of a distraction for the general good, he would puff deeply on his cigar to get the red-hot end burning more intensely. Then he would toss it in Mel's direction to signal his great disapproval of this unmanageable, *meshuggeneh* character. Brooks quickly became expert at dodging these fiery missiles and learned to make a joke of Liebman's taunts to lessen any sting of humiliation he might feel. Mel also turned a deaf ear to those many times when the exasperated producer shouted in disgust, "You're fired!" Brooks reasoned that Max's outburst of anger would pass, so why worry. After all, Sid was his almighty protector, and Brooks believed he could always redeem himself by bursting forth with another useful contribution to the show.

No matter what the career risks, the irrepressible, rebellious Brooks could not desist from sassing Liebman. One day, as Brooks recalls, Max and Little Mel were standing on the rehearsal stage. "I yelled, 'Pepper Martin sliding into second! Watch your ass!' And I ran straight at him at full speed and then threw myself into a headfirst slide. Slid right between his legs, sent him flying in the air, scared the shit out of him."

Such continual misbehaving by Brooks, the intractable juvenile, took its toll on the *Your Show of Shows* ringmaster. One day, Max Liebman's irritation with his unruly helper reached a breaking point. He exploded in a verbal torrent directed at his rebellious staffer. The diatribe ended with Max screaming at Mel, "You are nothing!"

To which Mel replied, "If I am nothing, then you are king of nothing!" With that, Brooks turned on his heels and left the scene of the latest confrontation. He knew better than to step on a good exit line.

11

Living on the Edge

What changed me was success and having to solve the problems of success. At that time of life, no matter what you do, you're getting your
education, what [novelist] Joseph Conrad called the bump on the head.
I got mine from the analyst and Mel Tolkin. Between them, they were
the father I never had.

—Mel Brooks, 1975

In early June 1951, during the summer break from *Your Show of Shows*,
Sid Caesar flew to the Windy City to appear live onstage. During the
week's engagement, he was scheduled to perform six to eight times daily
in a capsule revue presentation with his talented TV partner, Imogene
Coca. Sid's traveling companion aboard the four-engine Constellation
plane bound for Chicago was Mel Brooks. Somehow, during the several-
hour flight, the usually agitated Mel managed to remain relatively calm.
It was not until after the craft had landed in Chicago and Brooks had
solid ground beneath his feet that it suddenly hit him that he had actually survived what was, for him, a major ordeal. Mel was not a happy trav-
eler in the best of circumstances, and he always had great concerns about
flying, a mode of travel he avoided whenever possible. Being aloft in the
stratosphere triggered all sorts of fears in this hypochondriac: of not being
in control . . . of tempting death . . . of God knows what else. It was, as
Mel phrased it, his burden of "high anxiety." In later years, he would
recall that on his arrival at the Chicago airport he had literally kissed the
ground in joy at having outfoxed the fates and survived the perilous trek
from Manhattan.

• • •

On June 8, 1951, the *Your Show of Shows* revue debuted at the Chicago Theater. In the presentation, Sid and Imogene shared time on stage with other talent from their TV series: comedian Carl Reiner, singer Bill Hayes, and the Billy Williams Quartet (a vocal group). Backstage in Sid's dressing room, the star's entourage (including Caesar's older brother/ assistant, Dave) was coping with the high-strung Brooks. Mel was on hand to provide any last-minute jokes that Sid might need to freshen oft-repeated routines during the Chicago run. However, Brooks too often had too little to do to keep himself occupied while waiting to be needed.

It was not long before the antsy Brooks grew bored with being cooped up in the relatively small star's quarters at the theater. Often he paced the halls backstage to kill time and expend some of his surplus energy. He furiously chain-smoked cigarettes as his busy mind concocted new visual and verbal bits that his boss might or might not decide to use the next time he was on stage. With a quicksilver mind that was always working in overdrive, Mel was a nonstop comedy invention machine, unable to with-hold sharing his each and every wild, ridiculous suggestion with Caesar. Most of these absurd ideas Sid discarded with a slight back and forth shake of his head. However, the TV star knew that for every batch of un-usable material that spewed forth from Mel's frantic, fertile mind, there would be a gem that he could use—now or later—to amuse audiences.

If the hectic regimen of the many daily shows was a strain for Caesar, Coca, and the others, it soon grew intolerably tedious for the hyperactive Mel. After all, he was stuck backstage—away from the limelight—await-ing the great Sid to return to his dressing room between performances. These bleak periods gave Mel ample time to ponder—and then discard as imprudent, disloyal thinking—the question of why he himself wasn't performing onstage. After all, it was what he had always intended to do before he became a disciple, associate, and friend of the great Caesar.

At the end of each long day at the Chicago Theater, Sid—accompa-nied by Dave and the faithful Mel—returned to the Drake Hotel. There, Caesar, who had a voracious appetite, looked forward to a deluxe late evening meal delivered by room service. On one of these nights, Brooks was especially restless. On the way back to Sid's suite on the 18th floor, Mel kept urging Caesar to break the routine. "Let's go out and do some-thing!" he begged his boss. "Let's see the nightlife!" The repeated requests fell on deaf ears. Unlike Mel, Sid was married and already a family man. He had no interest—especially after the exhausting series of daily performances—to see the town. The shy Caesar was much happier unwinding in the privacy of his hotel. There he could devour his large repast in peace and quiet, away from the public's prying eyes.

But Mel was always itching for activity, and it was especially true this evening. Once a notion had popped into his mind, he rarely could let it rest—no matter how many impediments there might be to accomplishing his latest whim. Once back at Caesar's accommodations at the Drake, Mel continued harping at Sid, "Let's get out of here! Let's do something!" The self-contained Caesar vetoed or ignored each plea from his insistent sidekick.

When room service delivered the sumptuous dinner, Caesar sat down at the dining table to tuck in to his elaborate spread. Food was a great pacifier for the highly creative, volatile Sid, who expended so much energy on pleasing the public while all the time fighting a constant battle to keep his inner (childhood) demons at bay. The meal was delicious, and the comedian consumed it in great mouthfuls. Meanwhile, as Dave Caesar looked on, ensuring that his sibling had everything at hand to make his repast as pleasant as possible, Mel continued to frantically pace the room liked a caged ferret. Every few minutes he confronted Sid with his latest nudging request that they go out—now.

According to Caesar, he finally couldn't take the pestering anymore. Reluctantly, he set down his knife and fork. Next, with lightning speed, the tremendously strong Sid seized the bothersome Mel by the collar and the seat of his pants and stuck him out the open window of the 18th-floor hotel room. As Caesar dangled Brooks out over the street down below, Sid gibed, "How far out do you want to go? Is that far enough?"

Flailing in the wind and seeing fragmented moments of his life passing in front of him, the thrashing Brooks managed to timidly quip, "In would be nice. . . . In is good." Meanwhile, the powerfully built Dave came to the rescue. He slowly pulled the distraught Sid, and, in turn, the dangling Mel, away from the window. As he was doing this, Dave spoke soothing words to his enraged brother. Finally, the acrophobic Mel was retrieved from the clutches of death and was soon back safely inside the suite.

If this potentially near-death experience had deflated Mel Brooks's insistent need to partake of Chicago nightlife, it did nothing to dispel his great affection for the gifted Caesar. (Similarly, it did not damage the complicated friendship that Sid shared with Mel. As Caesar said of Brooks in his memoir, *Caesar's Hours*, "We were two close friends who genuinely loved each other and we had a relationship that was based on trust, affection and his relentless attempts to piss me off.")

As Mel rightly anticipated, the dangling episode soon became common knowledge and quickly turned into a show business legend (in which, as retold by many persons over the years, the setting of the incident kept moving up to higher floors at the Drake Hotel). This would not be the first or the last time that Mel would face such a traumatic physical or emotional situation. As he had already proven during his army service in World War II in Europe—and as he would countless other times during his extensive, multifaceted show business career—he was a born survivor.

12

On the Torturous Road to Success

I stayed with the game [i.e., working on TV with Sid Caesar] because the money got better and better. I always thought it was just something I would do until I found myself.

—Mel Brooks, 1966

B y 1952, Mel Brooks was in his midtwenties. Since officially joining the writing staff of *Your Show of Shows* he had received several healthy salary increases: jumps from $50 to $150 per week and then much higher. Brooks's pay raises reinforced a discussion Liebman had had with his junior staff writer some months before. Max had said, "You know, Mel, when I first saw you backstage at the Broadhurst Theater, well, I would say from that moment until this very moment, you were a kid." That is not to say that Brooks's unorthodox behavior still did not drive Liebman to distraction, but now he accepted that the young man had a fertile comedic mind and was a good addition to the *Your Show of Shows* company.

Also in this period there were changes in the writers' room. When Lucille Kallen went on maternity leave, the comedy writing team of Danny Simon and his younger brother Neil filled in for her. (The siblings departed when Kallen returned to work.) Later in the show's run, Tony Webster became the first non-Jew to join the ranks of the *Your Show of Shows* writing team. Another regular attendee at the writers' meetings was Carl Reiner, who had joined the lineup some months after the series debuted. Reiner, who had been born in the Bronx and was already a seasoned veteran of stage and TV shows, had a wonderfully inventive comic mind. He also displayed a flair for doing foreign-language double-talk— almost as well as the mighty Caesar. (What convinced Max Liebman to bring the multitalented Carl aboard was that he was slightly taller than Sid. This factor fulfilled Max's dictate that a show's support comedian— i.e., the second banana—should always be taller than the leading man.) Like Sid Caesar (and the less frequently present Imogene Coca), Reiner made solid contributions to the creation of the weekly skits. In short order, Carl became a close friend of Mel's.

Then there was Howard Morris, the third banana on *Your Show of Shows*. This New York–born actor was added to the cast of regulars in 1951. (Some have suggested that at one point, the aggressive Brooks hoped to win the acting post handed to the newcomer.) Previously, Morris had done occasional sketch work on *Admiral Broadway Revue*. In contrast to Reiner, Howard was short and physically quite slight. This provided an immediate visual contrast between him, Caesar, and Reiner when they performed together in front of the cameras. More important, Howard was sufficiently light of weight that the brawny Caesar could easily pick up the diminutive man and cart him about the stage—a gambit utilized to great effect on several *Your Show of Shows* sketches. Like Reiner, Morris made a habit of sitting in on the writers' meeting because (1) it was such fun and (2) it was a wonderful way to be in on the genesis of scripts and to learn all the nuances as the sketches developed. By becoming familiar with the material in this manner, these players had an easier time of learning their lines and the comic business amid the pressure of doing a weekly show. (Another of Liebman's dictates for his TV showcase was that no cue cards were to be used by the cast during the actual broadcast, just as no canned laughter was employed to "sweeten" the responses of the live studio audience.)

Brooks and Morris got off to a wacky start together. The madcap Mel thought it would be amusing to introduce himself to newcomer Morris by pretending to be a Frenchman visiting New York to observe the creative process on *Your Show of Shows*. For several days, Brooks kept up the charade, peppering his brief interchanges with Morris with a French word and relying on a great deal of pantomime. Howie, as most of his friends called him, could not make heads or tails of this absurd visitor from abroad who spoke broken English with such a heavy Yiddish accent. Then one day, the quirky Frenchman approached Morris and said in perfect English, "How the hell are you, Howie?"

In the coming months these two Jewish men, who both understood and loved the art of comedy, became good friends at and away from work. At least so the trusting Morris thought. One time the pair was strolling along a Greenwich Village street when, suddenly, Howie felt a sharp jab in his back. A voice growled, "Your money or your life!" Morris was caught totally off guard and swung around to see why his attacker sounded so much like Mel. Now standing face-to-face with the "robber," Howie saw that it was indeed Brooks. Unfortunately, there was no smile on the comedy writer's face. In fact, he had a strange, wild look in his eyes and a most determined set to his jaw. Morris was baffled by the situation and felt he should humor his "friend." He surrendered his watch, wallet, and other valuables. (According to some accounts of the bizarre incident, Mel tied up his perplexed victim before disappearing into the night.)

The next day, a mystified Morris questioned several others at work about this peculiar episode and how he should best handle the situation. He was reassured, "Oh, that's just Mel. He has these strange blackouts and one day he'll suddenly remember the incident and make everything right." True to their prediction, in the coming days, Brooks approached Morris, apologized for the episode, and returned all the taken items. Time passed and the occurrence was all but forgotten by Howie.

Many months thereafter, Morris and Brooks were enjoying a lunch break from the *Your Show of Shows* grind by renting a rowboat in Central Park. They ate their sandwiches and chatted about the day's events. Their boat was passing under a little bridge and Howie was lost in thought when all of a sudden he saw this crazy look pass over Mel's face. Before Morris could react to that strange stare, Brooks barked, "Give me everything you have or I'll kill you!" The "assailant" didn't look like he was kidding and the "victim" complied. Then Howie was ordered to get out of the boat and wade ashore. He did. Days later, Mel apologized to Howie and returned his possessions.

Such was life with the aberrant Mel Brooks, who rarely could resist indulging his antic sense of humor. Seemingly, he had little compunction about using anyone in his purview as a prop for his outlandish gambits. These larks usually were (subconsciously) constructed to make himself the center of attention.

• • •

Brooks's bond with Sid Caesar was far more complicated than the one Mel had with Howie Morris. Thanks to the *Admiral Broadway Revue* and *Your Show of Shows*, Caesar had achieved fame, power, and wealth. Being from a very humble background, he had great difficulty in accepting the fact that he earned in a week far more than his father (who died in 1946) had ever earned even in a good year. Somehow, Sid felt unworthy of his success, and he became increasingly guilt-ridden over his good fortune. Despite the soothing efforts of Sid's wife, Florence, the joy of their three children, and the emotional support Caesar received from his ever-present brother, Dave, and others in his inner circle, the star was a deeply troubled man. He would become so keyed up at work from the pressure of turning out a good show each week that when he came home at night, he found it almost impossible to unwind, and turned to several cocktails to calm himself down. By the time the exhausted man finally dragged himself to bed, he still could not easily fall asleep. He would lie there thinking about how to improve the coming week's skits, about how many people relied on his success for their daily livelihood, and about what might happen if he failed creatively and let down the network, the cast, and home viewers. Caesar's insomnia prompted him to start taking an escalating number of sleeping pills each night, which had an increasingly adverse effect, especially in conjunction with the growing amount of liquor he consumed daily. This led, in turn, to a routine of his taking stimulants in the morning to counter the grogginess of the prior night's lack of proper sleep and his injudicious use of pills and booze. The vicious circle escalated (and would continue for years until Caesar received successful substance abuse treatment).

Compounding Sid's major addictions was the mixture of his lifelong shyness, extreme moodiness, and a volatile temper. When the powerfully built Caesar erupted in sudden anger, he literally did not know his own strength, and anything could occur during these violent explosions. Sometimes Mel was an observer of such events, other times he acted as a court jester to pacify the rampaging star. On different occasions, he became the instigator of Sid's outburst (as with the infamous Chicago episode in 1951 during which Caesar dangled the bothersome Brooks out of an 18-story hotel window.)

One time, Caesar and Brooks drove down to Greenwich Village to see a club performance by entertainer Zero Mostel. They rode in Sid's new Buick, a luxury car of which the comedian was extremely proud. Sid parked on the street, carefully leaving plenty of space in front of and behind his auto. As they were crossing the street to enter the venue, Caesar noticed a man parking his car very close to his precious Buick. After a few moments watching the man maneuver into the space and brushing against his vehicle, Caesar stormed over to the man, explained that he was bumping against his new car, and asked him to desist. The man not only refused the request but grew sarcastic. Almost instantaneously, Sid boiled over, reached into the window of the offender's car, and attempted to pull the individual through the small opening. Thankfully, Mel rushed over and bit Sid on the arm, which caused Caesar to let go of his victim.

On another occasion, during a writers' room conference, Brooks suggested an anecdotal joke he had just developed and thought was a real winner. The premise concerned a snake who wanted to be freed from its cage because it couldn't stand to be imprisoned with others of its own kind. Sid did not find the joke funny, but Mel remained unrelenting in his insistence that it was a great bit and must be used. Later, Caesar and Brooks went out together for lunch. En route, bold Mel again brought up the subject of the snake joke. Once more, Sid vetoed using it on the show. Brooks grew increasingly belligerent in his reckless determination that this item must make it on air. He became completely caught up in getting his way and was, by now, punctuating his insistence by jabbing his index finger at the almighty Caesar.

In typical fashion, the star stood glaring at his pip-squeak adversary, who was carrying on frantically, oblivious that he had riled the much bigger man. Caesar could have easily pulverized this pest. Instead, he said very softly, "Shall I spare you?" Now attuned to his peril, Brooks replied, "Oh, yes, please, sire." This led Sid to say, "I'll let you live." (And he meant it!) Mel smiled ruefully and quickly changed the subject. Later, Caesar informed Brooks that if the noisome joke meant so much to Mel, it would be used in the broadcast.

On several occasions in the *Your Show of Shows* writers' room, the mercurial Sid would become enraged by the slightest thing that went wrong with his day. Sometimes, Caesar would vent his displeasure by slamming his fist through a wall. Other times, he might release his mounting tension by grabbing a heavy metal desk and lifting it one-handed into the air and then letting it fall back to the floor. At such tense moments, the clown of the group Mel Brooks would often come to the rescue by doing something particularly goofy to deflate his boss's boiling rage. For example, he might jump up onto Sid's back and ride him like a horse, all the while yelling, "Down boy, down!" Then Caesar would break into a grin and everyone knew they could get back to work.

Despite these (harrowing) antics, Mel remained a firm admirer of Sid Caesar's and considered him a good friend. (Some observers have suggested that in many ways Brooks subconsciously regarded the older Caesar as a father figure.) As time passed and Brooks became more established on *Your Show of Shows* and within the entertainment industry, the perimeters of his complex ties to Caesar shifted. One can read a lot into the situation that occurred one day when Sid, towering over Mel, laid his hefty hand on Brooks's head and said to the others in attendance, "This is *mine*." Nonplussed, Brooks reached over and grabbed Caesar's wallet from the star's pocket and said pointedly, "This is *mine!*"

•   •   •

Among Mel Brooks's *Your Show of Shows* confreres, he had particularly high regard for Mel Tolkin, who was both an agile comedy and songwriter and had the knack for being able to keep his collaborators largely in line to meet their weekly deadlines. (One of Tolkin's favorite sayings to alert his team that it was time to get back to the grindstone was, "It's Tuesday and hundreds of Jews all over America are waiting to see what we'll do [on Saturday night].") "Big Mel" was also a diplomat who knew how to stay on the right side of the mighty, short-tempered Caesar. One day, Tolkin presented Sid with the punch line to a sketch that he and the others had labored over for some time. As Caesar read it, a frown came over his face. "I'm not crazy about this joke," he announced. To punctuate his adverse reaction, the comedian lifted up a nearby piece of heavy furniture and then allowed it to slam back to the ground. In the silence following this outburst, Tolkin—with perfect timing—responded with a wry, "We're not married to it."

One of Tolkin's other attributes was that he was extremely well read in the classics, especially in the literature of his native Russia. It was he who first educated Brooks about the great Slavic writers, enthusing about the works of such Russian literary giants as Leo Tolstoy, Fyodor Dostoyevsky, Aleksandr Pushkin, and Nikolai Gogol. Such tutorials prompted Mel to read many of these authors' works, and it solidified his lifelong habit of enhancing his knowledge of literature, history, and so much more. Brooks was always grateful for Tolkin's efforts in prodding him to expand his cultural horizons.

Like many other bright, self-made individuals, Tolkin had overcome several obstacles in his strenuous efforts to succeed in life. This left him with unresolved emotional issues that, eventually, caused him to visit a psychiatrist and begin therapy. The sessions helped the writer to gain clarity and perspective to better deal with his problems. (In actuality, Tolkin was not alone among the creative forces at *Your Show of Shows* then undergoing analysis. Caesar regularly visited a therapist.) When Tolkin got to know Brooks better and learned more about his collaborator's emotional angst, he suggested that therapy definitely might help his colleague to adjust better to his life of increased responsibilities and demands.

Brooks had long been a strong believer in good physical health. His ongoing concern prompted him to seriously read medical literature so he could personally diagnose any possibly aberrant health symptom he might experience. Over the years, Mel subscribed to medical journals, pored through his personal library of medical dictionaries, and investigated a wide variety of innovative treatments for various serious ailments. He was convinced that such studies would help him to recognize—early on—any potentially dangerous health issues that might befall him. He believed that being so forewarned he would be forearmed and could prolong his time on earth. (As a result of this near-obsessive activity, Brooks became familiar with a wide range of medical conditions and was able to advise concerned friends when they consulted him about health problems they were experiencing or treatments they were undergoing.)

With all his medical reading, Mel had given little conscious attention to the state of his mental health. However, he knew something was wrong, and his knowledge/intuition suggested it was not of a physical nature. As he grew more successful and earned more on *Your Show of Shows* he found that, frequently, he would suddenly become panic-stricken at work. At such times, he'd have to leave a meeting quickly, or stop whatever else he was doing, and rush out into the street. Brooks described his plight: "I started having acute anxiety attacks. I used to vomit a lot between parked Plymouths in midtown Manhattan. Sometimes I'd get so anxiety-stricken I'd have to run, because I'd be generating too much adrenaline to do anything but run or scream. Ran for miles through the city streets. People stared. No joggers back then. Also I couldn't sleep at night and I'd get a lot of dizzy spells and I was nauseated for days." He also recalled suffering "bouts of grief for no apparent reason. Deep melancholy, incredible grief where you'd think that somebody very close to me had died. You couldn't grieve any more than I was grieving."

Following the suggestion of Tolkin and the example of his coworkers, Brooks visited a Manhattan psychiatrist. (This particular specialist had been analyzed by the renowned Theodor Reik, who, in turn, had been a protégé of Sigmund Freud, the founder of psychiatry.) Mel began treatment, visiting the doctor several times a week between 1951 and 1957. He found his analyst to be "kind and warm and bright." Many of his troublesome symptoms "disappeared in the first year, and then we got into much deeper stuff—whether or not one should live and why?"

As the exploratory process continued, the patient began to comprehend key causes of his internal turmoil. One of them was a fear of growing success. "When I was listed as a regular writer [on *Your Show of Shows*] and my pay went to $205 a week, I began to get scared. Writer! I'm not a writer. Terrible penmanship. And when my salary went to $1,000 a week, I really panicked. Twenty-four years old and $1,000 a week? It was unreal. I figured any day now they'd find me out and fire me. It was like I was stealing and I was going to get caught. Then the year after that, the money went to $2,500 and finally I was making $5,000 a show and going out of my mind. In fact, the psychological mess I was in began to cause a real physical debilitation To wit: low blood sugar and under-active thyroid." (Mel's suspicions as to the validity and durability of his career achievements were reinforced by his beloved, skeptical mother. Many times when Kitty Kaminsky's youngest son bragged of his show business success and mentioned yet again how much money he was being paid at *Your Show of Shows*, this cynical little lady asked him pointedly, "Have they found out yet?" Such statements guaranteed a deflation of Mel's self-confidence.)

In the therapeutic process, Brooks experienced other vital insights. He revealed, "You often hear, you know, that people go into show business to find the love they never had when they were children. Never believe it! Every comic and most of the actors I know had a childhood full of love. Then they grew up and found out that in the grown-up world, you don't get all that love, you just get your share. So they went into show business to recapture the love they had known as children when they were the center of the universe."

In later years, the highly successful Brooks would shrug off the seriousness of this siege of heightened emotional stress. He told a *Rolling Stone* magazine reporter in 1978, "I had low blood sugar, a chemical imbalance, plus the normal nervous breakdown everyone goes through from adolescence to adulthood. It comes from the suspicion that only an incredible amount of failure is there to greet us. But if you can fail between the ages of twenty and thirty, it's fabulous. Too much early success and the rest of your life becomes a measure of repeating it."

Meanwhile, in the early 1950s, as Brooks's therapy sessions helped to relieve the great weight on his mind, he made a concerted effort to turn his personal life around. That required him to make a concerted effort to bid farewell to his prolonged adolescence and to strive for emotional maturity. A great catalyst in the process was Florence Baum, a Broadway musical comedy dancer.

13

Broadway, Love, and Marriage

I was grieving about the death of childhood. I'd had such a happy child-hood, my family close to me and loving me. Now I really had to accept the mantle of adulthood—and parenthood. No more cadging quarters from my older brothers or my mother. Now I was the basic support of the family unit. I was proud of doing my bit, but it meant no longer being the baby, the adorable one. It meant being a father figure. Deep, deep shock. But finally I went on to being a mature person.

—Mel Brooks, 1975

Now that Brooks felt secure about his post on the writing staff of *Your Show of Shows*, he sought additional outlets for his spurts of creativity. One of these was to write a skit for *Curtain Going Up*, a Broadway-bound revue. The show tried out in Philadelphia in early 1952. Unfortunately, it failed to meet expectations and soon closed. A few of the project's numbers (including Mel's satirical sketch) were acquired by the veteran show packager Leonard Sillman to be used for his forthcoming revue, *New Faces of 1952*. The cast included such rising and new personalities as Ronny Graham, June Carroll, Robert Clary, Alice Ghostley, Eartha Kitt, Carol Lawrence, Paul Lynde, and Rosemary O'Reilly.

New Faces of 1952 bowed at the Royale Theater on May 6, 1952. It quickly proved to be a major winner. One of the highlights of the production was Brooks's lampoon, "Of Fathers and Sons," a parody of a recent Broadway drama (*Death of a Salesman*). The substantial success of *New Faces* gave Brooks a legitimacy within the theater community and reinforced his ambitions for a lofty future in the prestigious world of

Broadway. The show enjoyed a yearlong run and was then brought to the screen in early 1954 by Twentieth Century-Fox with most of its numbers intact, including Brooks's well-regarded "Of Fathers and Sons." Now Mel could boast that he had "conquered" three mediums: television, theater, and films.

· · ·

During the early 1950s, Mel was a devoted attendee of Broadway offerings (especially musicals) and had several acquaintances among the show business crowd. He therefore encountered many young women in the entertainment field. Thanks to his increased success as a television writer, his social poise had improved to a degree, and he discovered that women often found comedians/comedy writers to be, somehow, sexy. Among Brooks's circle of friends in the early 1950s were two dancers (Mary Katharine Martinet and Florence Baum) from the cast of the hit Broadway musical *Gentlemen Prefer Blondes*. Mel and Mary Katharine (known as M.K.) dated for a time. Even when the romantic aspect of their relationship ended, the two stayed friends. In early 1952, while Brooks was involved with the Broadway-bound revue *Curtain Going Up*, he pulled strings to get M.K. a part in the production. By 1953, Mel was dating M.K.'s good friend Florence Baum.

Florence's father, Edward, was a Londoner who had relocated to New York when he was about 20. He became an auto mechanic and soon had his own shop. In time, he met and married Lenore Douglas, a New Yorker. The couple's only child, Florence, knew at the age of four that she was "born to dance." A few years later she began ballet classes. Thereafter, she worked as an extra in Lewisohn Stadium opera productions. During World War II, she joined a group of youngsters who performed regularly for the USO. Around 1946, the teenager appeared on TV on *Places Please*, a talent/variety program. She then began working on Broadway.

At five feet five inches tall, this lithe, personable brunette with long, shapely legs proved to be an agile stage performer. She won out against strong competition to appear in a series of major Broadway musicals: 1947's *Allegro*, 1949's *Gentlemen Prefer Blondes*, 1951's *Top Banana*, and 1952's *Two's Company*. This last show was a revue starring Hollywood diva Bette Davis. When the cinema queen became seriously ill, the show closed in March 1953. Over these years, Florence had also danced on several major TV variety programs, including *The Colgate Comedy Hour*, *The Jackie Gleason Show*, *The Ed Sullivan Show*, and *Your Show of Shows*.

(It was in 1950, during Florence's tenure in the long-running *Gentlemen Prefer Blondes*, that she unwittingly helped create the tradition of the "Gypsy Robe," which became legendary among Broadway chorus performers. Bill Bradley, a fellow chorus member in *Gentlemen Prefer Blondes*, persuaded Baum to give him her well-worn dressing room gown. He wrapped the item ornately and sent it to Arthur Parkington on the opening night of a new Broadway musical, *Call Me Madam*. Bradley informed Parkington that the much-frayed robe had once been worn by all the *Ziegfeld Follies* beauties. In turn, Arthur cut a rose off a costume worn by the star of *Call Me Madam* [Ethel Merman] and sewed it on the robe. He then sent it to a friend in the chorus of the next main stem musical [*Guys and Dolls*] to open. The tradition continued over the decades right up to the present day, and the original gown, now much decorated and far heavier, has become greatly venerated as a good luck charm.)

• • •

The romance between Mel and Florence blossomed. On November 26, 1953, they were married in New York City in front of the library fireplace at the home of Rabbi Newman. Among the attendees were Mel's mother and three brothers (and their wives) as well as the bride's parents. For Brooks, in particular, the adjustment to married life was especially difficult. Having been brought up largely by a single parent, he had little to no frame of reference of what was required of him as a husband, let alone about how to act when he and Florence became parents. Later, Mel observed of his precipitous decision to marry Florence Baum that his wife thought she was marrying a man like her father. For his part, he had assumed that his new bride would be a younger version of the spunky, self-sacrificing, and always understanding Kitty Kaminsky. Such hasty assumptions soon propelled the newlyweds onto a distressing matrimonial path. Eventually, it led to escalating domestic disharmony.

14

Farewell, Caesar

I was aggressive. I was a terrier, a pit bull terrier. I was unstoppable.
I would keep going until my joke or my sketch was in the show. I didn't
care if anybody else's was in or out. All of us writers were like a litter of
pups, and we all fought for our little tit and struggled and screamed.
Sid [Caesar] was God, and if we could get his ear and he would smile
on us and say, "good," that was important. . . . We nearly got punching
each other. You'd hear, "Don't change that," and "How dare you!"
There were mighty big egos in a little room.

—Mel Brooks, 1989

On September 12, 1953, *Your Show of Shows* returned to the television
airwaves at its usual Saturday evening time slot, broadcast live from
the Center Theater at Sixth Avenue and 49th Street.

At the end of the 1952–1953 season, changes were in the works for
this well-established program, which many in the business felt was becoming a bit old hat for home viewers. To freshen up the show's lineup, some
of the regular support talent (such as Marguerite Piazza and Bill Hayes)
would be featured less frequently on the 90-minute program. It was also
agreed that every fourth week, NBC-TV would schedule its *All-Star
Revue* in the 9 P.M. to 10:30 P.M. *Your Show of Shows* time slot. It would
use a group of rotating hosts (including Martha Raye and Tallulah
Bankhead). In addition to these alterations to the venerable *Your Show of
Shows*, the NBC network executives tried to pressure Max Liebman to
permit more dramatic changes to the structure of his "baby." However,
the producer remained insistent about not tampering with a good thing.

Certainly, *Your Show of Shows* did offer an abundance of inspired ingredients in its recurrent sketch lineup. There were "The Hickenloopers" domestic routines, featuring Imogene Coca and Sid Caesar, as well as the troupe's elaborate spoofs of Hollywood movies (including *A Streetcar Named Desire, Shane*, and *From Here to Eternity*), American TV shows (such as *This Is Your Life*), and foreign art movies (such as Japan's *Rashômon*, Italy's *The Bicycle Thief*, and France's *Grand Illusion*). Also on the show's plus side were the inventive Caesar-Coca pantomimes, and the airport interviews with Carl Reiner as the roving reporter and Caesar as the buffoonish foreign professor.

During 1953–1954, Liebman exerted his authority over his beloved showcase by expanding the number and length of each episode's musical segments. He granted more air time for such guest talent as Nat "King" Cole and Lily Pons and allowed Coca more opportunities to headline song-and-dance production numbers. However, TV critics had grown increasingly negative toward this once highly lauded vehicle. For example, the *Washington Post*'s reviewer noted that the series' opening episode was "considerably uneven, ranging from excellent to pedestrian." *Variety*, once a great champion of the august program, complained, "The show is losing its peculiar distinctiveness and falling into the category of vaudeo [i.e., TV vaudeville]."

Of even more concern to NBC decision makers was the fact that as more geographic areas of the United States (especially the hinterlands) gained access to television reception, a greater portion of home viewers were unsophisticated, compared to the early 1950s when the bulk of TV stations broadcast only to large urban markets. Those changing demographics meant that many of the high-culture ingredients of *Your Show of Shows* were alien to an increasingly larger percentage of TV watchers. Many home viewers had never seen a foreign movie (the springboard for many of the show's spoofs) or cared little about opera and ballet, and were therefore not much interested in much of the fare provided on Liebman's show.

In February 1954, it was rumored that *Your Show of Shows* would not return for the following season. By May of that year, it was official: *Your Show of Shows* would end its run, and each of its three big talents (Caesar, Coca, and Liebman) would thereafter undertake separate projects for the NBC network. On June 5, 1954, the cast presented its 160th and final live broadcast of the landmark show that had become an acclaimed TV institution (and, later, would be credited with being the springboard for such future seminal television programs as *Saturday Night Live*).

As plans for the upcoming TV season began to be formulated, it was announced that Caesar, with a newly signed 10-year contract with NBC-TV that contained a $100,000 yearly minimum guarantee, would head-line his own series. Liebman would produce a series of color "spectacular" musical specials for the network. As for Imogene, the most upset of the three about ending the trio's years of collaboration, she was undecided as to just how she might fulfill her recently negotiated 10-year NBC pact.

In the wake of the demise of *Your Show of Shows*, the program's sub-ordinate talent was divvied up largely between the Caesar and Coca proj-ects. Writers Mel Tolkin and Tony Webster and actors Carl Reiner and Howard Morris were set to work on Sid's forthcoming new small-screen venture. Lucille Kallen chose to take time off to be with her family but agreed that she would be on tap to assist Coca in shaping a fresh TV showcase. As for Mel Brooks, he made a daring choice by announcing that he intended to explore his options and refused offers to join either camp. (It went without saying that there was no place for Brooks on Lieb-man's upcoming projects.)

There was some discussion of Brooks being in charge of writing a new TV show, but that did not come to pass. He seemed unfazed about all this, as he had grand visions of using his newfound freedom to become a Broadway playwright. However, he quickly discovered that after years of being part of a close-knit team of comedy writers, he lacked the requisite discipline or the inclination to work on his own—at least at this juncture. Weeks passed and he had to tap into his savings from the *Your Show of Shows* years so that he and Florence could maintain their Manhattan lifestyle.

• • •

Sid Caesar's new small-screen offering, *Caesar's Hour,* debuted on Fri-day, September 27, 1954, broadcasting live from Manhattan's Century Theater. The program received a generally warm welcome (more so for Caesar's return to the medium than for his current vehicle). Within his 60-minute showcase he chose to do a book show, using an extended sketch format to fill most of his hour on the air. The program eschewed those ingredients (such as classical music, opera, and song-and-dance production numbers) that had been so beloved by Max Liebman. On the series' premiere, the Italian movie actress Gina Lollobrigida displayed her sexpot charms as Sid's leading lady. The script was by head writer Mel Tolkin and his team (Tony Webster, Joe Stein, and Aaron Ruben), with, of course, the unofficial collaboration of Caesar and suggestions provided by Carl Reiner and Howard Morris.

A few days thereafter, on Saturday, October 2, 1954, Coca bowed in *The Imogene Coca Show*, a half-hour offering that seemed a rudderless shamble. *Variety* reported that there was "something frantic and almost desperate about the new so-called 'situation comedy,' which marks the premiere of Miss Coca as a TV star in her own right." The misguided project suffered from its star not having the oversized personality, ego, or inclination to grab control of her own show and give it much-needed focus and direction. Instead, she had fallen prey to network and agency executives who had tried, unsuccessfully, to thrust her into a format and persona that did not suit her admirable, unique talents. As a result, the series opener, written by Lucille Kallen, Max Wilk, and Ernest Kinoy, was a big disappointment to critics and home viewers alike.

Two additional writers (Hal Goodman and Larry Klein) were brought in to give Imogene's struggling property a new slant. After two weeks, the new scribes admitted defeat and left. At this chaotic juncture, the William Morris Agency (which had packaged the failing property), brought in yet another writer: Mel Brooks. He was already a big Coca fan and was very familiar with both her strong and weak points. Another impetus for Brooks was the healthy salary he was given for coming to his friend's rescue.

Unfortunately, things got off to a bad start for Mel on this assignment. With neither the strong-willed Caesar nor the well-disciplined Mel Tolkin to harness Brooks's unrestrained energy, Mel charged into the proceedings like a veritable loose cannon. While this was occurring, increasingly desperate network bigwigs ordained that Imogene's inauspicious showcase should switch its format. Thus, two weeks after the property's premiere, cast members Billy DeWolfe and Ruth Donnelly were let go. The sitcom was converted into a half-hour comedy/variety show, complete with production numbers, sketches, and guest stars. This changeover was not well received by audiences, and Coca's ill-fated show altered its setup again in February 1955—reverting to being a traditional sitcom. Now

Coca was presented as a newlywed (her spouse was played by Hal March) and the "amusing" misadventures they experienced with their neighbors (portrayed by Bibi Osterwald and David Burns).

Meanwhile, Mel's presence on Coca's writing squad had proved to be problematic. He was supposed to be the much-needed catalyst to push the failing program in a more satisfying direction. Instead, the boisterous, aggressive, and often undisciplined newcomer created dissension in the writers' room. Even worse, he failed to provide the hoped-for salvation for this sinking entity. Brooks seemed preoccupied with running to and fro at rehearsals, offering the cast and the director a rash of what proved to be unusable suggestions One of the show's creative team assessed the situation by saying Mel was "substituting energy and noise for any ideas."

When Brooks attended the show conferences in the writers' room, he was often overbearing and frequently tried to steamroll his ideas past the other participants. For those who had not worked with Mel before, the experience of dealing with this disorderly whirlwind force was unsettling. For Lucille Kallen, the show's head writer, Brooks's all-too-familiar gambit of being the juvenile show-off and a wild man was a time waster, especially when one was fighting to save a sinking project. It led to an inevitable flare-up between the already frazzled Lucille and the stubborn Mel.

At one of the writers' meetings, the dogmatic and overassertive Brooks— unwilling or unable to analyze the show's overall problems and make concrete suggestions about how to alter course—instead put forth for consideration one of his typical zany, off-the-wall jokes. On its own it was amusing. However, in the context of the sitcom it had no relevance. This led to a clash of wills between Lucille and Mel.

> Kallen: "That's very funny, Mel, but we can't use it."
> Brooks: "Don't you tell me what's funny, you just type."

This condescending remark angered Lucille so deeply that she could not even respond to her adversary. Instead, she rushed off to find the show's producer. After she recapped the distressing situation, she gave her boss an ultimatum regarding Mel: "It's come down to a point where it's either him or the rest of us." Eventually, a truce was reached between the opposing writing camps. It was decreed that Kallen and her squad should work together, while the disruptive Brooks would operate on his own. Each faction would exchange material but *only* in writing.

This splintered manner of script creation only furthered the chaos on *The Imogene Coca Show*. By June 25, 1955, the misfire had gone off the air. Nonetheless, the network had not lost faith in Coca's fey talents and set about fashioning a new vehicle for her—one that would *not* include the services of Mr. Brooks.

• • •

While Mel Brooks had been running amok on Imogene Coca's ill-advised program, Sid Caesar had been undergoing his own baptism under fire as the producer and star of *Caesar's Hour*, as well as an unofficial writer. By early 1955, his show had begun to dip seriously in the ratings. To counter the slide, Caesar abandoned the show's book format in favor of making it a comedy/variety outing. (Unlike *Your Show of Shows*, the sketches were the key ingredient of Sid's show, with the musical production numbers taking a distinct second position.)

While the delicious on-camera chemistry that Caesar had enjoyed with Imogene Coca would be hard to match, he found a viable substitute in Nanette Fabray. Fabray was a veteran of films and several Broadway musicals. Previously, she had appeared as a guest on *Your Show of Shows* (at a time when she was married to David Tebet, an NBC publicist turned network executive). When Nanette accepted the offer to be Sid's leading lady, she was just recovering from a nervous breakdown, triggered by learning that her persistent ear ailments might, one day, lead to permanent deafness. (Eventually, her condition was fully corrected through surgery.)

Just as Mel had missed the comforting familiarity and professional safety net of working for his alter ego and friend, so Caesar had missed both the zaniness and loyalty of his longtime comrade. The two parties bridged the delicate gap caused by Brooks's "defection" to the Coca camp, and Mel was contracted to return to Caesar's writing team. The arrangement allowed Mel to get back to work in an environment in which he knew he could function well. However, because Brooks was such a complex individual, his relief and gratefulness at returning to Sid's fold was mixed with an underlying, suppressed resentment over the fact that, once again, he had to be in his friend's orbit. At least he would now be assured of a steady paycheck, he hoped for a long time to come.

• • •

On September 26, 1955, *Caesar's Hour* launched its second year of broadcast. One of the opener's highlights was a new installment of "The Commuters," the domestic skit that paralleled "The Hickenloopers" routines from *Your Show of Shows*. This recurring husband-and-wife sketch allowed both Sid and Nanette to shine, and the story line provided sufficient small-screen time for Carl Reiner and Howard Morris as friends of the couple. The evening's other playlet was a satire on gangster movies, which interweaved club-style musical numbers into the proceedings.

For Caesar's new season, the writers' room (based in Sid's headquarters at the Milgrim building on West 57th Street near Fifth Avenue) was home to Mel Tolkin, Larry Gelbart, Sheldon Keller, Mel Brooks, and the group's lone female, comedian/writer Selma Diamond. With no Max Liebman in control and Caesar's production company signing everyone's paychecks, Sid ran the writers' room far more autocratically than before. (Appreciating their subservient position, the staff presented the star with a gold, throne-style chair in which Sid could hold forth royally while his writers sweated to put together that week's sketches.)

Typically, the writers congregated daily in their small office by about 10 A.M. Their plan was to get their creative juices rolling before Caesar arrived on the scene. As before, Brooks, the frequent insomniac, was always late. (It should be noted that his delayed appearance allowed him to stand out from the other writers, and it also served to postpone the moment when he would be under pressure to compete with his peers to please boss man Caesar.) Typically, Mel signaled his tardy arrival by having a bagel and coffee delivered to the smoke-filled writers' room. The snack would arrive well in advance of Mel's belated entrance. One day, Sid decided to teach Mel a lesson for being especially late. When Brooks walked through the writers' room door, Caesar signaled him to approach his throne chair. The boss quietly informed his persistently late staffer that he had already tipped the delivery boy for bringing Brooks's breakfast. Mel thanked Sid and handed him some change, thinking that would cover the cost of the order plus a very small tip. Not enough, said Caesar. Sid explained that he had given the boy $20 for the delivery. A disgruntled Brooks begrudgingly paid the difference. For a while thereafter, he was more conscientious about being on time to the office. However, he soon fell back into his old ways.

Usually, when Caesar strolled into the writers' room—always dressed in a neatly pressed suit, one with wide shoulders—he would be puffing on a big fat cigar. Typically, his first words to the staffers were "Show me the brilliance." This led the apprehensive writers to scramble madly into position to present their latest joke or suggestion for a new skit. Once Sid was seated on his throne chair (and often stripped down to his underwear so he wouldn't wrinkle his expensive suit), Caesar would glance over to ensure that Michael Stewart, the newcomer hired to type notes of these meetings, was poised at the typewriter (as Lucille Kallen had been in *Your Show of Shows* days). Stewart's unenviable task was to consolidate the wild chattering in the room into a semblance of written order. Thankfully, young Michael got some direction from the mighty Sid.

As the jokester gang shot forth ideas—aided and abetted by the show's second and third bananas (Carl Reiner and Howie Morris)—Caesar listened in rapt attention to the cacophony of noise. If he liked an idea one of the writers was shouting out, he signaled by nodding or by pointing a finger in Stewart's direction that he should take down this bit of comedic genius. If a joke displeased Caesar, he might shake his head. If he found the offered brilliance too far off the mark, he would adopt his posture as a gunner, shooting down the bad joke from the sky. (In the process, Sid provided the rat-a-tat sound effects of the machine gun blasting away at the offensive offering.)

Mel Brooks recalled (nostalgically) of those madcap, raucous sessions in the cigar smoke–filled writers' room (where a spread of food and candy was set out daily by Sid's brother, Dave), "We all thought alike. We all came from basically the same background, the second-generation Russian-Ukrainian-Jewish intellectual heritage." Of writing for, and with, the great Caesar, Brooks noted, "Sid was a natural philosopher. He very quickly passed the verbiage of intellectuality. We never dealt in polysyllabics. We talked. 'Why were we born? Why are we here?' Then we could write good material and we could portray characters that we knew very clearly. But without wit. We never adored wit." As to what were allowable topics for their comedy, Mel offered years later, "Whatever made us laugh was the only test of what would go into the hopper. I feel that the audience is always ready to absorb anything you have in your mind. They don't reject it based on their own sense of values." (One subject that was off limits on both *Your Show of Shows* and *Caesar's Hour* was topical politics. In the 1950s era of conformity and cold war paranoia, most TV shows had the same policy.)

Mel Tolkin had his own assessment of how this highly talented, frequently changing contingent of diverse personalities operated on *Your Show of Shows* and *Caesar's Hour*. "There was always, among the writers, a combination of competitiveness and anger, and an immense need to be loved by Max Liebman and Sid." The head writer pointed out, "There is a lot of anger behind comedy. There was so much violence, so much comedy in that room. A lot of jokes about death and murder, dirty language, quarrels, conflict, a lot of yelling. Sid punched the wall so much it was bent. You'd take a drink from a paper cup from the water cooler and the cups would be squeezed and thrown around. We'd throw pencils so they stuck in the acoustical ceiling. It was all creative anger, terrible competitiveness, trying to please Daddy. Sid of course was Daddy. And don't forget, we were asked not to be merely good but to be brilliant." In Tolkin's estimation, "To entertain is a search for love. Applause is a kiss, silence is a knife in the back. The comedian has to ask himself, or herself, 'How much love does the world want? How much do I have to prove?'"

Carl Reiner, who went on to produce, direct, and write TV sitcoms and feature films, was once asked how the writing squad at *Caesar's Hour* and the earlier *Your Show of Shows* could be funny at a given time within the nine-to-five workday. The second banana responded, "The answer lies in the nature of the comic beast. Professional comedy writers and performers will be funny wherever and whenever they are brought together. They are programmed to produce laughter, and when there is a job at stake, a professional reputation involved, and a wife or husband to be told on Saturday night, 'That's my joke,' the comedic motor quickly turns over. . . . All comedians are writers. Some are talking writers; others are writers who work for performers. The pros among them could no more turn off their fun-loving mechanism than a certified public accountant could suspend his knowledge of the multiplication tables."

As to the particular creative contributions of the perpetually tardy Brooks, Reiner recalled, "When Mel came to work a sketch would often be half written. He'd come in angry, and he'd listen to us and he'd say, 'All shit.' And he would start to try to destroy things that were written. Well, because Mel is really one of the funniest human beings in the world, he was able very often to improve on the jokes that were already written. He had to prove he could come in late and contribute at least his share or more. Mel coming in at one [P.M.] was a better commodity to have than a bum who came in early."

• • •

During these years, Brooks spent far more time with his collaborators at *Caesar's Hour* than he did with Florence, his wife. The day's work and shenanigans often spilled over into the evening, ending up with drinks and dinner with Sid after they had quit for the day or before heading back to the offices to repair an unsatisfactory sketch. (Sometimes the food/alcohol breaks were at Danny's Hideaway or at Lindy's restaurant.)

As at the office, the writing crew and the others in attendance had to deal with the vagaries of Caesar, who in recent years had become even more addicted to pills and booze. On one famous occasion, the group was seated around the dinner table, having just placed their orders. This evening, a particularly exhausted Sid was no match for the array of self-medication he had consumed that day. Suddenly, he fell over face forward, landing in a dish of coleslaw. The gang knew better than to arouse the volatile Sid from his stupor. Instead, for the next 40 minutes they played a variety of charades to disguise from the restaurant's patrons and staff that the mighty Caesar was unconscious. They performed ad-libbed routines and bits of business—such as "Let us all bend our heads down and pray"—waiting for Sid to eventually revive. He finally did so and continued on with his previous discussion, totally unaware that he had blacked out.

Not only were the demands and competition of work enough to keep Mel away from his home, but he also still felt ill at ease playing the role of husband. He was not sure what was truly expected of him and what he should require of Florence. In those first years they rarely ate at home. He preferred to be out and about in public surroundings. These settings avoided awkward domestic silences and gave him fresh locations and new audiences in which to be "on" and go into one of his nutty routines, which provided him with the attention he craved. (That these bouts of zaniness might be embarrassing to Florence or others caught in the situation never seemed to faze Brooks.)

Frequently, Brooks and his wife joined Sid and Carl and their wives for dinners, to see foreign movies (which was good fodder for their TV work), or to attend art exhibits. In the summer, Mel and Florence often visited Carl and Estelle Reiner at their Fire Island retreat and fell in love with the vacation spot, which had such a relaxed tempo and was populated with members of the show business crowd. Sometimes, the Brookses attended industry functions together. As always, no one knew what to expect from the attention-seeking Mel, who marched to his own beat.

There was the time (March 16, 1957) at the Colonial Theater when key talent of *Caesar's Hour* assembled for the Emmy Awards presentation, which was being televised by NBC. Sid Caesar, Nanette Fabray, Carl Reiner, and new cast regular Pat Carroll had won Emmy Awards for their work on *Caesar's Hour*. Sid's writing team was nominated in the Comedy Writing category. That year they were convinced they'd win the coveted prize. However, the victors proved to be Nat Hiken and his writing staff from *The Phil Silvers Show*. While the others from *Caesar's Hour* politely applauded their rivals' triumph, Mel could not contain his anger at this cruel slight. He jumped up on the dinner table and began ranting loudly, "Nietzsche was right! There is no God! There is no God!" Brooks's outrage did not abate on the taxi ride home with his wife. He asked Florence to borrow the manicure scissors she carried in her purse, and he began shredding his expensive tuxedo.

When they were first married, the Brookses lived in a walk-up apartment building on Manhattan's West 68th Street. Later, they moved to 33 West 70th Street, then to an apartment at 1056 Fifth Avenue, and then on to 125 East 72nd Street. Many of these relocations reflected Mel's escalating income as well as the salaries Florence earned as a dancer. Then they started a family (which led to Florence's abandoning her show business career) and required more room. The couple's first child, Stefanie, was born at New York's Lying-in Hospital on February 21, 1956. Their second child, Nicholas, "Nicky"—named after the Russian writer Nikolai Gogol—was born on December 12, 1957. Their third child, Edward, would be born on May 24, 1959.

Meanwhile, in the spring of 1957, unthinkable news spread about the *Caesar's Hour* headquarters. NBC was thinking of canceling the show, *unless* the increasingly intractable star would listen to (their) reasonings.

Mel Brooks and the others involved with *Caesar's Hour* all wondered the same thing: "What now?" For many of the troupe, such as Brooks, who had family responsibilities, the thought of suddenly being jobless was particularly frightening—especially if, like Mel, one did not have a large nest egg tucked away safely. Brooks wondered if he would ever find financial security in the roller-coaster ways of his chosen profession.

15

Unraveling

There were two me's. There was a glib, slick conscious me and a deep, brooding, disturbed unconscious me without a voice.

—Mel Brooks, 1996

When the American commercial TV industry was in its infancy in the late 1940s, it occurred to very few people that a popular personality who appeared on the airwaves too frequently could actually wear out his welcome with home viewers. Yet such a seeming impossibility did happen to Milton Berle with his weekly variety series, which ended its run in June 1956. He had been on the airwaves constantly since 1948 and, in the process, had become old hat to home viewers, who became enthusiastic fans of new programming.

Sid Caesar suffered the same ignoble career fate as "Uncle Miltie," an unfortunate situation exacerbated by other issues. For one thing, at the end of the 1955–1956 season, his weekly program lost the valuable services of Nanette Fabray who recently had requested a substantial pay raise. Rather than meet her financial demands, Caesar chose to go with a new leading lady. The assignment went to song-and-dance movie actress Janet Blair, a pleasant but bland talent who had once appeared with Sid on the big screen (in 1946's *Tars and Spars*). Sadly, the give-and-take between Caesar and Blair in front of the cameras proved to be less than inspired, and that had sorely damaged the show's energy level. Another debilitating factor in the 1956–1957 season was that NBC had switched *Caesar's Hour* from its Monday-night berth to Saturday evening in the nine to ten time slot. Now the program had to compete with the already very popular *The Lawrence Welk Show* on ABC-TV. As the year progressed, bandleader Welk and his Champagne Music captured an increasingly bigger chunk of the Saturday night audience ratings. Meanwhile, the overhead at Caesar's weekly hour kept escalating and now had reached more than $225,000 per episode.

NBC tried to reason with Caesar that he must adapt his offering to meet TV audiences' fickle interests, and especially find some way to freshen the program's overly familiar format. Caesar did not take kindly to such suggestions from on high. He believed he was too potent a force for the network to contend with, especially since he possessed a long-term NBC contract. Caught up in his hubris, Sid ignored management's insistence that he trim the show permanently into a half-hour presentation. As an alternative, it was recommended that *Caesar's Hour* be repositioned in the 1957–1958 season to an every other week or every few weeks schedule (or better yet, have Sid concentrate on a succession of occasional specials). When Caesar (struggling with his swelling substance abuse) continued to balk at the options put forth on the bargaining table, NBC took unilateral action: the network canceled his show, and it went off the air on May 25, 1957.

• • •

During Sid Caesar's fall from TV grace, Mel Brooks realized anew that, somehow, he must expand his show business work options so he would not be fully tied to Sid's purse strings. Thus, he readily accepted an offer to help smooth out the book (i.e., the story line and dialogue) of an upcoming Broadway show, *Shinbone Alley*.

The property was based on the late Don Marquis's well-liked tales about archy (a cynical cockroach) and mehitabel (a randy alley cat). In 1953, composer George Kleinsinger and lyricist Joe Darion (who went on to write the lyrics to the huge Broadway hit *Man of La Mancha*) adapted the popular stories for an album. The Columbia Records release featured narration by David Wayne, with vocals by Eddie Bracken and Carol Channing. This, in turn, led to a December 6, 1954, concert presentation of the adaptation at Manhattan's Town Hall by Thomas Sherman and the Little Orchestra Society. Among those who attended that Monday evening performance was stage producer Peter Lawrence. He was intrigued by the concert's subject matter and acquired an option on the offbeat property. He believed that the material could be turned into a captivating musical. In the coming months, Lawrence raised $220,000 to fund the Broadway-bound venture, which was first known as *Back Alley Opera* and then was retitled *Shinbone Alley*.

Initially, filmmaker/actor Orson Welles was touted as likely to direct the vehicle, which was to costar Eartha Kitt and Eddie Bracken (with Chita Rivera and Tom Poston assigned as understudies). But Welles dropped out of the enterprise, and actor/director Norman Lloyd took over. When Joe Darion (responsible for both the show's libretto and the song lyrics) was unable to resolve the script's plot-heavy second act, Brooks was hired to work out the kinks in the story line.

Shinbone Alley was scheduled to open on April 13, 1957, at the Broadway Theater, without benefit of an out-of-town tryout. A week before it was to bow, Norman Lloyd left the project, telling the *New York Times* that he was departing because of "a great difference of opinion regarding the approach to the show" between him, producer Peter Lawrence, and the writers. Thereafter, Peter Lawrence unofficially took over the directing chores on the troubled production (which featured the fine choreography of Jacques D'Amboise, Allegra Kent, and a sturdy ensemble).

Shinbone Alley managed to open on schedule, but the critics were not impressed—especially by the quality of the show's book. Brooks Atkinson (of the *New York Times*) wrote, "Not much of the humorous comment on human nature is left in the libretto of *Shinbone Alley*. A librettist would have to be the equivalent of Don Marquis to bring it into the theatre. What Mr. Darion and Mr. Brooks have done on their own account is not a satisfactory substitute. Taking the line of least resistance on the musical stage, they have portrayed archy as being in love with mehitabel . . . this is hard to accept. A cat and a cockroach do not make attractive lovers." The other New York critics were in agreement. Tom Donnelly (of the *New York World-Telegram* and *The Sun*) missed the presence of "a coherent narrative," while John McClain (of the *New York Journal-American*) pointed out that there were "long lapses when the story falters." One of the few champions of the book was Robert Coleman (of the *New York Mirror*), who thought the coauthors had done an "amazing job in adapting the esoteric essays of Don Marquis." Most of the reviewers devoted their attention to praising the talents of the captivating Eartha Kitt.

Shinbone Alley closed after a meager 49-performance run. Looking back, Brooks analyzed, "It should have been at a little off-Broadway theater," but instead it opened at a big venue and "was lost on that stage." (In 1970, the property was adapted into *archy and mehitabel*, a two-hour PBS-TV special headlining Tammy Grimes and Eddie Bracken. The next year, the stage vehicle became an animated cartoon feature released by Allied Artists Pictures. The low-budget entry utilized the voices of Carol Channing, Eddie Bracken, John Carradine, and others. It quickly came and left theatrical distribution.)

The show's failure, and Mel's association with the misguided production, exacerbated Brooks's growing doubts about the viability of his show business future. It was hard for him not to become panic-stricken. Brooks's usual optimism was sorely tested by this professional failure.

• • •

With Sid Caesar off the air and *Shinbone Alley* a flop, Mel Brooks had to really scramble for new work in the summer of 1957. Grabbing at proverbial straws, he signed on as a producer/writer for *The Polly Bergen Show*, which debuted on NBC-TV on September 21, 1957. One of the other writers on this 30-minute musical variety series for the singer/actor was Michael Stewart, another *Caesar's Hour* veteran.

Once Brooks was aboard this modest new show, he was approached by his friend Lee Adams, a lyricist and writer. Adams was then unemployed, and Brooks—in a mood of largesse since he was now ensconced in a new industry job—suggested that Adams work for free on the new show in the capacity of an assistant writer. Mel explained that this would undoubtedly lead to Lee's being placed on staff at a likely $100 weekly salary. (It is also likely that Brooks decided it would make good sense to have loyal friends aboard the project.) Adams followed through with his benefactor's proposition, and Brooks liked the ideas Stewart presented. The newcomer happily anticipated soon becoming a paid part of the team, a transition he hoped would occur at the upcoming Friday staff meeting.

That day Adams waited for Brooks to emerge from the conference. When Mel did, he looked exceedingly glum. Lee quickly grasped the situation and said to his pal, "Look, you tried. I really appreciate it, Mel. Maybe sometime . . ." Brooks waved his hands and said, "You don't know what happened." Lee replied, "Sure I do. You pitched me for the job and they said no." Mel shook his head and said with a sardonic grin, "Not exactly. Before I got to that, I was fired."

• • •

While Brooks was dealing with a rash of show business defeats, Sid Caesar was contemplating his own uncertain professional future. Not being an active part of the television scene was anathema to the toppled comedy king, and he pondered his next career step. His solution was to approach Imogene Coca (then completing a summer stage tour of the comedy *Janus*) and suggest they reunite on air. She loved the idea, and soon Sid's representatives were approaching the various networks for a production deal. NBC and CBS passed on the idea, but the less prestigious ABC offered the duo a half-hour weekly program to begin in early 1958. Caesar swallowed his pride at being forced to accept a 30-minute time slot (which he felt was far too short in which to properly present sketches). Coca followed suit and also signed for the new series.

Sid quickly assembled a writing staff drawn from the ranks of his past creative teams—all of whom were anxious to re-create the magic of *Your Show of Shows* and, equally important, to keep afloat in the increasingly perilous waters of show business. The hired scribes were Mel Tolkin, Neil Simon, Mel Brooks, Mike Stewart, and Danny Simon (plus Larry Gelbart for the opening episode). It seemed like old times (especially with Carl Reiner aboard as the program's second banana). Helena Rubinstein Cosmetics agreed to sponsor the relatively well-budgeted offering, which bowed on January 26, 1958. The media hyped the premiere as the "major comeback" of these two small-screen legends. *Variety* reported, "Even though the opening show was way off, lacking much of the brilliance and wit of some previous excursions, it wasn't too important to a Caesar-Coca fan."

Initially, the program did sufficiently well in the audience ratings, buoyed by curious viewers who wished to share in the nostalgia of Sid and Imogene working together again. However, the reunion soon lost its novelty to home audiences, and the series fell prey in the rating wars to its competitors in the Sunday 9 P.M. time slot: CBS's *General Electric Theater* (an anthology drama showcase) and NBC's *The Dinah Shore Show* (a musical/variety entry). As a result, *Sid Caesar Invites You* went off the air on May 25, 1958, after a mere four-month run.

At this juncture, the British Broadcasting Corporation (BBC) network approached Caesar and Coca and lured them to London to repeat much of their material from *Sid Caesar Invites You* for home viewers in the United Kingdom. The new edition of *Sid Caesar Invites You* debuted abroad on July 23, 1958. As had happened back in the United States, initial good ratings quickly tapered off, and the half-hour program departed the BBC lineup that September after only a 13-program run.

It was now clear to most everyone—except to the substance-abusing Sid Caesar, who vainly remained in denial—that his reign as a major prime-time TV star was over.

• • •

Distressing as it was for Mel Brooks to watch the gifted Sid Caesar thrust aside by the TV industry and the viewing public, Brooks was preoccupied with his own mounting number of career crises. For over a decade he had allowed his show business ambitions to be funneled through the talented Caesar, his great protector and pal. While Brooks had gained many benefits from his professional and personal association with the gifted Caesar, it had also stymied his growth as an entertainment talent.

Now Mel was cut loose from his regular work ties to Sid and had the scary task of largely fending for himself. True, there were occasional TV network specials that Caesar undertook in 1959 and 1960 for which Brooks and Mel Tolkin teamed with Sydney Zelenka to write the sketches. For a few of these small-screen offerings in the late 1950s, a young Woody Allen was brought aboard as a junior member of Caesar's writing staff. Years later, this gave rise to a widespread misconception that Allen had been part of the stellar writing crew that had contributed so admirably to Sid's *Your Show of Shows* and *Caesar's Hour*.

Moreover, the brief collaboration of Brooks and Allen with others on Caesar's specials gave the media a convenient springboard to compare and contrast the success and talent of these two men. It reached a point at which, seemingly, neither individual could be judged on his own merits. Rather, the press—and increasingly the public—assumed that both writers were creatively linked beyond the facts that both were Jewish, grew up in Brooklyn, boasted the outsider's comedic slant on life, and had worked for Sid Caesar. By the late 1970s, Mel had grown weary of the endless comparisons being made between him and Woody. It prompted

Brooks to make his own statement about the so-called similarities between him and his "counterpart." Said a peevish Mel, "He [Woody Allen]
feels that his art is his life. And more power to him. The difference is that
if someone wants to call my movies art or crap, I don't mind."

• • •

During this transitional career period, Brooks's income, which had risen
to nearly $5,000 a week on *Caesar's Hour*, had tumbled precipitously.
This abrupt economic free fall—and the accompanying negative effect
on his self-confidence—played havoc with Mel's already shaky marriage.
Temperamentally ill-prepared for being a husband, the still emotionally
immature Mel had even less understanding of how to be a model parent
to his three young children.

The escalating domestic stress in this difficult period led Mel and
Florence to undergo several trial separations. Then the unhappy couple
split on a more permanent basis. By now Mel could no longer afford his
expensive therapy sessions, and he felt truly alone in the world. As various aspects of his life seemed to be falling apart, he tried to mask his
growing panic by being more of a bon vivant and zany nut. His desperate masquerade may have fooled some people, but in moments of self-
honesty, he knew his fluctuating run of luck had finally petered out. Try
as he might to ignore facing the reality of his depressing situation, years
of therapy had made avoidance of self-examination less and less viable.
During these recurrent somber periods of self-reflection, personal insight
made clear the stark truth that he could no longer depend on others to
kick-start his flagging career or to reorder his muddled personal life. The
only person who could redeem Brooks was Mel himself.

16

A Wacky Man for the Millenniums

More than anybody, it was Sid [Caesar]. He was from another planet. I am the funniest man America has ever produced and I wasn't a comic. I wouldn't go onstage for nine years, because there was a greater talent out there, an outlet that satisfied me and my talent for writing. When he left he almost *forced* me on stage. The amount that was demanded of Sid . . . I don' t know why it didn't kill him.

—Mel Brooks, 1982

Often, in the entertainment industry—as in other arenas—successful ventures are the result of a sequence of fortuitous events. Naturally, without a solid foundation of creativity, individual chance incidents might never lead to a great artistic and/or commercial triumph.

• • •

During the 1948–1949 run of the Broadway revue *Inside U.S.A*, actor Carl Reiner shared a dressing room with fellow cast member Louis Nye. Reiner described, "To entertain ourselves, I used to play the part of an interviewer, asking questions and breaking up over the brilliant answers he came up with. I am by nature an interviewer, an aural learner. Whenever I hear somebody say something funny or informative, I immediately start asking questions to get more laughs or more information. It started as a comedy routine when Louis and I were in the Army and did a bit built around the rolling of a field pack."

By 1951, the versatile Carl Reiner was a regular on *Your Show of Shows* and had become friendly with Mel Brooks, who had recently bull-dozed his way into becoming an official member of the program's writing staff. Both of these Jewish men came from humble backgrounds and both adored the world of show business. They also shared an antic sense of humor that could veer into the raunchy, a thirst for knowledge on a wide range of topics, and, most of all, an unquenchable inner urge to always be "on." With this voracious craving to be in the limelight, they thrived on entertaining others—as well as themselves—whether at work, a business meal, or a social function.

Carl's innate curiosity and his knack for improvisation made him admirably suited to play the inquisitive roving reporter on "The Professor" sketches performed on *Your Show of Shows*. In these memorable routines he volleyed questions at the bumbling expert (performed by Sid Caesar), typically a pompous eccentric from abroad. It was Brooks who provided much of the material for these classic TV question-and-answer comedy skits.

One day, Reiner, a regular attendee at the writers' meetings, stormed into the smoke-filled think tank headquarters. He was deeply perturbed. The night before he'd seen an episode of a news-style TV program which utilized re-creations of important world events and the key people in-volved to provide viewers with a sense of "being there." This particular segment dealt with the escalating cold war and had the host overhearing in a bathroom Russian leader Joseph Stalin predicting the likelihood of a nuclear war between the East and West. Carl was enraged at such irre-sponsible TV journalism. In his fuming state, he suddenly turned to Mel, who was seated nearby. Reiner thrust an imaginary microphone in Brooks's direction. Out of nowhere, Carl inquired of Mel, "I understand you were at the Crucifixion?"

Caught off guard, Brooks thought for a few split seconds, then launched into a humorous reply as if he were a nearly 2,000-year-old man. "Christ," he responded, "was a thin lad, always wore sandals. Hung around with 12 other guys." The others in the writers' room were amused. The favorable response to the verbal give-and-take gambit led to repeats of the routine, usually featuring new questions and fresh answers. Soon the team was doing their shtick for friends at parties. (Occasionally, when

Reiner was unavailable, Brooks would do the "act" with Mel Tolkin, the head writer of *Your Show of Shows*, substituting. Once in a while, Brooks would even venture to do a solo performance. According to Tolkin, one evening at a gathering when Reiner was not there, Brooks did a monologue, but could not come up with a good payoff line to finish his routine. He finally broke off in midsentence and walked out of the room. The guests waited, but Brooks failed to reappear. Tolkin went in search of him. It developed that Brooks had departed the scene in self-disgust. He had left a scribbled note on a table, "A Jew cries for help!")

In his performance guise, Mel's Methuselah-like alter ego came across as an all-knowing—albeit eccentric—elderly sage who had observed literally everything in the continuum of world history (including the time cavemen first discovered that they were different from women). Over many centuries, this "wise" person had encountered nearly every famous person known to mankind, including Joan of Arc (once his girlfriend) and the legendary Robin Hood, who "stole from everybody and kept everything." This self-impressed old soul was eager to share his colorful opinions on what's what in the world, from the start of time to the present day . . . and beyond. He gladly offered his (amusing) thoughts to the roving reporter on how music first developed, and excitedly expounded on the many delights of nectarines: "Half a peach, half a plum. It's a hell of a fruit!"

From the start, Mel employed a rather heavy Jewish accent for his eccentric, funny old man. He said later that he had based the opinionated but lovable character on his uncle Sol, the type of man who asked, "Why do we need these big, six-story buildings? God never intended people to live so far from the street. Why do we have to be above two floors from the street?" . . . According to Brooks, Sol "was crazy, he was wild. I loved his energy. The 2000 Year Old Man is a purveyor of these same large truths—I don't wanna call them lies. He mocks the things that we all are to become, just as I see my kids making fun of me and my ways. But someday they're gonna end up with their own kids mocking them. . . . I never forgot his voice. That sound meant a great deal to me—safety, protection, strength, that loud, vigorous voice with the Jewish accent. When I redid it, when I listened to the tapes the first time, it was amazing, it was incredible. I went right back to being 6 years old with my mother's family."

Brooks also acknowledged another reason he gave his character such an ethnic, old-country voice. "It's easier to hide behind accents. Once you're playing a character you have more mobility, more freedom. I suppose it's also cowardice on my part. I can say anything I want, and then if people question me, I say, 'Don't blame me. Blame the old Jew. He's crazy.'" Another time, in 1966, when talking to *Playboy* magazine, Mel told interviewer Larry Siegel of his by-then famous alter ego: "It's not a Jewish accent. It's an *American*-Jewish accent. And in 50 years it will disappear. I think it'll be a great loss." Brooks emphasized, "Unless Jews do Jews accurately, I consider the whole thing to be in questionable taste."

• • •

In 1953, Carl Reiner, always a great enthusiast for new gadgets, purchased a recently marketed Revere audio recorder. Carl began capturing these unrehearsed skits he played out with Brooks. He thought they might be fun to listen to in later years.

Already, Reiner and Brooks were celebrated in their social and business circles for their wacky, off-the-cuff 2000 Year Old Man skits. During their unrehearsed interviews, Carl, the ever curious reporter, often confronted other characters played by Mel. (Brooks's other personae ranged from a newborn baby to a hip musician to a slightly mad accountant.) In Reiner's estimation, these other figures being questioned by the intrepid newsman were more artistically satisfying than the 2000 Year Old Man because the premise of such alternate sketches could expand in so many more fresh creative directions. However, listeners expressed their preference for Mel doing his oddball but lovable old codger.

What appealed to Mel so much about these impromptu performances was that the situation challenged his creativity. He felt like a student who had waited until the last minute to prepare for an important test and suddenly must deliver the goods in an exam. It gave Brooks a tremendous adrenaline rush to respond with crazy logic to the probing questions of his insistent interrogator. It literally made Mel think hard and fast on his feet. If he faltered a bit in answering due to his panic about providing amusing and irreverent responses to Carl's queries and verbal retorts, so be it. It gave their routines an edge and spontaneity that seemed to heighten listeners' pleasure.

Brooks enthused, "I loved how much Carl laughed, and how much I laughed. We loved how much we got hysterical and they [i.e., the audience] got hysterical. It was like spreading joy. Then it became a challenge, to see whether or not I could field anything Carl could throw at me. A cat-and-mouse game . . . [in which] I would dig myself into a hole, and Carl would not let me climb out." Early on in these Q&A sessions, Reiner had discovered it was not an easy task to be a straight man to the nimble-minded Brooks. "As soon as he starts answering, I've got to start thinking about the next question. I'm listening with my third ear so I can give him the follow-up, and I'm looking for the moment where it's needed. You never know when Mel is finished with a thought, because he'll get five jokes on the way to the one that's in his mouth."

• • •

In 1959, Carl Reiner was making his feature film debut in *Happy Anniversary*. In this celluloid comedy, he costarred with David Niven and Mitzi Gaynor. Mel attended the wrap party for the movie's cast and crew, which was held at a Greenwich Village restaurant. At the star-studded gathering were Broadway playwright/director Moss Hart and his singer/TV personality wife, Kitty Carlisle. From across the crowded room Mel recognized the legendary Hart (who was also a veteran of working in the Jewish Catskills). Without giving it more than a second's thought, Brooks maneuvered his way over to Hart's table and stood there frozen until he had gained Moss's full attention. Then the brash interloper said loudly, "Hello. You don't know who I am. My name is Mel Brooks. Do you know who you are? Your name is Moss Hart. Do you know what you've written? . . ." Without waiting for the listener to respond, Brooks recited a list of the other man's many stage credits. Then he shouted, "You should be more arrogant! You have earned the right to be supercilious."

At first, Hart was nonplussed by this apparent lunatic, who was causing a commotion with his ranting. Then Moss's attitude changed. He concluded that Mel was being zany and not just a "nutcase" on the loose. He smiled benevolently at Brooks and the two chatted briefly. Later, at the same party, Brooks and Reiner ad-libbed a skit involving the 2000 Year Old Man and others in their growing repertoire of characters. Hart and the rest of the crowd were amused by the verbal virtuosity of the performing team. This created further word of mouth for the pair. (Also in this same period, Mel and Carl presented their interview act at Danny's Hideaway, a restaurant that catered to show business folk. It gave them further currency with the New York in crowd.)

A few months later, on October 23, 1959, Moss Hart was the subject of a party to celebrate the publication of his memoir, *Act One*. He suggested that Brooks and Reiner be invited to regale the 300 A-list guests with their unique 2000 Year Old Man routine. At the book soirée, held at Mamma Leone's (a famous Italian restaurant on Manhattan's West 48th Street), Mel Brooks and Mel Tolkin (standing in for Carl Reiner, who was fulfilling a work assignment in Los Angeles) provided 14 minutes of mirthful verbal exchanges. The pair was a big hit with the VIP crowd. Kenneth Tynan, the well-known English drama critic, author, and theatrical executive, who years later wrote a lengthy profile of Brooks for *The New Yorker*, said of that memorable evening: "All I knew as I left Mamma Leone's that night was that his [i.e., Mel Tolkin's] stubby, pseudo-Freudian partner [i.e., Mel Brooks] was the most original comic improviser I had ever seen."

By 1960, Carl Reiner was back in southern California to write for Dinah Shore's variety/music TV series. Brooks was again at loose ends in his life and came out to the West Coast to see if he could generate any work assignments. When playwright Joe Fields, a longtime admirer of Mel and Carl's interview act, learned that both men were now in Los Angeles, he hosted a large party in their honor. He made one stipulation: the duo *must* perform their 2000 Year Old Man patter. The guests of honor agreed. Among the notables on hand that night were talk show host/author/songwriter Steve Allen, movie star Edward G. Robinson, and veteran comedian George Burns.

Allen was highly enthusiastic and said the two must seriously consider making a comedy album of the 2000 Year Old Man. While Mel and Carl appreciated the kind thought, they explained that they were concerned that the very ethnic character portrayed in their most popular sketch would not likely appeal to the general public who bought such recordings. Later at the gathering, Burns, a star then in his mid-60s, warned the two performers, "Listen, you better put that on a record, because if you don't, I'll steal it." With such enthusiastic feedback, Brooks and Reiner agreed to allow Allen to use his record industry connections to determine if there was real interest for such an album. Steve even offered to finance the recording session.

According to Reiner, "A few days later, Mel and I walked into a studio at World Pacific Records [in Los Angeles] and ad-libbed for over two hours" [in front of a small invited audience]. The edited results—which deleted occasional digressions, any too-lengthy pauses between answers, and any overly bawdy material—was released in an LP format in late 1960. The album (*2000 Years With Carl Reiner & Mel Brooks*) retailed for $4.98. It slowly gathered momentum through word of mouth from comedy aficionados, who found the album's routines intriguing, irreverent, off-the-wall, smart, and endearing. Soon several talk radio stations around the country began airing cuts from the record, and sales zoomed even higher. Before long, World Pacific could not keep up with orders for the album, and Capitol Records took over distribution of the product. A whopping 1 million copies of the album were sold, making this classic album a huge success—in the same league with the comedy platters of then genre favorites like Bob Newhart, Bill Cosby, and Mike Nichols and Elaine May.

This success could not have come at a better time for Brooks, who was struggling to find his professional self now that he was no longer working full-time as one of Sid Caesar's TV show writers. Said Reiner: "That was a turning point for Mel. . . . It gave him an identity as a performer for the first time." (Writer and cultural analyst Kenneth Tynan assessed of this lucky turn of events for Brooks, "It gave him a comic persona [i.e., the 2000 Year Old Man] that at once embodied and exorcised his own deepest anxieties; for the main point about this jaunty survivor—more than twice as old as Methuselah and still going strong—is that he has conquered death. By playing a character who was immortal, Brooks may have staked his principal claim to immortality as a comedian."

Brooks and Reiner's debut album was nominated for a Grammy Award, and led the team to return to the recording studios on May 26, 1961, to create *2000 and One Years With Carl Reiner & Mel Brooks*. Like their original album, the new one divided its attention between the venerated old man (who was now given more time to rant and ruminate) and several other characters: the nutty tax expert, a newborn baby, a conclave of bizarre psychiatrists, and a man of verse.

Reiner described the making of this follow-up album: "At that second recording we had Brendan Behan, the famous Irish playwright, and Mel didn't know he was there. I'll never forget this. I'd asked Mel, 'Did you have a national anthem?' He said, 'Yeah, every cave had a national anthem'— he didn't know I was going to ask him that, and he sang ['Let them all go to hell, except Cave 17']. . . . And Behan came up after the session and said, 'You know, I've got a new motto now,' and he said something to me in Gaelic. I asked, 'What does that mean?' He'd translated Mel's anthem. Now, that is exactly what flags, what nationalism does. Everybody should go to hell as long as we're OK. That's what I mean—Mel hits the absolute truths."

This Capitol LP was also Grammy nominated and further cemented the comedic reputations of the madcap Brooks and Reiner. However, there were a few critical dissenters to the latest album. For example, Thomas Lask noted in the *New York Times*: "There's a frantic side to Carl Reiner and Mel Brooks's *2000 and One Years*, which tends to overwhelm the material. The wisecracks are sprayed like buckshot, one voice frequently covers the other, studio laughter covers both and there is never a second's respite to savor any of it."

• • •

From the start of the public success of the first 2000 Year Old Man album, Brooks and Reiner began receiving a slew of requests for the duo to perform together on TV. It led to their joint appearances on shows hosted by Steve Allen, Ed Sullivan, and Andy Williams, and later on, the *Hollywood Palace* variety series. On the first such outings, Mel and Carl appeared on camera wearing suits. Thereafter, Steve Allen suggested that Mel don an identifiable outfit. His costume evolved to include a black cape, an impressively large black fedora hat, and a black cane. (Sometimes Brooks wore a white wig to make himself look more aged.) Reiner often sported a reporter's trench coat as he had on *Your Show of Shows* for "The Professor" skits.

While Reiner was used to appearing on TV in an assortment of acting guises, this was a new experience for Mel. He soon grew quite adept at selling himself and his 2000 Year Old Man character to the public. However, neither he nor Carl was happy with the limitations that the television medium placed on their humorous act. First of all, the duo was restricted to a condensed amount of air time and could not afford to ad-lib questions and answers freely for fear that that might not mine gold in their allotted on-camera minutes. Then too, because of still-strong censorship rules controlling TV broadcasting, the team had to carefully avoid saying anything too risqué. To resolve such performance restraints they memorized their routines, and this spoiled (for the performers) the spontaneity of their presentation.

In 1962 came the third album: *Carl Reiner & Mel Brooks at the Cannes Film Festival*. It allowed for the introduction of several colorful showbiz characters (e.g., Frederico Fettucini), as well as a not-so-closeted Nazi type (i.e., Adolph Hartler) and, of course, the 2000 Year Old Man, who was now two years older than when he first reminisced and whined on vinyl.

After that it was not until August 25, 1973, that the duo—preoccupied in other show business arenas—came back again to the recording studios, this time under the aegis of Warner Bros. Records. *Carl Reiner & Mel Brooks: 2000 and Thirteen* was taped on a soundstage at the Burbank Studios in southern California. There, an array of guests lounged on 200 sofas and were provided with snacks and drinks. The purpose of this was to help Brooks, in particular, get over his concerns that he might not come up with really good, zany responses to Reiner's questions. The intent was to relax the performers by making the ambiance more like a party in an oversized living room than a recording studio work session.

After an absence of so many years from doing their first such recordings, the costars decided to meet ahead of time to review (past) routines and ideas that could be springboards for their new album. According to Reiner, "A couple of hours before, upstairs, I had little cards and I'd ask him a question. And if the question was good, I'd put it down and say OK. He'd say, 'Those are no good, don't ask that,' and I threw those into my valise. . . . At least he knew what the question was—I didn't know what the answer was, nor did he. But I could see his eyes flashing something would come. At the end of an hour, they were roaring, and I said, 'Let's try some of this garbage.' All the garbage turned out great, because his mind was clicking. I knew Mel could do it. We go to dinner together. There's always four or five things he says that nobody else would."

Brooks recalled of the occasion: "Carl's son Robbie [i.e., actor turned film director Rob Reiner] got very excited when we said we were going to do another record and he sat down right in the front, and I was scared. I didn't think I had the rhythm, the thoughts, the sound, the wisdom for this. But the minute he started laughing, I was off and running." Reiner noted, "We knew we were going to have to do two sessions. It was like spring training, you're rusty. The second session, it was like back 20 years. This guy was wailing. It was just wonderful." Mel remembered, in particular, of this recording session, "You know, it's hard to fall off a chair, but it's easy to slip off a couch. I remember seeing a lot of empty couches and thinking that people had left. But I heard the screams of laughter. They had actually fallen off the couches and onto the floor. They obviously liked the character."

On January 11, 1975, CBS-TV aired a special titled *The 2000 Year Old Man*. The half-hour animated cartoon entry was made by filmmaker Leo Salkin and featured the off-camera voices of Brooks and Reiner. Salkin planned a follow-up special, but it never materialized. However, a much delayed new album, the fifth in the series, was released in 1997. Titled *The 2000 Year Old Man in the Year 2000*, this Rhino label CD covered a plentitude of subjects for the old philosopher to vent his opinions on. The topics ranged from "Famous People" to the "Seven Wonders of the World" and "Wives and Famous Women." Simultaneous to this most recent release—which earned the costars a Grammy Award—HarperCollins published a companion book to the disk. (This led to *The 2000 Year Old Man Goes to School*, a 2005 HarperCollins book/CD set geared for readers in the fourth to eighth grades.)

Over the many years that Mel Brooks and Carl Reiner did their 2000 Year Old Man routine in different media and venues, the partners maintained such a high level of performance that it made them the envy of generations of comedians. For Brooks, the great success of the act helped to restore his self-esteem and bank account at a time when life was crashing down upon him. It also provided Mel with a forum to vent (and, sometimes, excise) his deepest fears about mortality and the meaning of life. Most of all, it gave the public an opportunity to experience a side of the irreverent Brooks of which previously only friends and business associates were aware.

Without the 2000 Year Old Man coming to Brooks's timely and remarkable rescue, Mel might never have had the impetus and opportunities that led to his noteworthy filmmaking career.

17

A Season of Many Changes

I kept yelling about how great I was, and Jerry [Lewis] and the others said, 'What do you mean, great? When the world says you're great, you're great.' They were right.

—Mel Brooks, 1977

Before Mel Brooks's show business career took an upturn in 1961 thanks to his 2000 Year Old Man persona, he was at very loose ends in all facets of his life. His income had dropped from a $5,000-a-week high to an $85-a-week low in really bad weeks. To pay some of his many bills, Mel had to scramble for any writing assignments available. The occasional Sid Caesar TV specials (for NBC and then CBS) in 1959 and 1960 were brief respites from Brooks's career doldrums. However, these occasional programs were churned out relatively quickly and were only a temporary career/financial stopgap for most of the individuals involved.

Meanwhile, the birth of the Brookses' third child, Edward, in May 1959, had not helped to resolve the chronic domestic troubles between Mel and Florence. (As before, the chief problem was Brooks's inability, at the time, to handle his responsibilities maturely. Seemingly, he found it too difficult to avoid falling back on familiar adolescent behavior.) During one of the couple's several breakups, Mel took an unfurnished fourth-floor walk-up on Perry Street. He paid a monthly rent of $78 for this modest Greenwich Village apartment. Then, with his meager income stretched by several new financial obligations, he found he could no longer afford even this place.

Then Irving "Speed" Vogel came to Mel's rescue. Vogel was the son of a well-to-do family and had grown up in Manhattan. (He earned the nickname "Speed" because he was just the opposite of speedy in many things he did in life.) A man of many talents, Vogel had once been a herring taster at Zabar's, the gourmet food shop on the Upper West Side. Later, he became a furniture manufacturer. When he retired at a relatively early age from that business, he turned to expressing himself artistically through sculpture and painting.

Vogel first encountered Brooks in the early 1950s at a small party in Manhattan hosted by actor Stanley Prager. Speed's first sight of the offbeat Mel was of the latter holding forth at the gathering with an impromptu entertainment. In a bid for attention, Brooks was impersonating the Queen Mother of England ordering her son (the king) not to leave the palace without benefit of a warm cloak. (As was Mel's wont, the routine was replete with a Jewish accent and Yiddish words.) The two men met again the next summer when Speed and his wife had a vacation home at Ocean Beach on Fire Island. Mel's rented house was nearby. Vogel and Brooks became good friends.

In the coming years, Vogel's marriage fell apart. He moved to a small apartment on Central Park West and maintained a studio on West 28th Street as a haven to work on his art projects. During this period, Speed became a father confessor of sorts for Mel, who could not make up his mind about how to cope with his recurrent domestic turmoil. Frequently, Brooks the insomniac persuaded Vogel to accompany him on long late-evening walks, during which Mel would regale Speed with all the reasons why he wanted to leave Florence and how he worried about the effect that would have on their three youngsters.

Speed liked the amiable Mrs. Brooks and hated being caught in the middle of the couple's unresolved conflicts. Nevertheless, Vogel soon found himself stuck in that ticklish position. One evening, Brooks remarked that Florence was repeatedly telling him that he should follow his often expressed wishes to leave home once again. Speed wanted to be sympathetic to his pal's woes and found himself saying—without thinking of the consequences—that this was kind of a "demeaning situation" for Brooks to be in. Perhaps, he suggested, it would be best if Brooks did move out of his home. In a flash, Mel was asking, "Will you bring your car and help me pack? Can I move in with you?" The obliging Speed said yes, although he instantly regretted it, because he was aware that insomnia was not Mel's only current neurosis.

For the next three increasingly impossible months the two men were roommates. In *No Laughing Matter*, a 1986 memoir Vogel coauthored with his novelist friend Joseph Heller, Speed wrote of Mel, "He was the worst. We were living in rather close quarters, which did not improve matters. Mel's insomnia didn't help either. He had a blood-sugar problem that kept us a scintilla away from insanity, and his brushstroke of paranoia had me on the verge (more than twice) of calling Bellevue to come and collect him."

There were times when the hyper Mel would answer the phone at Speed's art studio with such loony statements as "Mr. Vogel can't speak to you now. He's working on his horsey and he cannot be disturbed." Even worse was the morning Vogel awakened to find the white walls of his studio covered with graffiti. Mel had appropriated tubes of his host's best-quality oil paints to smear on the walls "You snore, you son-of-a-bitch! Yes, that's what you do! All night! Snore! Snore! Snore! You fuck!" Adding further insult to the situation, the obtrusive, phobic houseguest had taken to borrowing Vogel's luxury dress shirts and imported underwear to replenish his own depleted wardrobe. Despite each new infraction perpetrated by Brooks, the good-natured Vogel thought it would be uncharitable to evict his distraught guest. However, Speed finally reached the end of his patience.

When Brooks went off to Los Angeles in 1960, Vogel decided it was his golden opportunity to cut loose from this untenable situation. He hastily called Florence Brooks and begged her to forgive him for having helped Mel leave home. Speed offered to make amends for his interference in their private lives by moving Mel's things back to the Brookses' apartment. He suggested that, thereafter, "You guys can do whatever you think best without me in the picture."

According to Vogel, Florence listened to Speed's extended apology with polite silence. When he finished relating his idea that Mel should move back home, she let loose with: "Are you crazy? Where did you get such a dopey idea? If you can't stand him anymore, throw him out. What do you want from me?"

With that avenue of salvation cut off, a desperate Vogel decided to meet his pressing problem head on. He phoned Mel in Los Angeles, where he was staying at the Beverly Hills Hotel. A flustered Speed gently began his opening salvo that would, somehow, lead into his telling Brooks that he was at his wits' end with having Mel as a roommate. Speed had barely gotten out a few words before Mel interrupted him. "I know. . . . You want me to leave, right?" Brooks laughed and asked his caller, "Will you help me pack and move?" A much relieved Speed sighed, "Sure! *This* time it'll be a real pleasure."

Thus, the disastrous roommate situation ended on a positive note, with Mel and Speed remaining good pals throughout the coming decades. The fiasco also had an aftereffect: it provided the inspiration for the characters and plot of Neil Simon's 1965 smash hit Broadway play, *The Odd Couple*.

• • •

Over the years, Mel Brooks had seen Jerry Lewis perform (with and without his once partner Dean Martin) and thought he was a terrific clown. Their paths also crossed socially and, occasionally, professionally. (Like Brooks, Lewis had worked as a tummler in the Jewish Catskills.) Now a freelancer anxious for work, Mel accepted an offer to cowrite Lewis's comedy/variety special that aired on December 10, 1959, on NBC-TV. Both parties were pleased with their working association on this production. It led to Lewis's inviting Brooks to Los Angeles to collaborate on the script for Jerry's *The Ladies' Man*, the prankish star's upcoming comedy vehicle for Paramount Pictures.

Brooks was used to the freewheeling work environment that he experienced on *Your Show of Shows* and *Caesar's Hour*, where the writers' room was filled with mayhem and anarchy but the scribes always had the attention and respect of management and the stars. Mel had no real inkling that working with Jerry Lewis would differ from the good old Sid Caesar days.

Since Lewis's hugely successful show business partnership with Dean Martin had ruptured in the mid-1950s, Jerry had become a solo act starring in his own Paramount screen vehicles. He made two or three movies a year. He soon took on the added chores of being producer, director, and sometime songwriter for these screen showcases. Thanks to his string of highly lucrative movie hits, he was king of the Hollywood film lot and could do pretty much as he wished. In such an exalted position, Jerry had become accustomed to having his movie team be a loyal work force who understood that in all areas their boss had *the* first and final word—and every one in between.

Knowing none of this, the unsuspecting Mel arrived in Los Angeles in the summer of 1960 prepared to begin his scriptwriting chores on *The Ladies' Man*. One can only imagine how Mel must have felt initially to be working for a major Hollywood studio and for the industry's then biggest comedy star. Brooks must have concluded that he indeed had come a long way from his days of street corner antics in Williamsburg and his summers in the Catskills, where he had frantically sought to amuse the demanding resort guests.

It was soon made clear to Brooks that he would work in tandem with writer Bill Richmond and Lewis, and that Jerry would set the speed and direction in which the group composed their screenplay. Eager to be accommodating in order to receive his weekly paycheck, Mel agreed to the setup. However, it was not long before Brooks discovered that Lewis was a supreme egotist who felt he knew far more than anyone else about most things related to moviemaking. In addition, because of the star's continued movie success, no one interfered with his fiefdom or dared to question his inflated outlook on the world. The more Mel realized the extent of the restricting situation in which he had gotten himself, the more he bridled. For a while, he managed to hold his tongue in order to keep the job.

By September, Lewis, Richmond, and Brooks were deeply involved in an ongoing series of story conferences on *The Ladies' Man*. As always, Jerry was in total control of these meetings. He autocratically made creative suggestions and expected his coworkers to jump at his every command. He might change direction on the script from day to day and leave his writing team perplexed, but that was the big boss's prerogative. Lewis was accustomed to yes-men, and he shortly discovered that Brooks did not easily fall into this category, and increasingly was being obstinate in his refusal to follow the boss's demands. Jerry would discuss a plot point or character development in the embryonic screenplay and Mel would have his own thoughts. By now he was expressing his divergent opinions, not always in a diplomatic way. It did not help the tenuous situation that Brooks was unused to structure or discipline at work. At the time he found it difficult to understand that on a movie lot, the script was the basis for big expenditures and needed to be created on time, in an orderly manner, and according to protocol.

The more Mel offered suggestions that he thought appropriate from his viewpoint as a writer, the more he got slammed by the domineering Jerry. Because Lewis had a very sentimental outlook toward his screen characters and screenplays, he wanted the story line to reflect a gentle, almost sweet approach. This sensibility was alien to the cynical Brooks. (Actor Gene Wilder later said of Brooks, his pal and coworker, "There's not much white sugar in Mel's veins. . . . He would never ask an audience for sympathy.") Such opposing points of view further widened the gulf between Mel's and Jerry's approaches to the film.

Before long it was evident that Jerry the boss and Mel the hired writer were on a collision course. As the friction escalated between the two men, the story conferences on *The Ladies' Man* became increasingly tense. Soon, Lewis was lecturing Brooks with sarcastic pronouncements on the proper scriptwriting process.

Eventually Lewis dismissed Brooks from the project. Mel received a total payment of $46,900 for his labors over a 13-week period. When *The Ladies' Man* was released in June 1961—with the usual excellent box office results for a Jerry Lewis caper—Mel's name was *not* among the picture's credits. Rather, Jerry Lewis and Bill Richmond were the only ones listed as the film's coscripters.

Looking back on his Tinseltown fiasco with *The Ladies' Man* in the mid-1970s (by which time he was himself the new king of Hollywood comedy), Brooks said, "That didn't go well. I gave him [i.e., Jerry Lewis] the material and he and another writer took it and went on a boat and rewrote it. I'd always had that privilege, with Sid Caesar of being consulted, you know. My work was highly respected. So I was incensed." Brooks, the industry's prized new funster, also observed of Lewis, his one-time boss, whose glory days had long since passed, "He was an exciting, dynamic creature, and I learned a lot from him." Nonetheless, Mel could not resist pointing out that, "high-key comics like that always burn themselves out. Lewis could do thirty-one different takes [i.e., physical reactions], and when you'd seen them all, that was it. Low-key, laid-back comics like Jack Benny are the ones that last." By 2004, a more mellow Brooks was telling interviewers of his decades-ago professional misadventure with Jerry Lewis, "I didn't get along with him too well. I thought he was silly. Today, I think he's funnier."

．　．　．

Brooks was back in New York in the late fall of 1960. He had already recorded the first of the 2000 Year Old Man albums with Carl Reiner, but he had no concept yet of how successful it would become. Meanwhile, Mel had to find new living quarters, since neither his wife, Florence, nor his pal Speed Vogel desired him as a roommate. No matter how he tried to ignore the implications of their rejection of him, it was obviously a personal embarrassment for him not easily diverted and covered over by any of the usual Brooksian bravado.

Making the situation even more awkward for Brooks, by February 1961, he was in New York Supreme Court being questioned by Justice Vincent A. Lupiano about the state of his finances. Florence was then suing Mel for a legal separation and seeking temporary alimony of $1,000 per week from Mel to support herself and their three children. Brooks explained to the judge that TV industry trends had changed and comedy writers were no longer in great demand. (He noted that of his $87,000 gross income for 1960, only $40,100 had come from television work.) The trade paper *Variety* published an article about the breakup of the show business couple, noting that the plaintiff "charged Brooks committed adultery with 'many women of various repute while in Hollywood.'" After hearing testimony from both parties, the court awarded Florence Brooks $400 a week in temporary alimony for the support of herself and their three children.

Mel Brooks and Florence Baum divorced on January 20, 1962. "We had married too young," Mel assessed later of their domestic incompatibility. He frequently repeated the glib statement "I expected I would marry my mother and she expected she would marry her father." He explained further, "It reached the point where it was irreparable, and the best thing to do for the entire family was to separate. It was done mutually."

At first after the divorce, Mel saw his children frequently. ("For myself. I wasn't doing anyone a favor. I had to see them.") However, changes in his private life and career soon altered that situation and it was largely left to his ex-spouse to rear their three youngsters. By the mid-1970s, when Mel and Florence's children were 18, 17, and 15, Brooks had enough distance from the painful reality of his broken marriage to acknowledge of his ex-wife, "I think she did a splendid job with the children. They're healthy, terrific kids and it's all due to their mother's upbringing." In 1975, he also admitted that "the thing that sickens my heart the most" was the physical distance that separated him from his children. "I live in California and my three children, who are of an age now to really be my friends on a more adult level, are living in New York and I can't see them enough. We're lucky if we see one another three times a year for a week or so at a time. It's not enough. I really enjoy being with them. They've helped me with everything I've written. I bounce ideas off their good, young, supple minds and they say 'bullshit' or 'sensational.' They don't think I'm a kook. They know I'm a serious human being who is a humorist." Then, in typical Mel style, he sidetracked from revealing further uncomfortable honest feelings to the interviewer by resorting to a quip: "Think what a barren existence it would be without the constant asking for money and the sarcasm and the laughing at you."

18

A Remarkable New Love

She [Anne Bancroft] understood, she laughed. She loved my mind. . . .
[Then] finally, over time, my face, my body. First my mind, which was
much more beautiful.

—Mel Brooks, 1993

I had never derived so much pleasure so quickly from being with another
human being. Right away, I wanted him [Mel Brooks] to enjoy me as
much as I enjoyed him."

—Anne Bancroft, 1974

The failure of Mel Brooks's collaboration with Jerry Lewis and his team
on the screenplay of *The Ladies' Man* had not soured Mel on moviemaking. Brooks had never outgrown his childhood love of the glamorous
medium. He still cherished a firm belief that one day, somehow, he
could be a legitimate part of the still exciting motion picture industry.

Actually, as far back as the mid-1950s, Brooks had been suggesting to
Sid Caesar, his TV star friend and boss, that they should relocate to Tinseltown, where they could make great pictures together. Sid rejected his
pal's suggestion because NBC had just upped Caesar's salary to induce
him to star on *Caesar's Hour*. Later in the decade—by which time Caesar's TV career was sagging badly, Sid had ended his NBC network pact,
and he was fumbling for a new career direction—Brooks again suggested
they give Hollywood a try. Still Caesar said no. Somehow, Sid hoped to
reestablish himself in the medium of television, which he knew best and

in which he felt most comfortable. Therefore he remained based in his hometown of New York, as did Mel.

What neither party appreciated—or was willing to concede—was that the era of live television based in New York was fast becoming a thing of the past. Already, huge TV production facilities had sprung up in Los Angeles, and most of the industry was now based on the West Coast, where nearly every show was being taped or filmed for on-air distribution.

For Mel's part, he remained reluctant to leave the excitement and comforting familiarity of New York City life. He had so many ties to the metropolis: his mother and brothers; his three youngsters, who lived with Florence, his estranged wife; and, of course, his wide assortment of (show business) cronies and acquaintances. Thus, in early 1961, Brooks was still hanging on in Manhattan, frenetically networking with friends and past associates for possible writing assignments to keep himself afloat financially.

• • •

One of Mel Brooks's many acquaintances from the good ol' *Your Show of Shows* days was Charles Strouse. The latter, about two years younger than Brooks, was also Jewish and had been born in New York. After Strouse graduated from the Eastman School of Music, he studied with the esteemed composer Aaron Copland and the elite French music teacher Nadia Boulanger. Later, Strouse became a piano player for dance bands. Sometimes, he had worked as a rehearsal pianist for *Your Show of Shows* while waiting for one of his song compositions to catch on with theater producers and/or the public. In late 1960, Charles had enjoyed a solid Broadway success with *Bye Bye Birdie*. For this hit musical he provided the music, and his writing partner, Lee Adams (another friend and former coworker of Mel's), wrote lyrics for the show's songs. Even in these recent years of Strouse's growing recognition, he earned extra money as a rehearsal pianist. Not long ago one of his gigs had been at the Actors Studio, where he'd worked with the film, television, and stage actress Anne Bancroft, who was practicing her presentation of song numbers. She wanted to prove her performing versatility and indulge her penchant for singing.

One day while Mel was visiting Charles Strouse at his apartment, Bancroft dropped by for a few minutes to discuss song rehearsal matters. After Anne chatted with Strouse, she swept out of the room. Even from that brief glimpse of the classy two-time Tony Award winner, Brooks was entranced by her natural beauty and exuberance. Thereafter, Mel—by now separated from but not yet divorced from Florence—pestered Charles to arrange a real introduction between him and the tantalizing Miss Bancroft.

Strouse did not think this was such a wonderful idea. He knew Mel fairly well, and Anne less well. However, his intuition suggested that these two seemingly disparate individuals were *not* likely to hit it off. As it was, she was far more successful in her career than Mel had been in his to date. Her achievements included a wide range of impressive performances, especially on stage and on TV. On the other hand, Brooks was a formerly well-employed TV comedy writer whose recent bid for a place in the show business sun was his recent album (*2000 Years with Carl Reiner & Mel Brooks*), which had yet to prove itself a winner. Mel was prone to a crude sense of humor and was happiest when he was the full center of attention—no matter what outlandish zaniness was required of him to grab the spotlight.

Physically, Anne was a good inch or two taller than Mel. This brunette with Mediterranean features boasted a pleasing profile and a fine figure. In contrast, Brooks was neither handsome nor well built. Bancroft was Italian Catholic and Brooks was Jewish. It was hard to envision these two as either a love couple or even good friends.

• • •

One day—February 5, 1961—Strouse decided once and for all to end Brooks's constant pestering of him to arrange a meeting with Anne Bancroft. That cold winter day, as Strouse, Lee Adams, and Mel Brooks walked briskly along a crowded Manhattan Street, Charles suggested they stop by the Ziegfeld Theater, where singer Perry Como was rehearsing for one of his upcoming TV shows. The trio entered the theater, and, as Strouse knew, Bancroft was there to rehearse her guest spot on Como's program. As the three men arrived, Anne was on stage rehearsing a song number, "Married I Can Always Get."

Brooks found it hard to contain his enthusiasm now that he was once again in Bancroft's presence. When the number ended, he and the others applauded enthusiastically—Mel loudest of all. Without waiting for Strouse to make a formal introduction, the determined Brooks boldly rushed up on stage, marched over to the actress, and said jauntily, "Hey, Anne Bancroft; I'm Mel Brooks."

•   •   •

Anne Bancroft was born Anna Maria Louisa Italiano on September 17, 1931, in the Bronx, New York. She was the second of three daughters of Michael and Mildred (DiNapoli) Italiano. Her father was a dress pattern maker, and her mother helped the close-knit family stay afloat during the Depression by working at Macy's department store as a telephone operator. As a child, Anna was a ball of energy who happily entertained loved ones at family picnics and gladly gave impromptu song performances in the neighborhood. Later, she recalled, "I was the personality kid. When I wasn't sick, I was singing."

Having been richly pampered by her adoring family, Anna found it difficult to adjust to the regimented academic life at school. One area, however, in which Anna shone at school was in performing snappy song numbers. Her teachers were so impressed with her verve that she was often shepherded from one classroom to another to demonstrate her song-and-dance skills for her peers. Mrs. Italiano took notice of Anna's special gifts as a performer and decided the plucky girl should have tap dance lessons, even though money was very scarce in the household. Anna began classes, and soon became so devoted to her terpsichorean studies and her desire to transform herself into a lithe ballerina that she lost her appetite for eating. This upset her mother, who withdrew her child from the strict training. As Anna grew older, she maintained her interest in performing at school, at church, and at neighborhood functions. By now, she was developing into a striking young woman.

It was actually a family friend who launched Anna's show business career. He worked at a tiny radio station in Peekskill, a little town about 40 miles north of the Bronx. He happened to mention that his station was having difficulty in filling a gap in its Saturday morning broadcast schedule. Anna jumped in and suggested that she and her pals could put together a program of condensed dramatizations that would fill up the

15-minute time slot. Before long, Anna and her group—who named themselves the Radcliffe Radio Players—were performing on air each weekend. The newcomer decided she needed a fancier name for her radio work. She grandly billed herself as Anne St. Raymond.

By the time Anna reached her senior year at Christopher Columbus High School, her passion for drama had turned into a strong desire to become a lab technician. She envisioned gaining fame within the medical field. Then the young woman developed a powerful crush on a classmate with whom she had been in school plays. He mentioned that he intended to enroll in the American Academy of Dramatic Arts after graduation. In a flash, Anna decided that this institution was her destiny and she begged her parents to let her attend the Manhattan acting school. The ever-obliging Mrs. Italiano found the funds to pay for her girl's tuition at the American Academy.

Anna graduated from high school on an accelerated program. Now she found herself the youngest member of the entering class at the American Academy. She also discovered that, at the last minute, her boyfriend had chosen not to matriculate at the school. To help pay for her classes, Anna held a variety of jobs (including working at local drugstores and giving English lessons to the exotic Peruvian singer Yma Sumac, a talent who became famous for her amazing five-octave range).

A few weeks before completing her intensive studies at the American Academy, Anna was in a school rehearsal hall preparing a scene. One of her teachers (Frances Fuller) happened to wander into the room and was deeply impressed by the student's performance. Fuller referred the pupil to her husband (Worthington Miner), the creator/director of the TV drama anthology series *Studio One*. Anna made her debut on the live program on April 17, 1950, and acquitted herself well in her dramatic role. She was now billing herself as Anne Marno. This appearance led to several other TV assignments, including a recurring role on the popular comedy series *The Goldbergs*. By 1951, Anne was not only a busy television performer (and receiving good notices), but she had acquired a new boyfriend. He was actor John Ericson, another graduate of the American Academy. The tall, handsome talent had gained prominence in the film *Teresa* and was then appearing on Broadway in the hit drama *Stalag 17*.

During the summer of 1951, an East Coast representative of Twentieth Century-Fox Pictures asked Anne if she would make a screen test with a young actor they were considering signing. She said yes. Ironically, the studio decided against Anne's coplayer but wanted to hire her. At age 19, her professional future seemed secure. She agreed with Ericson that when his New York play run was over, he would join her in Los Angeles and they would wed. (Unfortunately, during their time apart, John fell in love with another woman. By the time Ericson came to Hollywood in 1953 under an MGM contract, he had married his new girlfriend.)

Once in Hollywood, Anne was immediately processed through the production mill at Twentieth Century-Fox. The new contractee was ordered to take a less ethnic professional name and agreed to become Anne Bancroft. Her debut was in a melodrama, 1952's *Don't Bother to Knock*, but all the attention went to the picture's leading lady, Marilyn Monroe. Through trial and error, in such lesser films as 1954's *Gorilla at Large* and *The Raid*, Anne learned her craft.

At first, Anne was thrilled by the mere fact of being in the land of palm trees and swimming pools and being part of the seemingly glamorous film industry. "When I went to Hollywood under contract to Fox, I thought I had arrived; on a clear day you could've seen my swelled head from Pasadena!" Later, she recalled of her new hometown, "I thought it was the cat's meow. Here I was, in the movies! Hey, I thought it was the best thing that could ever happen to a little girl from the Bronx. And it was a dream come true for me. What did I know? I wore spangles. And somebody did my hair every day, and put my makeup on. And brought me coffee, and Kleenex when I sneezed. What a life! And when you're nineteen years old, that's great."

However, as Bancroft adjusted to the glitzy moviemaking lifestyle, it lost a bit of its sparkle. Meanwhile, she was growing increasingly unhappy at the studio, where she worked diligently in one (mediocre) picture after another but never seemed to get a key part that would truly launch her career.

Bored with the not-so-merry round of picturemaking, she found solace in the Tinseltown nightlife and became a frequent face at the Sunset Strip nightclubs. Then she met Martin A. May, who came from an oil-rich Texas family. He was a law student at the University of Southern California. The couple began dating and, eventually, they decided to wed. (In retrospect, Bancroft said she was very discouraged with her professional life at the time. She had decided that marriage was her only option and "just about anybody would have done." The couple wed in a civil ceremony on July 1, 1953. However, the groom insisted they keep their marital status secret until he had the right opportunity to break the news to his mother back in Texas. Thus, for several months, they maintained separate residences, and Anne gained a reputation in the film colony for being a bit ditzy due to her vague answers about the state of her relationship with May.

May's legal career did not materialize and he turned to a career in real estate development. By this point, the couple had realized they were ill-matched as a domestic team. (For one thing, Anne was amazed to discover that her husband slept with a loaded revolver under his pillow. It made her nervous, but she assumed all men had that strange habit.) To please Anne's parents, the couple remarried in a Catholic ceremony back in New York. Eventually, they separated and, in February 1957, they divorced. Bancroft explained the breakup with: "Call it different temperaments. He's blond and I'm brunette. . . . He's from Texas and I'm from the Bronx. Texans will never understand Latins, and vice versa."

Later, May said of his ex-wife, "Annie was intense about everything. She'd lie on the floor and watch television by the hour, or she'd fry an egg, standing there leaning over the skillet staring as if the fate of the city depended on that egg. She was either a hungry tiger or a lovable lap dog." Another time May revealed of his displeasing marriage: "She worked from 4 A.M. to 6 P.M. She came home and couldn't talk. Once she wouldn't talk to me for three weeks. There was a lack of companionship with millions of people tracking into the house. She tried to combine two loves— one a marriage and the other a career. The career turned out to be the greater of the two."

Anne's film contract at Twentieth Century-Fox had expired in the mid-1950s. Thereafter, she kept busy both with freelance movie assignments (such as playing a mixed-race Native American in the 1956 Western *Walk the Proud Land* and the female love interest in the 1957 film noir entry *Nightfall*) and doing TV parts. One of these roles was on a segment of the esteemed *Playhouse 90* TV series. Later, Richard Basehart, her costar in that episode, auditioned for the male lead in an upcoming Broadway play, *Two for the Seesaw*. He suggested to the playwright (William Gibson) and the director (Arthur Penn) that they audition Bancroft to play opposite him. Anne met with the creative team, but no decision was made about hiring her. Not long after this, Basehart dropped out of the project, and Anne thought that would squash her chances of playing the juicy stage role.

By now Bancroft was more than fed up with West Coast life. She explained, "I was beginning to have a lot of lonely times out there when there was nothing to do, and I would have to look at myself—at the thoughts that came into my mind—and it was a very dangerous time. I was going steadily down-hill in terms of self-respect and dignity: I was completely demoralized by the time I left Hollywood." Then came the turning point. "Someone must have hollered at me too loud because I just went home, packed my bag, and asked someone to phone my mother Millie to say I was returning to New York. That was the first time in my life I made a decision entirely on my own. And that was when I was ready to be an actress!"

Anne returned to New York. She enrolled in acting classes at Herbert Berghof's prestigious HB Studio, convinced she had to unlearn some of her film and TV technique in order to fulfill her dream of becoming an accomplished stage performer. Meanwhile, she continued to campaign hard for the coveted play assignment, which still had not been cast. However, all final decisions on the show were in abeyance until a suitable male lead (with box-office appeal) could be signed. Finally, veteran stage and film star Henry Fonda agreed to do the project. Thereafter, Bancroft was contracted for the cherished part of the kooky Gittel Mosca, life's "born victim." After many pre-Broadway tribulations, *Two for the Seesaw* opened at the Booth Theater on January 18, 1958. It proved to be an enormous hit and earned Anne her first Tony Award. According to Bancroft, "For the first time in my life I was a star, an honest-to-gosh star in an important production. There was a tremendous sense of achievement in me and I really felt like an actress."

Anne cemented her status as the toast of Broadway by headlining in another new drama by William Gibson. She gave a searing performance as Annie Sullivan, the visually impaired teacher who taught the deaf and mute young Helen Keller (played by Patty Duke) to communicate with the world. *The Miracle Worker* bowed on October 19, 1959, at the Playhouse Theater (where almost a decade later Mel Brooks would film the musical play within the movie sequences for his movie *The Producers*). *The Miracle Worker* was a tremendous success and won several major awards, including another Tony for Bancroft.

• • •

By now Anne had the professional fame and success that had so eluded her during her Hollywood years and the making of 15 feature films. She was earning around $150,000 a year and had invested her money in real estate, a Texas oil well, and a California bank. (She spent $96,000 to purchase a brownstone apartment building at 260 West 11th Street "because I got tired of paying exorbitant New York rents." There, she could live life on her own terms.)

Soon after Bancroft reestablished herself in New York City, she began regular visits to a psychiatrist. She hoped to learn how to better deal with her frustration over the seemingly pointless Los Angeles years and the unhappiness of her marriage, which had left her so distrustful of men. (She quipped, "The only men in my life from now on will be my father, my agent, my press agent, and my psychiatrists.")

At this point, the very outspoken Anne made it quite clear to the men she dated, to her family, and to the media that she had no interest whatsoever in remarrying. "I had had one disastrous divorce which I knew from the wedding day was not going to work. So when I got divorced, I had everything from my panties to my umbrellas monogrammed 'AB.' That was it. I don't even think of getting married," Bancroft said. "I've got too many character quirks to eliminate before I can expect a man to marry me." Summing up her situation, Anne assessed, "I was lonely, but I could pay that price too. I escaped into the work, but also I had a good time. I could have gone along that way." (Despite her protestations of happiness at being a confirmed bachelorette, Bancroft kept asking herself why she couldn't have "a mature relationship based on trust, respect, and recognition.")

Anne continued her determined lifestyle for several months. One day, in a session with her therapist, she told him she had put a piece of a friend's wedding cake under her pillow. He answered sarcastically, "At last you're taking active steps."

19

Back to Broadway and Beyond

I never leave show business. It's in everything I do. That's because, to me, in a world where we know we're all going to die, the show business thing—to sing and dance, laugh and shout—is the most courageous emotional banner a human being can wave. That's why I love show business and performers so much.

—Mel Brooks, 1983

Mel Brooks was so excited at being in the presence of the sparkling Anne Bancroft on that momentous February day in 1961 that he was not about to let her out of his sight.

After Anne chatted briefly with Mel at the Ziegfeld Theater, she mentioned that she was off to meet with her talent agent at the William Morris Agency. She thought that would be a polite way to end the impromptu meeting. But Mel refused to be brushed off. He replied that, coincidentally, he was heading over to the same agency to see his representative there (although his agent was not based at that impressive firm). The two agreed to share a cab, and during the ride they exchanged further pleasantries. Once at their destination, Mel escorted Anne to the agency offices. Later, when she came back out to the reception area, lo and behold, there was the persistent Mel. They left the building together and continued their conversation. The next day Brooks brought Bancroft a copy of his recent *2000 Year Old Man* album. This prompted a conversation between them on TV comedy, and Bancroft mentioned that she had long been a fan of Sid Caesar's.

In the coming days, through great ingenuity and determination, Mel learned where Anne would be dining or attending a function that particular evening. Then he would appear there and feign surprise at the twist of fate that had brought them together once again. On each such occasion he did his utmost to entertain the star and keep her attention. Finally, he summoned the courage to ask her out on a real date. Since his funds were low, he suggested they dine at a quaint little restaurant downtown and then see a movie at an art house theater, where the price of tickets was reasonable. As Anne continued to see Mel, she realized that his finances were meager. So she frequently suggested that he come by her place so that she could cook a traditional Italian meal. It soon became a habit for Mel to spend a great deal of his free time at Anne's West 11th Street residence. Mel was ecstatic at his sudden good fortune.

• • •

Producer Edward Padula had endured over 80 backers' auditions for possible investors to raise the $290,000 needed to finance *Bye Bye Birdie*, which opened on Broadway in April 1960. The play was a remarkable success, playing through to October 1961. During its lengthy run, Broadway/film director Joshua Logan saw a performance of the popular show. At intermission Logan encountered Padula in the lobby and told him how much he was enjoying the evening and hoped that they could work together one day. Padula used the occasion to mention a property he had long wanted to convert into a new musical for the American theater, Vladimir Nabokov's novel *Pnin*. The plot concerned a Russian-born professor who comes to teach in the United States and must adapt to the strange culture of his new homeland. Padula's representatives had approached Nabokov for the rights, but the author had refused all offers. Then the producer found Robert Lewis Taylor's 1950 novel, *Professor Fodorski*, which dealt with much the same matter. The rights to that work were acquired rather easily. Thereafter, Padula assigned the *Bye Bye Birdie* songwriting team of Charles Strouse and Lee Adams to the new project. In turn, the duo suggested Mel Brooks as a good bet to adapt the Taylor book for the upcoming musical. Mel jumped at the offer without fully thinking through what would be required of him. Instead he focused on the more appealing aspects of the job. Not only would his fee help to tide him over during these tough financial times, but he remained determined to earn a solid Broadway credit. That, he reasoned, would prove to everyone that his last stage venture, *Shinbone Alley*, was not truly representative of his talents.

Logan became intrigued with the developing stage production and arranged for Padula and his creative team to convene at Joshua's country home in Stamford, Connecticut. At the meeting, the group bandied about ideas for giving the satirical story line a proper structure to support the musical comedy. In the course of the day, Mel expressed his ideas, some of which seemed promising. When the get-together ended, it was agreed that Logan would seriously consider coming aboard the Broadway-bound venture. At the time, everyone believed that the elitist Joshua was the proper person to helm this production. After all, his Broadway credentials included such successful musicals as *Annie Get Your Gun*, *South Pacific*, *Wish You Were Here*, and *Fanny*. While Logan rushed off to Hollywood to make films and ponder his possible participation on the show, the others got down to creating the musical.

Unlike *New Faces of 1952* (for which Brooks had provided a humorous skit) and *Shinbone Alley* (for which Mel had only undertaken rewrites of Joe Darion's book), this time Brooks was responsible for the *entire* libretto. Under the best of circumstances this was a challenging assignment. What made it more difficult for Brooks was that he was used to writing (or better yet, talking) in "committee" as he had done on both *Your Show of Shows* and *Caesar's Hour*. There, each member of the writing squad spurred on the others, and, if a sketch proved too unwieldy, it could always be discarded. If weekly script deadlines seemed perilously close to being missed, there was always head writer Mel Tolkin to corral the comedy writers (including Brooks) back onto schedule. However, on this new stage venture, Mel was virtually on his own in structuring the libretto, and he had little background and too little discipline to handle such a demanding situation successfully. As he submitted drafts (which he either handwrote or dictated and had transcribed) and was told they required substantial revamping, he grew progressively less enthusiastic about the project, for which he was not the final arbiter.

Besides, at this time, Mel had many distractions. The dissolution of his marriage to Florence Baum was going through the legal process and causing him great pangs of guilt, frustration, and annoyance. Meanwhile, his romance with the distinguished Anne Bancroft was building and re-quired his constant attention to keep afloat. In addition, there were his financial responsibilities (including monthly support payments to Florence and their three children), which left him with little ready cash. (While the growing sales of his comedy albums were starting to provide royalties, they hardly yet solved all his monetary problems.) To replenish his mea-ger bank balance, Mel undertook an increasing number of TV appear-ances, both guest shots to promote his 2000 Year Old Man persona as well as brief stints on panel shows and talk programs. They paid relatively little, but every bit helped.

Over the course of several months, as Strouse and Adams constructed the show's many songs, Mel drafted several versions of the book—none of which seemed to solve the structural problems of the story line (espe-cially in the overly complicated second act). While these creative strug-gles were going on, Josh Logan finally committed to directing the property (which was now called *Fodorski*).

The production team's jubilation at bringing Joshua Logan on board (which would give the musical useful prestige and attention, and attract more backer money) quickly turned to concern. It soon became apparent that Logan did not see eye to eye with the others. As Charles Strouse pin-pointed the problem, "Josh was from a different generation, he looked at America, college, the youth culture in ways that were different from ours." In addition, Strouse said, "Many times, later on, he told me he felt he had put his finger into the show in the wrong way. He had seen in it more of the flesh and blood realities of the characters than we had, and, because of that, their physicality became more important than the satiri-cal point of view we had initially envisioned." As Brooks perceived the emerging situation, it was as if Logan had come into the party "and sat on our birthday cake."

This conflict over artistic intention between Logan and the others became painfully clear when it came time to hire a leading man on whose shoulders the focus and success of the production heavily rested. Early on, the core creative team had agreed that Zero Mostel would be excellent in the pivotal part. However, Logan vetoed the idea, insisting that the oddly built, strange-looking, and inelegant Mostel would not be right as the romantic lead for this musical comedy. Another top candi-date was Britisher Ron Moody (who had recently scored on the London stage as Fagin in the musical *Oliver!*). Logan and some of the others flew to England to discuss the project with Moody, but negotiations fell through. Others considered to play the immigrant professor were Danny Kaye, Peter Ustinov, and Victor Borge.

Mel Brooks had an even better idea for the key role: Jacob Pincus Perelmuth. As Jan Peerce, this New York–born Jewish singer had gained great fame at the prestigious Metropolitan Opera. There he was a leading tenor and displayed a strong stage presence. The interesting suggestion fell on deaf ears with Logan, who decreed that he, himself, had finally found the ideal Fodorski: Ray Bolger. The latter was a well-known stage and film dancer. The lanky performer with the hook nose profile was best known for playing the Scarecrow in the classic film *The Wizard of Oz*. Later, Bolger enjoyed a great Broadway success in the musical *Where's Charley?* However, that was back in 1948. Since then, his only New York stage appearance had been in a brief 1951 revival of the same show.

Padula feared angering Logan and reluctantly went along with the choice of Bolger as leading man. (One of the producer's concerns was that the star's overprotective wife might try to interfere creatively on the new show as she had done on *Where's Charley?*) In due course, Bolger, then in his late 50s, arrived in New York for rehearsals. In his mind, he was still the toast of Broadway and egotistically demanded that the production be reshaped to better suit his particular talents. This led Logan, who suffered from periodic bouts of depression and anxiety, to rationalize that the easiest course was to side with Bolger against the others—including Mel, who considered Bolger all wrong for the show.

On the other hand, the cast of the production (which soon changed its title to *All American*) featured many talented performers: Eileen Herlie (a dignified stage star who had been effective in the recent musical *Take Me Along*), Ron Husmann (the handsome young performer who had used his deep, crisp voice to good effect in the Broadway song-and-dance entries *Fiorello* and *Tenderloin*), Anita Gillette (a pert young talent who had participated in such musicals as *Gypsy* and *Carnival*), and Fritz Weaver (a versatile, experienced stage actor who was cast as the villain in *All American*).

Rehearsals for *All American* were held at the Fraternal Clubhouse Rehearsal Hall on Manhattan's West Side. As work progressed, it became obvious that most everything Josh Logan told Ray Bolger during the day to help shape his pivotal character and his presentation was being undone at night by Bolger's interfering wife. Increasingly, this problem created confusion and unhappiness among the cast and the others involved. As the time approached for the out-of-town tryout in Philadelphia, everyone's nerves were thoroughly frayed.

Orders came down to Mel that the book, especially the still unresolved second act, needed substantial revamping. By now, Brooks was almost tapped out of fresh ideas for this project, in which he was in over his head. Often, he would leave rehearsals promising to go home and meet the challenge of repairing the still-cumbersome second act. Just as often, he'd return the next morning with little new to share with his collaborators. When they expressed disappointment at Mel's lack of progress, he would nervously launch into other topics of conversation, such as how he was going to marry Anne Bancroft (a concept that amazed the others). Even harder for the others to believe was that Brooks was hard at work writing a novel called *Springtime for Hitler*, in which he was dealing satirically and comically with the odious late German dictator. The idea was so bizarre that his confreres passed it off as just another wild brainchild of the ever boastful Mel, one that was clearly much too absurd to ever materialize into anything viable.

In the first weeks of 1962, the cast of *All American* headed to Philadelphia, hoping to work out the show's many kinks during its pre-Broadway tryout at the Erlanger Theater. The musical opened there to mixed reviews, at best. This prompted Bolger to become even more arrogant and demanding. He determined that he required a special number—as he had enjoyed in *Where's Charley?*—to bolster the show (and, of course, to emphasize his position as its star). Strouse and Adams concocted "I'm Fascinating" to appease Ray. Meanwhile, the winning ensemble number ("Physical Fitness"), which had literally stopped the show during Philadelphia playdates, was, for a time, dropped from the musical's lineup, for reasons that never made sense to others in the cast beyond Bolger.

If there was chaos backstage and onstage at *All American*, it was mild in comparison to a late-night brouhaha that occurred at Philadelphia's stylish Warwick Hotel, on Locust Street. That was where many of the key contributors to the show were lodged during the tryout engagement. Late one night, in Logan's spacious suite, Josh, Charles Strouse, Lee Adams, and Mel Brooks were hard at work trying to resolve the musical's ongoing creative problems. Suddenly, the door to the suite's living room burst open and in rushed Rita Almaviva, one of the show's investors. She had a

wild look in her eyes, and her hair was noticeably disheveled. Her unexpected late-evening appearance was sufficient to upset the already stressed
group. However, what stunned the surprised men even more was that the
woman was wearing only a sheer nightgown, which was on the verge of
falling off. The creative team froze in a panic at how to handle this peculiar situation. While they pondered, Miss Almaviva launched into a verbal attack. She pointed in Mel's direction and said, "You have no talent!"
She continued her salvo against the nonplussed Brooks with: "You can't
write a line! You can't tell a joke! You can't smell what an audience lis-
tens to—you're a No Talent. You stink!" In turn, she lambasted the others, accusing each of them of being ill equipped to make a Broadway
show come alive. The stunned assemblage was rescued by the timely
arrival of one of Logan's associates, who convinced the distraught woman
to return to her room. *All American* remained in Philadelphia for six
weeks, with Strouse and Adams writing several more songs as tunes were
added and discarded. Brooks struggled through providing yet new versions of the book.

Creatively, the show was still in a very unsettled shape when it limped
back to New York City for its March 19, 1962, debut at the Winter Garden Theater. When it bowed, Howard Taubman (of the *New York Times*)
carped, "With a rangeful of choice targets in sight, *All American* has
managed the amazing feat of hitting none. The principal trouble with
the marksmanship of the new musical is that it can't make up its mind
what it's shooting at." Taubman also noted, "The story Mel Brooks has
drawn . . . is diffused and heavy-handed."

Several of the other reviewers were equally dissatisfied. Richard Watts
Jr. (of the *New York Post*) found that the production "bounces back and
forth between the agreeable and the embarrassing," while Walter Kerr (of
the *New York Herald Tribune*) reported, "The show then is schizoid, half-
sentimental and half desperate enough to send a squad up and down the
aisles passing footballs over the customers' heads." *Newsweek* judged, "The
Mel Brooks libretto bites off much that it should eschew." The critic for
Theater Arts magazine chided, "Where the book exhibits its worst mis-
conceptions, however, is the area of verbal wit." John Chapman (of the
New York Daily News) was one of the few New York critics to find something positive to say about the show: "There are many impish moments in
this jolly story—as when the ad genius is shooting pictures of Whistler's
mother holding a giant bottle of whiskey."

All American struggled through 80 performances before mercifully closing. Most of the talent involved with the misfire was glad to be finally finished with the ongoing agony. Quipped Brooks of the over $400,000 flop, for which he had failed to rise creatively to the occasion, "We had an unfortunate stroke of luck, it opened in New York when there was no newspaper strike."

• • •

If Broadway apparently did not need Mel Brooks, others did. The rising sales of the 2000 Year Old Man albums had made Mel and Carl Reiner cult favorites. While their fame was growing in the comedy record arena, Reiner was busy nurturing his CBS-TV sitcom *The Dick Van Dyke Show* (1961–1966). However, Mel was at liberty and continued to write for the occasional TV specials that came his way and made guest appearances (with and without Reiner) on small-screen specials and talk shows (including the opening installment of *The Tonight Show Starring Johnny Carson*).

Then, out of the blue, it was announced that Brooks would be teamed with TV writer/personality Dick Cavett in a series of radio commercials for Ballantine beer. It was a timely job offer that Mel was in no position to reject. Brooks enthused/rationalized of this gig, which had him do spiels in the guise of a 2,500-year-old man (a variation of his comedy album persona), "They gave me carte blanche. I had complete script approval. Although, truthfully, we never used scripts. My interviewer, Dick Cavett, and I started with a premise and then winged it. We made all kinds of tapes, but they used only the ones that we liked." When Mel was asked what prompted the unlikely combination of the brash Brooks and the mild-mannered Cavett, he explained, "Dick is a marvelous foil for me. He's innocent and guileless, and he just aches to be cut to pieces. He reacts beautifully during the interviews, especially when I call him 'company rat,' 'pusher,' 'marshmallow,' 'fluffy,' 'sellout.'"

The Ballantine commercials were a solid hit and did much to enhance Mel's standing in both the entertainment industry and in the advertising world, as well as with the public at large. (In analyzing Brooks's success with this venture as a spokesman, Madison Avenue copywriter Alex Kroll pointed out, "That's why you have a Mel Brooks. Because he can give you that flash of genius. He doesn't use punch lines so much as he uses startling non-sequiturs which get better with repeated hearings. It's much more long-lasting than the typical comic-type of surprise-ending humor."

•   •   •

Mel remained in a flurry of activity throughout 1962, hoping that one or more of his scattershot creative efforts would pay off royally. He tried his hand at writing a screenplay based on his failed marriage to Florence Baum, but there were no buyers for *Marriage Is a Dirty Rotten Fraud*. That fall, Brooks returned to Philadelphia to help out on another Broadway-bound musical. It was *Nowhere to Go But Up*, a Prohibition-set tale of two undercover law enforcers (Martin Balsam and Tom Bosley) coping with bothersome bootleggers (including a hoodlum played by Bruce Gordon). The show's book and lyrics were written by James Lipton (much later the host of cable TV's *Inside the Actors Studio*), and the music was by Sol Berkowitz. The expensive musical ($480,000) was being produced by, among others, Kermit Bloomgarden (the Broadway figure who years earlier had promised to audition Mel Brooks the actor but failed to follow through). Sidney Lumet was directing the show and decided the unsatisfying libretto required fresh repairs.

Brooks journeyed to Philadelphia to doctor the book, but his efforts were to little avail. The production received poor notices and did only fair business at the Shubert Theater. Then the production moved to New York, where it bowed on November 10, 1962, at the Winter Garden Theater (the site of Mel's prior Broadway effort). The reviewers quickly nailed the lid on the coffin of the new musical, and it closed days later, on November 17—despite the effort of 235 irate backers who picketed the theater to prevent the producers from shuttering their costly investment.

Fortunately for the resilient Mel, this latest of many career setbacks would soon be supplanted by new show business opportunities that proved that Brooks, indeed, had nowhere to go but up.

Mel Brooks earned his first official TV credit as a member of the writing team on *Your Show of Shows* (1950–1954), a variety series costarring Sid Caesar and Imogene Coca. *Courtesy of JC Archives*

Florence Baum, a successful dancer in Broadway musicals and on TV variety programs, in the early 1950s. She and Mel Brooks wed on November 26, 1953. *From the author's collection*

The stellar members of the Writers' Room on TV's *Caesar's Hour* circa 1956. Front row: Gary Belkin, Sheldon Keller, Michael Stewart, and Mel Brooks. Back row: Neil Simon, Mel Tolkin, and Larry Gelbart. *Courtesy of NBC/Photofest*

Anne Bancroft, Cary Grant, and Mel Brooks attending the Hollywood premiere of Bancroft's screen vehicle *The Miracle Worker* (1962). *Courtesy of Photofest*

A mid-1960s TV appearance by Mel Brooks as the venerable 2000 Year Old Man and Carl Reiner as the intrepid reporter. *Courtesy of JC Archives*

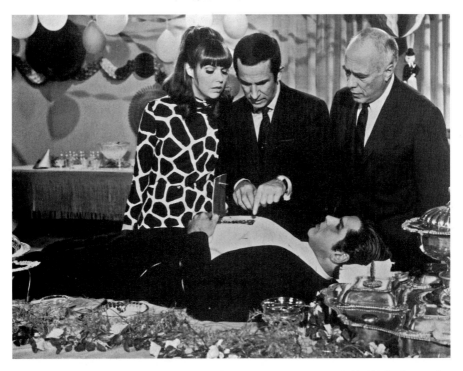

Mel Brooks cocreated the hugely successful TV series *Get Smart* (1965–1970). Pictured are four of the show's regulars: Barbara Feldon, Don Adams, Dick Gautier (lying down), and Edward Platt. *Courtesy of JC Archives*

Moviemaker Mel Brooks gives Dom DeLuise a few pointers for
The Twelve Chairs (1970), shot on location in Yugoslavia.
Courtesy of JC Archives

Mel Brooks wore many hats in
his breakthrough film, *Blazing
Saddles* (1974). He is seen here
in one of his roles in the comedy
hit—a Yiddish-speaking Native
American chieftain.
Courtesy of JC Archives

Gene Wilder (as Dr. Frankenstein) gives Peter Boyle (as the monster) a helping hand in *Young Frankenstein* (1974). *Courtesy of JC Archives*

Bernadette Peters, Mel Brooks, Sid Caesar, and Dom DeLuise hope for the best in a scene from *Silent Movie* (1976). *Courtesy of JC Archives*

Mel Brooks and Madeline Kahn disguise themselves as an elderly Jewish couple to elude airport security in *High Anxiety* (1977). *Courtesy of JC Archives*

Mel Brooks as the French monarch Louis XVI proves why "it's good to be the king" in *History of the World: Part I* (1981). The object of his lust is the buxom Pamela Stephenson. *Courtesy of JC Archives*

Anne Bancroft and Mel Brooks teamed on camera in *To Be or Not to Be* (1983). They played the stars of a Warsaw acting troupe involved in underground activities in Nazi-occupied Poland during World War II. *Courtesy of JC Archives*

Filmmaker Mel Brooks at an industry screening in Hollywood of his new picture, *Life Stinks* (1991). *Photo by Albert L. Ortega*

Amy Yasbeck, Mel Brooks, and Cary Elwes costar in *Robin Hood: Men in Tights* (1993). *Courtesy of JC Archives*

Nathan Lane (as Max Bialystock), director/choreographer Susan Stroman, Matthew Broderick (as Leo Bloom), and writer-producer Mel Brooks on the set of *The Producers* (2005), the film adaptation of the megahit Broadway musical. *Courtesy of Universal Pictures/Photofest*

20

Becoming the Critic

Credit is part of the whole business of affirming yourself. You start as a little boy, scratching your initials in your desk. You're saying, "I was born. I am here. I live." I began by making noise. "Ya! Ya! Ya! Here I am!" I yelled but nobody cared. I discovered you had to find a form for that noise if people were going to notice. So my next noise was as a drummer, then as a comedian and tummler. But I wanted the noise to last longer, so I became a writer.

—Mel Brooks, 1977

While Mel Brooks was wildly making forays into many areas of show business in 1961 and 1962 and hoping for the best, Anne Bancroft was being more selective (for better or worse) in her career choices. After ending her run on Broadway in *The Miracle Worker*, she returned to film-making. Although she lost out on re-creating her stage role in the screen adaptation of *Two for the Seesaw*, Bancroft was given the opportunity to portray Annie Sullivan in the movie adaptation of *The Miracle Worker*. This 1962 release was largely shot on the East Coast. Thereafter, the in-demand Bancroft was offered other stage and film parts, but nothing in particular appealed to her. As a lark, however, she appeared on a mid-1962 "All-Star" edition of the TV game show *Password*, as well as turning up on television talk shows, which she found fun to do. In 1963, she starred on Broadway in a production of *Mother Courage and Her Children*, a somewhat misguided venture that lasted for only 52 performances.

Because the down-to-earth Bancroft was such a high-profile and distinctive personality, the media was constantly eager to interview her. To one columnist the celebrity admitted that she was experiencing a pleasantly expansive period of her life and felt less restrained by any emotional baggage. She acknowledged that, through therapy, "I learned to uncork my thoughts, if nothing else." She also mentioned, "I feel that if my artistry is based on my neurosis, well then, my artistry will just have to go out the window. Because I think a human being is the finest thing that's ever been put on this earth, and it's bigger and better than anything else it can produce." She summed up her emotional goals by stating she would rather be a "healthy human being . . . not necessarily a happy human being."

Since Mel Brooks was still officially married, Bancroft played down his ongoing role in her private life, and focused on discussing with the media her general likes and dislikes about the opposite sex. To illustrate her feelings on the topic, she referenced an unspecified male suitor: "He kept opening doors for me and trying to help me on with my coat. I'm not the kind of woman who needs those gestures, and I can't stand being forced to accept them. I can't stand any man trying to make me behave like his image of me. . . . Women don't need doors opened for them anymore. That's an old social custom that has no more meaning. As women are becoming liberated and independent, they need men who find other ways to prove they're men."

She informed the press: "I have a very active [social] life. I find that the more I am with—of course, it may be just the role that I'm in—but the more I have to do with people, the more eager I am that night to give what I got that day on the stage." On the subject of ever remarrying, she explained to another scribe, "It's not best for any woman. I will marry, but certainly my husband has to understand that sometimes I must work from 4 A.M. to 6 P.M. —but not always."

• • •

Besides keeping company with Anne Bancroft, Mel had several other constants in his New York social circle of the early 1960s. For one, there was Alan Schwartz, an attorney (born and raised in Brooklyn) whom Mel first met in 1962 and who became an integral part of Brooks's career team as well as a good friend. Schwartz recalled, "Mel had just written a play called *All American*, which was a disaster. He had no money—zero. He was getting a divorce. He had three kids. And he would come to my office in New York with a cup of tea and a walnut-and-cheese sandwich from Chock full o'Nuts and talk about the future. Our law firm carried him for a long time; he couldn't pay his bills."

Schwartz has described the Brooks of this period as "a street kid" with a "'little Jew' mentality about the way the big WASP world feels about him." The lawyer found the complex man to be full of interesting surprises, and sometimes, contradictions: "Here's a guy with very little edu- cation and sophistication who . . . [over the years became] . . . a wine ex- pert." The lawyer observed, "Mel was surprisingly resilient. My impression was that he felt rejected, but expected that." [Part of his childhood legacy was] "a very realistic view of the way the world behaves."

According to Schwartz, "By Mel's standards, an improviser isn't class. He wanted to be classy. Writing is classy. A screenplay is classy." Over the years, this lawyer's other clients included such illustrious writers as Joseph Heller, Peter Shaffer, and Tom Stoppard. As Schwartz saw it: "Mel is as intelligent as any of them. He must have a fantastic IQ. But sometimes, if he's with playwrights or novelists, he feels he has to prove that he's a serious literary person. When he met Shaffer for instance, he kept saying things like 'pari passu' and 'ipso facto.'"

Other key people in Brooks's life during this transitional phase were the members of the Gourmet Club (aka the Oblong Club). As legend has it, this colorful group evolved as the result of a party hosted by Speed Vogel in the summer of 1962 at his West 28th Street studio. Among the guests were Zero Mostel (who had a studio in the same building), Joseph Heller (whose novel *Catch-22* had been published the prior year), Ngoot Lee (a painter and a calligrapher of Chinese parentage who also lived in Vogel's building and was a gourmet cook), and Mel Brooks. These five men found they enjoyed the evening so much they agreed to celebrate the occasion by reassembling every Tuesday thereafter for food and talk. Club "meetings" were generally held at inexpensive restaurants in the heart of Chinatown.

Over time, various of the charter members brought others to these sacred gatherings, but it was understood that the newcomers were ineligi- ble to become official members of the group. Among the visitors allowed to attend one or more of these Chinatown meals and wide-ranging gabfests was a diamond dealer whom Brooks knew. This particular guest entertained the others with odd impersonations of movie notables. Among Heller's personal invitees was George Mandel, a novelist who happened to have a steel plate in his head as a result of an injury he suffered at the Battle of the Bulge. At a later Gourmet Club assemblage, Mandel recited the particulars of his World War II combat wound as the others listened respectfully in silence. Then, out of the blue, Mel said, "I'm sure glad that happened to you, and not to me." (Heller assessed of Brooks's abrupt remark, "He wasn't being cruel, he was being honest. He just blurted out what we were all thinking but didn't dare to say.")

In turn, Mandel brought another writer, Mario Puzo (who later authored the best-selling *The Godfather*), to a Gourmet Club outing, and Puzo soon became a frequent attendee at the gatherings. Among other "approved outsiders" were Mel's longtime friend Carl Reiner and writer Joe Stein. (Stein had been an early member of the *Caesar's Hour* writing team. Later, he adapted Reiner's novel/memoir *Enter Laughing* for the Broadway stage and wrote the book of the musical *Fiddler on the Roof*, which became a major hit for its star, Zero Mostel.)

Reiner, who could only attend sporadic congregations of the Gourmet Club due to the demands of his screen and TV work on the West Coast, observed that this formidable group had several standing rules. "You are not allowed to eat two mouthfuls of fish, meat, or chicken without an intermediate mouthful of rice. Otherwise, you would be consuming only the expensive food. The check and tip, and the parking fees, if any, are equally divided among the members. It is compulsory, if you are in New York, are not working nights, and are in reasonable health, to be present at every meeting. The members are very polite. Once, I had a seat facing the kitchen door and I looked through and saw a rat strolling across the floor. They immediately offered me a chair facing the other way." Carl also allowed, "I would put that group up against the [celebrated 1920s and 1930s literary/Broadway gatherings at the] Algonquin Round Table and bet that, line for line, they were funnier. The speed of the wit is breathtaking. It just flies back and forth." (Regarding that evaluation, Brooks noted, "I'm sure we're funnier than the Algonquin crowd, but we're not as bright.")

Anne Bancroft proved to be a onetime visitor to the Gourmet Club outings. She had heard so much about the group from Mel that she was intrigued to know firsthand what actually transpired at these gatherings. What really whetted her appetite was the fact that women were not welcome at the meetings, whose locations were a closely guarded secret, known only to certified members. One evening, by happenstance, Anne came across a notepad on which Mel had jotted down the address of that night's Gourmet Club rendezvous in Chinatown. Bancroft surprised the clan with her unexpected arrival. Although everyone was polite to her, it was clear to the show business star that she was not to make another such impromptu appearance at these cherished men's nights out.

Over the years of the Gourmet Club's many get-togethers, Joseph Heller got to know Brooks quite well. (In fact, variations of Mel's persona appeared in Heller's novels *Something Happened* and *Good as Gold*.) Later, after Brooks gained international fame in the mid-1970s, Heller was asked to describe Brooks for a *New Yorker* magazine profile of Mel. In a blend of shrewd observation, sly wit, and unabashed fun, Heller pointed out about his longtime pal, "Mel has always had plenty of resentment and aggression that he can sublimate into creativity. He's usually at his best when he's envying people more successful than he is. Now that there's hardly anyone more successful, what will he do? . . . He likes to see his rivals fail, but not his friends. Provided, of course, that *he's* succeeding."

When the *New Yorker* interviewer asked Heller if he believed fame had truly changed Brooks, Heller answered teasingly: "Not a bit. He's just as nasty, hostile, acquisitive, and envious today as he ever was." He explained further: "You have to distinguish between Mel the entertainer and Mel the private person. He puts on this manic public performance, but it's an act, it's something sought for and worked on. When he's being himself, he'll talk quietly for hours and then make a remark that's unforgettably funny because it comes out of a real situation. You might say that he's at his funniest when he's being most serious. He has a tremendous reverence for novelists and for literature in general, because it involves something more than gag writing."

To illustrate the "real" Mel Brooks, an amused Joe Heller recounted for the journalist a prank that Joe had once pulled on Brooks. On that occasion Heller had exaggerated the fee he was then earning for teaching creative writing courses at City College of New York. He told Mel that he was receiving $68,000 a year for his efforts. Soon thereafter, Brooks met with his accountant (who also had Heller for a client). The comedy writer promptly launched into a tirade: "Why am I in the entertainment business? Why aren't I teaching and earning seventy thousand a year like Joe Heller?" According to Heller, the highly competitive Mel "was out of his mind."

• • •

Back in the early 1950s, when Mel Brooks bullied his way onto the writing staff of *Your Show of Shows*, he was thrilled—at first—to receive screen credit for his contributions to the program. Then he began to suffer pangs of self-doubt. He told himself, "My God, I'm not a writer, I'm a *talker*. I wish they'd change my billing on the show so that it said, 'Funny Talking by Mel Brooks.' Then I wouldn't feel so intimidated."

In that and other instances thereafter, he found a way to deal with and survive the professional pressures of being a comedy writer. A decade later, when Mel set out to write his novel, *Springtime for Hitler*, he had to stifle anew his many fears about his true abilities as a writer. He sought to overcome his trepidation with a pep talk. He vowed to himself, "One little word at a time, but, by God, I was going to do it."

In the coming months, between bread-and-butter writing assignments and performing gigs related to the 2000 Year Old Man, Mel forced himself to toil on his book project. It proved to be a very slow and frustrating process. Meanwhile, assorted distractions kept cropping up, including his latest creative brainstorm, which he'd had one Manhattan evening in the spring of 1962. Brooks was about town doing one of his favorite things: attending a movie. Besides the feature, the cinema's program included a short subject. It was a surrealistic abstract cartoon made by Norman McLaren, the noted Canadian animator. According to Brooks, "Three rows behind me there was an old immigrant man mumbling to himself. He was very unhappy, because he was waiting for a story line and he wasn't getting one."

Brooks could not help but eavesdrop on the noisy patron, and from the man's rambling an idea sprang into Mel's fertile mind. Within a short time, Brooks contacted a friend, Ernest Pintoff, who had written, directed, and sometimes produced short subjects (such as *Flebus* and *The Shoes*). He asked his pal to provide the visuals for a McLaren-type cartoon. After Pintoff agreed to the request, Brooks warned him, "Don't let me see the images in advance. Just give me a mike and let them assault me." With the help of Bob Heath (as animator-designer), producer-director Pintoff fulfilled that task. Next, Brooks went into a screening room—without a script—and viewed what Ernie had prepared. Said Mel, "I mumbled [in a Russian Jewish accent] whatever I felt that that old guy would have mumbled, trying to find a plot in this maze of abstractions. We cut it down to three and a half minutes and called it *The Critic*." The result was a product of Pintoff's company and Brooks's newly formed Crossbow Productions (an entity created for tax purposes and, as a side benefit, for Mel to feel that he was becoming a more prestigious figure within the show business world).

In May 1963, the short subject opened at the Sutton Theater on Manhattan's East Side. Within *The Critic* a series of geometric patterns flow across the screen. On the sound track there is a running commentary by a cranky and clueless old Jewish man who has obviously wandered into the art house cinema and cannot fathom what he sees on the screen. As the elderly Russian seats himself in the theater, he wonders aloud, "I don't see a poyson heah. What is it, a squiggle? It's a fence. It's a little fence. Nope, it's moving. It's a cockaroach. I'm looking at a cockaroach. I came to see a hot French picture with a little nakedness; what am I looking at here?" Later, he mutters, "Vat da hall is it? . . . I don't know much about psychoanalysis, but I'd say this was a 'doity' picture." Relying on the same type of comedy patter that made his 2000 Year Old Man performances and his Ballantine beer commercials so popular, Brooks turned this relatively brief footage into an engaging piece of satire.

The Critic benefited from playing at the Sutton Theater on the same program as a new Peter Sellers comedy, *Heavens Above!* That British film was held over at the art house cinema, and during the coming weeks, many moviegoers had the opportunity to view Brooks's amusing spoof of the pseudo-art film. By then several movie critics had already endorsed this Brooks-Pintoff offering. Bosley Crowther (of the *New York Times*) applauded the "cheery" entry, calling it "good for a few rich laughs." The *New York Herald Tribune* scribe judged *The Critic* to be "brilliant . . . the epitome of wit."

To everyone's astonishment, *The Critic* began winning plaudits at assorted film competitions, including a prize at a West German film festival and a trophy from the British Academy of Film and Television Arts. To Brooks's and Pintoff's great pleasure, *The Critic* was nominated for an Academy Award in the Best Short Subject—Animation category. At the April 13, 1964, ceremonies, held at the Santa Monica Civic Auditorium, Mel was on hand with Anne Bancroft (who had won an Academy Award the previous year for *The Miracle Worker* but had not been able to attend the ceremonies because she was working on Broadway at the time). To the nervous couple's joy, *The Critic* won an Oscar.

Later in life Brooks wisecracked that *The Critic* and "Fruit of the Loom were the best shorts ever made." Nevertheless, Mel was elated to have finally begun his filmmaking career and to have made such a positive impression on the industry and the public alike. Possibly, he speculated, his long-held ambitions of becoming a Hollywood mover and shaker might have a legitimate chance of occurring.

21

Getting Smart

[Anne Bancroft] . . . was my patroness. We were living separately, and then I moved in with her. I always saved enough money to pay for dinner. I was not quite a gigolo. I always paid for the food, even though I didn't pay for the rent. . . . But she was paying for a lot of other stuff that I don't bring up. Like laundry and dry cleaning.

—Mel Brooks, 1997

When Anne Bancroft fled Hollywood in 1957 and retreated to New York to begin a new life as a Broadway performer, she felt extremely vulnerable in her private life due to her recent bad marriage. That sour experience had made her defensive and suspicious and led her to remove herself somewhat from the social scene. "I guess men were afraid of me, of the character I represented then, since no one dared dating me," she later told a friend. As Bancroft underwent therapy and became more self-confident and emotionally open, she found that, over time, she had attracted two serious suitors: comedian turned stage/film director Mike Nichols and Mel Brooks. Anne recalled to the same confidant about these two audacious bright wits who dared to infiltrate her emotional wall, "I admired Mike Nichols for his talent, but Mel had a lethal weapon: he made me laugh to death. I fell instantly in love with him." (In fact, Bancroft told her psychiatrist soon after meeting Brooks: "Let's speed this process up—I've met the right man.")

Anne did her best to make Mel feel less self-conscious about the fact that she was earning a very good income while he was struggling mightily to make ends meet. (Years afterward, Brooks kidded of their temporary role reversal in which she was the breadwinner, "When we went to a Chinese restaurant, she'd slip the money under the table so I could pay the bill. And she'd say, "Don't leave such a big tip; it's my money!'"

After his divorce from Florence Baum in 1962, Mel moved fully into Anne's West 11th Street brownstone home. They were seen about town as a pair and now made no pretense of hiding their relationship (even in an era when unmarried couples were still not readily accepted). However, neither of them, particularly Bancroft, would commit publicly to when she and her comedian boyfriend might marry.

By the fall of 1963, Anne Bancroft was in London preparing for her demanding role in the upcoming screen drama *The Pumpkin Eater*, which was to costar Peter Finch and James Mason. During Anne's time away, Brooks frequently flew to England to be with her. When filming ended, Bancroft returned to the United States. In the spring of 1964, she attended the Academy Awards, at which she was a presenter. More important to her, she wanted to be at Mel's side as his animated short subject, *The Critic*, had been Oscar nominated. While in Hollywood, Anne renewed her acquaintanceship with the Tinseltown press. Bancroft informed veteran newspaper snoop Louella Parsons that she had already completed six years of psychoanalysis, adding, "I'm at that time in my life where you stop looking for the man on the white horse and settle for another human being."

Bancroft and Brooks were now into the fourth year of their romantic relationship, and they had settled many of their differences of opinion. She had learned to trust this wildly funny man, who, like her, came from a humble background, had survived an unhappy first marriage, and badly wanted to gain self-identity through substantial show business success. By now, Bancroft had become less fierce in her consuming drive to be a self-sufficient career woman, while Brooks accepted that his beloved was far too talented to become "just" a conventional housewife. Anne summed up their give-and-take domestic negotiations with: "Like so many problems, we found that they really didn't exist except in our minds. I don't know why—maybe my thirtyish 'maturity' solved it. I simply found myself working only when the role was exactly what I wanted with time and emotion left for other things in life."

Once those barriers were largely resolved, the couple still had to deal with the issue of her being Catholic and his being Jewish. Having an interfaith marriage did not bother the twosome, but they were concerned about how each of their strong-willed mothers would react to news of the impending marriage. Anne noted, "When I brought Mel home, my mother said, 'You could do better.' We still laugh about that." As for Mel, he claimed, tongue-in-cheek, that when he and his intended visited Kitty Kaminsky to tell her of their imminent nuptials, he had a hard time conversing with his mother. "Her head was in the oven, I couldn't hear a word." Later, on a more serious note, he countered his oft-told joke with: "The truth is, my mother was so delighted and proud that I married such a wonderful, beautiful girl. You know, when somebody becomes a star, they're no longer, you know, Jewish or not Jewish. A star is a big thing, you know, six points is better, but a star! You know, my wife . . . my wife was a star. My mother was very happy."

Bancroft claimed that Brooks never actually proposed to her, but that she asked him to get married and he finally said yes. Thus, on Thursday, August 6, 1964, the duo arrived at city hall at noontime to be wed in a civil ceremony. (No one there seemed to recognize the famous actress.) A man they encountered on the way into the clerk's office served as their witness. Although the pair had thought to obtain a marriage license, neither party remembered to bring wedding rings for the ceremony. (Bancroft improvised by taking off one of her silver earrings and using it as a substitute.) Later, the radiant bride quipped of her groom, "My mother was so happy I got married, it could have been an orangutan."

When the media first reported on the offbeat union, actress Patty Duke, Anne's teenaged costar in *The Miracle Worker*, said, "It wasn't a surprise to me that she and Mel Brooks married—of course she would marry that crazy man!" However, much of the public was puzzled by two such seemingly disparate individuals becoming a legalized couple. Many onlookers felt that crazy—meshugge—Mel was definitely getting the better end of the deal: wedding a beautiful, talented, and successful performer. Some less kind souls labeled the offbeat couple Beauty and the Beast.

Despite the public's surprise about this out of the ordinary celebrity marriage, each of the newlyweds was genuinely happy with his/her choice of a new life partner. Bancroft said, "People think we're an unlikely couple. Wrong; we're perfect. He's terribly funny all the time. I'm not above competing, and at first maybe I would try to top him. Now, I'd rather just sit back, laugh and enjoy, y'know? Maybe 'cause I discovered early, I couldn't." Anne summed up her feelings about Mel with: "He makes me laugh a lot. I get excited when I hear his key in the door. It's like, 'Ooh! The party's going to start!'" Brooks observed facetiously, "We're so close we interchange roles. I can become the wonderfully statuesque, feminine Anne Bancroft, she becomes the Yiddish Mel."

Not that over the years the couple didn't have their share of normal, everyday arguments. One time, Mel Brooks arrived for a dinner meeting of his beloved Gourmet Club. He was in a rage. When asked what the problem was, he explained that just before he was leaving for his repast with the boys, Anne had said, "Mel, when you die, where do you want me to put you?" He had retorted, "In the kitchen, under the table. And what makes you think I'm going to die before you?" Now he was stewing because he knew his wife had knowingly taunted him about his greatest fear in life—dying. On another occasion Bancroft and Brooks were in the midst of a flare-up that was quickly turning into a heated argument. Anne noticed that Mel was beginning to clench his hand into a fist. She shouted, "Don't you dare touch me, my body is my instrument." To which Mel replied, "Oh, yeah? Then play Melancholy Baby."

To Bancroft's way of thinking, such disputes were a normal part of any marriage. She reasoned, "Hostility is basic to both sexes. It's part of the business of sex appeal. . . . We all have hostility in us. I think it's dangerous to repress it. Gorillas never do." Even with their recurrent differences of opinion, Mel knew for certain that "God was very good to me. God said, 'Here, I'll give you one present for your life. I'll give you Anne Bancroft.' I said, 'OK, that's enough. That'll cover me,' you know."

• • •

After their marriage, Mel and Anne continued to live at her West 11th Street house. In the next two years she chose to work only infrequently. On film, she costarred in 1965's *The Slender Thread* and replaced an ailing Patricia Neal in 1966's *Seven Women*. On stage, she appeared in the 1965 Broadway drama *The Devil*, a short-running mishap in which she was miscast. Meanwhile, Brooks continued to make TV appearances as the 2000 Year Old Man, was a frequent comedic guest on *The Tonight Show with Johnny Carson*, and turned up on such other small-screen fare as *Open End*, David Susskind's syndicated discussion series.

Back in 1963, Mel had scripted a pilot for ABC-TV. It was titled *Inside Danny Baker*. Its rather thin premise focused on a precocious son of a dentist who hopes to earn funds to buy a fishing boat by turning his Ping-Pong table into a work of modern art. It featured actor Roger Mobley and New York Yankees pitcher Whitey Ford. The half-hour entry failed to inspire network interest, and the project was shelved.

Then, in 1964, Brooks was contacted by TV personality/producer David Susskind. He and his partner, Daniel Melnick, who owned Talent Associates, had had a brainstorm for a new television series. It would play off the then current James Bond craze that had begun with the success of 1962's *Dr. No* and had built tremendously with its follow-up (*From Russia with Love*). Another Bond entry (*Goldfinger*) was due for late 1964 release. Meanwhile, several movie producers were already jumping on the superspy craze with their own film productions and TV series.

Susskind and Melnick thought the revitalized espionage genre was now ripe to be satirized on TV, where the spy series *The Man from U.N.C.L.E.* was already a big hit. The producers also believed that in this era of President Lyndon Johnson and the increasingly unpopular Vietnam War, much of the American public was becoming fed up with the restrictive, often blundering U.S. government. This led the Talent Associates partners to conclude that a good number of home viewers would be amused to see a show that poked fun at the red tape of the American governmental bureaucratic structure.

Initially, Talent Associates contacted comedian Mike Nichols about this project because of his recognized flare for satire. They asked if he would write and direct the pilot. Negotiations got under way, but then Nichols became committed to several other ventures and had to drop out. Melnick and Susskind were anxious to get their idea into motion, as they feared that their spoof premise might occur to another TV producer or that the spy genre craze could become passé. The executives turned to Mel Brooks.

At this point in time, Brooks was having great difficulties getting his *Springtime for Hitler* to come together as a novel. Again, he badly needed to improve his cash flow situation, so he quickly accepted the offer from Talent Associates. Melnick, who had been a high-ranking executive at ABC, contacted that network and pitched them this idea of a Mel Brooks–created project. The network's decision makers soon green-lighted the concept.

Despite all Mel's show business experience to date, he remained a talking writer who was best at coming up with a volley of wild and sometimes viable ideas. He still lacked the requisite discipline and organizational ability to sit down and turn out a script on schedule. He also had deliberately not yet learned to type, reasoning from past experience on TV shows that on a comedy writing team that "the one who typed got tied down. I wanted to be the one who ran around and acted it out." (Then too, Brooks was still determined, somehow, to finish his book, and that took up a good deal of his time.)

Talent Associates quickly realized they needed to provide Brooks with a collaborator *if* this venture was to materialize in the relatively near future. (Fortunately, Mel allowed himself to be persuaded of the wisdom of this practical decision.) The producers' choice for Mel's potential team-mate was Buck Henry Zuckerman. He was a New Yorker and a Dartmouth graduate. As Buck Henry, the acerbic young man had made an impact on television by writing for (and sometimes acting in) such TV fare as *The Garry Moore Show* and *That Was the Week That Was*. Like Mel, Buck had already made a foray into films, having cowritten and played a role in the independent feature *The Troublemaker*.

The producers arranged for Mel and Buck to meet at the production company's midtown offices. Brooks detailed, "They had a pool table at Talent Associates, and he [Buck Henry] was a very good pool player. I grew up in a pool hall, so I said, 'This is the guy.' Anyway, Buck was immediately brilliant, smart, very sharp, satiric, you know, a truly witty mind." The two men hit it off. Over the next four months, the duo played a good deal of pool and bounced ideas off each other.

From the start, the iconoclastic Brooks insisted that this show must not fall into the category of the then typical TV sitcom. He explained, "I was sick of looking at all those nice, sensible situation comedies. They were such distortions of life. If a maid ever took over my house like Hazel [the title character of the 1961–1965 series starring Shirley Booth as a busybody domestic], I'd set her hair on fire. I wanted to do a crazy, unreal, comic-strip kind of thing about something besides a family. No one had ever done a show about an idiot before. I decided to be the first."

The wacky premise soon fell into place. The male lead would work for CONTROL, a U.S. intelligence agency based in Washington, D.C. The organization's chief mandate was to outmaneuver KAOS, a global organization dedicated to dominating the world. The "hero" would be a bumbling do-gooder. He would repeatedly exasperate his boss (the Chief) and would often be prevented from screwing up a top secret mission by his levelheaded and beautiful female partner. Brooks came up with the name Maxwell Smart for the clumsy protagonist, who also went by his code name of Agent 86. (That particular number was suggested by Melnick, playing off the slang term "to eighty-six someone" because of drunken, obnoxious behavior.) It was Henry who decided that 86's attractive partner would be known merely as "Agent 99." The show was to be called *Get Smart*, a title selected because it had various meanings on different levels.

The writers came up with other inspired lunacy for the program. Maxwell's trademark gadget would be a shoe phone. (Reputedly, this particular idea was based on the time that several phones were ringing all at once in Brooks's office, and it prompted him in crazed reaction to take off his shoe and answer it.) Not to be outdone, the hard-working and inventive Henry suggested the Cone of Silence, a plastic dome that could be lowered from the ceiling at CONTROL headquarters so the Chief and Agent 86 could discuss vital matters in secret. (Naturally, the Cone never operated properly and the two men were always forced to shout at the top of their lungs, thus giving away the contents of their top secret discussions.)

With the pilot episode of the daffy situation comedy mapped out, the next chore was to cast the lead characters. At first, Orson Bean was considered to play Maxwell Smart. Mel suggested that he might be right to portray Agent 86, but that idea never triggered great momentum with Talent Associates. When the pilot script was presented to ABC, the network decided that Tom Poston, who had gained currency on *The Steve Allen Show* (especially with his role as the goofy "Man on the Street") and on panel programs, was the right choice to be Maxwell Smart. While this notion was being bandied about, ABC executives voiced concerns about the overall tone of the pilot script. They claimed they did not realize it would be so antic . . . so antiestablishment. Network management suggested that Agent 86 should have a mother (seen on the show) and Max should reveal his tender side by being the thoughtful owner of an appealing canine. Brooks and Henry rebelled at such conventional sentimental notions. In retaliation, they added a pooch for Maxwell, but called him Fang, and made him a rather disheveled dog. As to a mother for Smart, the writers said, "Absolutely not!"

Soon thereafter, a displeased ABC shelved *Get Smart*. Talent Associates wanted to shop the project elsewhere but had to return the $7,500 development money to the network. The duo scraped together the necessary sum, and *Get Smart* was again their property. Through Grant

Tinker, an NBC executive on the West Coast, Talent Associates was able to convince that network to shoot a pilot. NBC "suggested" that the acerbic comedian Don Adams (whom they had under contract) be cast instead of Tom Poston in the pivotal role. (Brooks agreed to this decision because he thought he and Adams shared a physical resemblance—especially with their close-set eyes—and each had a biting sense of humor. It was Adams who contributed many of the personality traits and character business for the Maxwell Smart character, some based on past routines he had performed.) Rounding out the show's lead players were Barbara Feldon as the sexy, intelligent Agent 99, and Edward Platt as the harassed Chief. The pilot was shot in black and white by Brooks's onetime *Your Show of Shows* and *Caesar's Hour* colleague Howard Morris.

Get Smart debuted on NBC-TV on September 18, 1965, in the 7:30 P.M. time slot. The show quickly gathered momentum with critics and the public alike. *Variety* reported, "It is broad and unadulterated hokum, usually played to the hilt." *Time* magazine quipped of the new half-hour offering, "It dares to be healthily sick while the competition is sickeningly healthy." *TV Guide*'s Cleveland Amory endorsed, "Credit the developers of *Get Smart*, Mel Brooks and Buck Henry with at least getting down to that serious business of being funny right from the start." In contrast, Jack Gould of the *New York Times* was far less enthusiastic: "Having begun with a whale of a concept, the program promptly proceeded to lay on the slapstick much too heavily and, on the premiere at least, spoil just about everything. . . . The use of a dwarf in the part of 'Mr. Big' was indicative of an undercurrent of tastelessness. With a massive dose of restraint, however, *Get Smart* might still make it."

The TV show gathered steam through the year and rode a rising crest of popularity. Many of the show's catchphrases caught on with home viewers, and before long, such expressions as "Would you believe?" "Sorry about that, Chief," "I asked you not to tell me that," "Missed it by that much," and "The old so-and-so trick" entered the lexicon. *Get Smart* ended the season as America's 12th favorite TV series. Analyzing the program's hearty endorsement from the public, Brooks sounded off with, "We're doing a comic strip. Smart is a dedicated boob whose heart is in the right place, but whose brains are in his shoes. We don't pretend that Smart himself or the situation he's involved in is plausible. It's the broadest kind of satire. It succeeds because it's bright, witty, refreshing—and lucky enough to be on opposite low-rated shows."

Mel grew expansive as he sounded off on the winning qualities of this highly commercial hit. "It's a funny bird. It's the Big City protest. It's the only witty show on TV today. . . . I think *Get Smart*, incidentally, is a man's show, the first one in a long time. All the TV shows today, y'know, are for women. Or for kids. Women and kids, they rule TV. It's a matriarchal society. But *Get Smart* is for men."

During the first season, Mel Brooks wrote three episodes (numbers 1, 8, and 16), for one of which he was Emmy nominated in the Comedy Writing category. But then, involved in many other potential projects, he grew tired of his *Get Smart* scripting chores, which demanded far more concentration, organization, and discipline than he cared to invest. (He reasoned, "It's hard to capture one's vision and dream in 23½ minutes." Another time, he reasoned, "When you are doing a series, of course, it's terribly hard to avoid repetition. If I tried to write *Get Smart* every week, I'd run dry very soon—I could put a couple of things together, but the juice, the chemistry wouldn't be there.") Thereafter, Brooks served largely as just a consultant to the ongoing program. (This less taxing job required him to commute to the West Coast at least once a month.) Naturally, as one of the show's creators, he received royalties and other allied income.

Long before the end of the first season, Brooks and Buck Henry had a serious falling-out. It stemmed from the show's credits crawl, which read "By Mel Brooks with Buck Henry." Henry felt he deserved equal billing with Brooks, and it irked him greatly that Brooks was receiving the lion's share of media attention. Mel insisted that the "misunderstanding" was a result of his agents pressuring him to take senior credit on the show because of his array of industry credentials, and that he deeply regretted the rift it had caused with Henry. Brooks also asserted that his representatives had originally wanted only Mel's name listed as a creator of the series, and it was Brooks who fought to gain Henry his due. (A decade later, Brooks spoke sharply about the still frosty situation with Henry: "Buck envied me because of the hit I'd made with the Two-Thousand-Year-Old Man. I'd galloped like a greedy child, and got ahead and taken off. I had a reputation for being a crazy Jew animal, whereas Buck thought of himself as an intellectual. Well, I was an intellectual, too. . . . What Buck couldn't bear was the idea of this wacko Jew being billed over him. The truth is that he read magazines but he's not an intellectual, he's a pedant.")

Get Smart, under the strong stewardship of executive producer Leonard Stern, remained on the air for five seasons, the last two under the aegis of CBS. The cult favorite, which had been so heavily merchandized with all sorts of tie-ins, returned as a feature film, *The Nude Bomb* (aka *The Return of Maxwell Smart*) with only Don Adams among the lead players re-creating his TV role. The movie was a box-office flop. In 1989, the property emerged again as a TV movie, this time reuniting Adams with Barbara Feldon, and such others from the original series as Dick Gautier (as Hymie the Robot) and Bernie Kopell (as Conrad Siegfried). Six years later, the Fox network revived *Get Smart*. This time around, Andy Dick had the lead, playing the son of Agent 86 and his wife, Agent 99. The lame rehash came and went in early 1995. A decade later, Warner Bros. announced that it would film a big-screen version of the cult TV series.

Despite the financial rewards and high industry visibility that *Get Smart* provided Mel, he was relieved when the show finally went off the air. For one thing, he had a great concern that *Get Smart* would force him to remain in the small-screen medium. It led him to say years later, "You know they can't pay you enough for the aggravation you go through in television. I went through six years [in one capacity or another] of *Get Smart*. The costs are always a factor. They would have preferred making that show by putting two people in a closet with a naked light bulb talking to each other for 13 weeks." Thereafter, each time he was offered his own TV series, he declined because television "grinds you up, makes a sausage out of you every week." However, over the coming years, circumstances would prompt the mercurial Brooks to change his mind about participating again in the hectic arena of television series.

22

Flaunt It, Baby

The best way to stay alive as a good writer is to run a bulldozer through your conditioned values, learn to live frugally—which I haven't—and take all the time you need to develop your ideas. You can't do that if economics are smashing you to the wall. Movies and television are so mechanized now that if you've got a little bit of talent there are a lot of fellas in shiny suits waiting to grab you and chain you to a typewriter. Pretty soon you're thinking the way they're thinking. Or a television producer wants you to write a story about a bird with a broken wing or some other piece of idiocy which people don't have to watch at all—they can just hear it kind of subliminally. This is what you've got to resist.

—Mel Brooks, 1966

By the mid-1960s, Mel Brooks had gained cult status as the 2000 Year Old Man and was enjoying high visibility in the entertainment industry and with the public as the cocreator of the thriving *Get Smart* TV series/franchise. Mel's elevated professional status allowed him the luxury of being more selective in choosing his projects. Meanwhile, he and Anne Bancroft were enjoying the fruits of their respective professional successes. In late 1965, the Brookses purchased a summer home at Lonelyville on Fire Island. When asked what inspired the new real estate purchase, Anne explained, "There are no autos and few phones on Fire Island. If I stayed home [in Manhattan] I couldn't get any rest. I'll do nothing for an entire month. Fire Island has the best beach I've ever seen. It is a narrow island with the bay on one side and the ocean on the other. From our house you can see both."

Bancroft also updated the media on life with the zany Brooks: "I'm a moody person. When I'm in a bad mood anything can make me angry: if I'm in a good mood nothing bothers me. I'm hard to live with and so is Mel hard to live with. But my husband is one of the funniest men who ever lived. Sometimes I laugh at him until the tears roll out of my eyes."

• • •

In the mid-1960s, Brooks occasionally found himself hired as a "script doctor" for floundering Broadway plays. It was the type of task that meshed with Mel's then helter-skelter work habits. Such assignments generally required no protracted commitment on the part of the consultant, but only to step into the fray and spew forth ideas that others on the production team would execute. If the last-minute counsel proved at all helpful, it enhanced the script doctor's behind-the-scenes reputation; if the efforts failed, no serious fault could be attributed to the consultant, who had merely tried to salvage what proved to be an untenable situation.

For *Kelly*, which cost nearly $650,000 (a whopping sum at the time), Mel was one of three writers (including Leonard Stern of *Get Smart* fame) brought in during the messy pre-Broadway tryout. The show's producers (*Get Smart*'s David Susskind and Daniel Melnick, as well as independent film mogul Joseph E. Levine) paid Brooks to help rescue this floundering musical about the legendary Steve Brodie, who had once jumped off the Brooklyn Bridge. The troubled show opened and closed at Manhattan's Broadhurst Theater in one night during February 1965. Thirteen months later, Brooks was involved in a similar capacity with *The Best Laid Plans*, which bowed and folded in New York within two days. Mel insisted to the press that he had not rewritten Gwen Davis's comedy but had merely helped director Arthur Storch in an advisory capacity.

With much more success, Mel was a cowriter on *The Sid Caesar, Imogene Coca, Carl Reiner, Howard Morris Special* that aired on CBS-TV on April 12, 1966. The nostalgic reunion of the gang from *Your Show of Shows* did well in the ratings. Along with Sam Denoff, Bill Persky, Carl Reiner, and Mel Tolkin, Brooks shared an Emmy Award in the category of Outstanding Writing in Variety. (At the same June 1967 Emmy ceremony, Brooks's *Get Smart* coworker, Buck Henry, shared an Emmy with Leonard Stern in the category of Outstanding Writing in Comedy for a particularly funny Maxwell Smart segment.)

In his capacity as a TV personality, Brooks was still much in evidence on the small screen. He was a guest in 1966 on such game shows as CBS's *The Face Is Familiar* and NBC's *Eye Guess*. In May 1967, Mel paired with Carl Reiner as hosts of (and performers on) *The Colgate Comedy Hour*, a 60-minute variety show designed to resurrect the 1950s series of the same name. The NBC-TV pilot failed to generate sufficient network interest for any continuation. Also, Mel served as a dapper guest cohost on the syndicated *Mike Douglas Show* in late 1967.

Back in 1963, Brooks had written, directed, and appeared in the trailer to *My Son, the Hero*. This promoted a dubbed edition of *The Titans*, a European-made costume "epic" overhauled for U.S. release by Carl Reiner. Mel's amusing promotional piece earned more attention than the actual film. Now, in 1965, Brooks was scheduled for a role in *Easy Come, Easy Go*, a low-budget comedy for Paramount Pictures to be directed by Barry Shear and to showcase British comedian Terry-Thomas and the singing act of Jan (Berry) and Dean (Torrence). However, on August 5, 1965, in Chatsworth (in the West San Fernando Valley outside of Los Angeles), a freight train being filmed for the picture slammed into a flatcar carrying several of the production's acting and technical team. Twelve people were injured, including the 24-year-old Berry, who fractured his left leg, and director Barry Shear, 42, who suffered internal injuries. During the impact, a camera worth over $10,000 was thrown to the ground and smashed. The picture was canceled before Mel even got in front of the camera.

Amid these myriad activities, Mel found time to talk with Larry Siegel for *Playboy* magazine. The results appeared in the October 1966 issue. The offbeat Q&A session labeled Brooks as that exceedingly amusing comedic writer who had now turned the usually staid forum of the print interview into a fresh and irreverent art form. In the course of this classic dialogue, the madcap Mel was witty, gregarious, and always ready to throw the writer off track with such non-sequitur interjections as: "How much are you paying me for this?" When asked about his recent trip to the Continent he shot back, "Europe is very near and dear to my heart. Would you like to see a picture of it?" The highly mirthful article was so popular it led to a second *Playboy* interview showcase for Brooks a few years later.

• • •

While Brooks had many professional, financial, and personal distractions in early to mid-1966, his mind was always on his pet project, *Springtime for Hitler*. At first, the satire about Germany's dictator emerged in the form of a long anecdotal novel. It focused on key adventures in the despot's life that led to his becoming the dastardly leader of the Third Reich. By the time of Mel's travails on the Broadway musical *All American*, the long-brewing work had morphed in a new direction. Now the fiction highlighted a faded White Way producer (based on a man Brooks had worked for in the 1940s) who had mounted a string of flop shows, all of them financed by his wooing and bilking vulnerable old ladies. As Mel further developed the plot line, he utilized the gimmick of having the sleazy producer overfinance his latest production (a show glorifying Adolf Hitler) and hoping it will be a flop so that none of the backers—let alone the Internal Revenue Service—will be any the wiser. (A variation of this plot premise had been used in the past, including in the RKO screen comedy *New Faces of 1937*, costarring Milton Berle and Harriet Hilliard. Then, too, the gimmick of mocking Hitler to belittle his importance had been employed in the 1950s by Brooks's old pal, comedian Will Jordan. Later, shock comic Lenny Bruce weaved a variation of Jordan's routine into his own unorthodox club act and it appeared on his comedy album, *The Sick Humor of Lenny Bruce*.)

As Mel labored off and on for a long period over his efforts, he showed his work in progress to various people in show business. Several critiqued that it was too dialogue heavy and would be better served as a play. Anxious to get the property off the ground, Mel followed this advice and tried to adapt his narrative into the new format. However, when he had completed a rough draft, he was now informed by those who saw it that the revamped work had far too many scenes to be feasible as a play. "So, what is it?" Brooks wondered. "A screenplay," he was advised.

By the mid-1960s, *Springtime for Hitler* was taking shape as a film script. Mel worked on it at home, as well as at his place out at Fire Island, and, increasingly, at an office on Manhattan's West 46th Street. The latter premises belonged to producer Lore Noto, an acquaintance of Mel and his helper, Alfa-Betty Olsen. (She was transcribing Brooks's handwritten drafts and notes into a typed format and, later, would serve as casting agent and assistant on the film.) Olsen remembered, "In return for looking after Noto's mail and things, we had an office, and that's where we wrote it. Lore would come in after lunch and then, around two o'clock, the phone would ring, and it would be Anne Bancroft. Anne would get Lore on the phone and ask him, 'Is my husband there?' That's how it went. We also cast the movie out of that office. Everything was kind of makeshift. . . . And it was just evident Mel wanted it very much. You could feel him reaching for the brass ring. Writing . . . [this property] . . . was Mel creating himself, he wanted to declare himself to the world."

Eventually, Brooks had a polished 30-page screen treatment and various drafts of his ever-developing screenplay. He began to peddle it to different movie studios, but almost invariably he was met by rebuffs from executives who were flabbergasted that Mel could expect any Hollywood lot to produce an unorthodox comedy that dared to highlight Adolf Hitler in such a lighthearted manner, let alone include a slimy Broadway producer who seduced elderly women for their life savings.

The fact that these conservative movie executives had missed the obvious satirical thrust of Mel's work was all the more infuriating to Brooks. There was, however, one Hollywood top honcho, Universal Pictures' Lew Wasserman, who said he might actually take a chance on Brooks's shocking frolic. But Wasserman demanded that the author agree to substituting the "less" odious Benito Mussolini—Hitler's Italian dictator/ally—for der Führer in the narrative. Much as Brooks wanted his much sweated-over property to become a film, he could not conceive of his very personal work becoming *Springtime for Mussolini*.

A dejected Brooks returned to New York. He wondered if his film would ever become an actuality. Then an associate introduced Mel to producer Sidney Glazier. Glazier, born in Philadelphia of Russian Jewish immigrant parents, had endured a very difficult childhood. After serving in World War II, Glazier relocated to New York City. For a while he was the night manager of a bar. Later, he became an apprentice jeweler, then a salesman of bonds for Israel. Eventually he emerged as the executive director of the Eleanor Roosevelt Cancer Foundation. After Mrs. Roosevelt's death in 1962, Glazier produced a documentary on the late humanitarian. The 1965 film won an Academy Award.

Mel made an appointment to meet Glazier at Manhattan's Hello coffee shop. When Brooks walked into the restaurant, Sidney was eating a tuna fish sandwich and drinking a cup of coffee. Brooks immediately launched into his hard-sell pitch, in which he dramatically acted out highlights from *Springtime for Hitler*. Brooks's all-out presentation so amused Glazier that soon the producer was choking with laughter—and spitting out bits of tuna and a spray of coffee. When Sidney finally regained his composure, he informed Mel, "I vow to get this movie made. The world must see this picture."

True to his promise, Sidney Glazier set to work locating the necessary backing for the unorthodox feature film. He raised over $400,000 himself and then turned to industry sources for the balance of the needed money and the all-important theatrical distribution deal. He took Mel with him to a battery of meetings with industry big shots. At these conferences, Brooks provided a condensed account of *Springtime for Hitler*, along with copies of the screen treatment. The two enthusiasts met with little success until they visited the New York City offices of Avco Embassy, the filmmaking/distribution corporation run by Joseph E. Levine. (This self-made man had gained his fortune in the movie business with a series of Italian-made cloak-and-sandal features, as well as with such art-house imports as the Oscar-winning foreign film *Two Women*. Levine was the same powerful moneyman who had been a backer of the 1965 Broadway fiasco *Kelly*, for which Mel had provided script rewrites.)

Much to the great surprise of both Brooks and Glazier, who had endured so many rejections on this politically incorrect project, Levine agreed to complete the financing of *Springtime for Hitler* and to distribute the resultant movie comedy. However, he made a few demands. The film's budget could not exceed $941,000 on the planned two-month shoot. Also, the picture's name must be changed because, Levine argued, many theater chains would not exhibit a picture with "Hitler" in its title. After much debate, the men agreed to call the movie *The Producers*.

When Levine asked Brooks and Glazier, "Who do we get to direct?" Mel replied brazenly, "Me. I know everything about this picture. I know where every character has to stand." After some negotiation, it was arranged that Brooks would audition for the director's assignment by helming a TV commercial with Alfa-Betty Olsen serving as his casting director. If the results proved successful, Mel would be given the green light to direct *The Producers*. The ad was done for Frito-Lay products and proved to be sufficiently professional. As Levine had promised, Mel got the go-ahead to make his feature film directing debut.

While the financing arrangements were being completed, Mel further polished his long-in-the-works screenplay. He knew that the story line required an original song for the stage show within the movie, but he kept procrastinating about trying his hand at such an unfamiliar task, and considered finding a real tunesmith to create the number. One day, Brooks's wife, Anne Bancroft, said to him, "You're musical, you're a good singer, and besides, you've been talking my head off ever since I met you about how much you want to be a songwriter. So take a pad, a pencil, go into the next room, and I'll bet within an hour you'll come out with a nice song."

According to Brooks, "I took a pad, a pencil and went into the next room. And lo and behold, one hour and one month later came out with 'Springtime for Hitler.' (I had come up with not only the lyrics but also the tune, which I'd heard in my head, picked out on a piano, and then hummed into a tape recorder—a full 32-bar song that a musicologist friend of mine then transcribed into actual notes on actual music paper, a method of composing I've since used for all my songs.)" Mel also wrote another number for the upcoming film. He called it "Prisoners of Love" (coincidentally, the final words of a lengthy prison sketch done on *Caesar's Hour* years earlier). Later, Brooks said, "I can't tell you how thrilled I was to see the first copies of the sheet music of my songs and the credit in the upper-right-hand corner: 'Words & Music by Mel Brooks.'"

•   •   •

Over the years, as Brooks was developing his cherished screen project into its final shape, he had one actor in mind to play the seamy Broadway producer, Max Bialystock. That was Zero Mostel, Mel's larger-than-life compatriot from the Gourmet Club. Like Brooks, Mostel had been born in Brooklyn and was Jewish. Even more so than Mel, Zero had suffered a roller-coaster career. He was an intellect and multitalented artist (including being a painter and a sculptor) who was encased in a strangely shaped body and possessed of an odd-looking face. Mostel was a righteous liberal, and his political affiliations had led to his being blacklisted during the anti-Communist hysteria of the late 1940s and early 1950s.

As a result, Mostel's promising career as a movie character lead fell apart. Thereafter, he struggled to find work in the New York theater. He made a great comeback in the early 1960s starring on Broadway in *A Funny Thing Happened on the Way to the Forum* and *Fiddler on the Roof*. When Brooks showed "Z" (as he fondly called Mostel) the script to *The Producers*, the latter said no, it was not right for him. However, Mel was prepared for this reaction and had already sneaked a copy of the screenplay to the actor's wife, Kate. She convinced her husband that he would be totally crazy to reject this meaty screen assignment.

Initially, Mel thought of British comedian Peter Sellers to play Leo Bloom, the timid accountant who accidentally provides Max Bialystock with the great scheme to swindle his way to financial success. Brooks contacted Sellers's representatives. The actor expressed an interest in this film project, and Mel arranged to meet with Peter when the latter next passed through New York City. The day of the meeting Sellers insisted on dragging Brooks to Bloomingdale's for a shopping excursion. As they went from counter to counter, Mel kept bringing up *The Producers*. At every available opportunity, Brooks tried to capture Peter's attention—to explain the role of Leo Bloom and reiterate yet again how excited Brooks was at the prospect of the great Sellers interpreting the part. Brooks recalls, "I'd be in the middle of a very important moment—where Bialystock says to Bloom, 'Do you want to live in a gray little world, do you want to be confined, don't you want to fly?'—and he'd say 'You like this buckle? What do you think of this buckle.'" This was typical of Sellers's scattered state of mind, in which he would fasten on a particular thing for the moment and "get lost in it" and then, just as quickly, move on to a new passing interest. Eventually, even the persistent Mel gave up trying to get through to the British comedian. Brooks realized he would have to search elsewhere to find his Leo Bloom.

While Brooks had been in vain pursuit of the elusive, vague Sellers during 1963, he also was spending many evenings backstage at the Martin Beck Theater on West 45th Street, where Anne Bancroft was starring in *Mother Courage and Her Children*. One of the supporting players in this serious drama was the young Gene Wilder, in the role of the Chaplain. It was not a funny part, but somehow the actor found comedic elements in the character. Each night, Wilder came offstage bemused as to why his performance had drawn laughs from the audience. Mel took sympathy on this meek, rather neurotic actor and explained to the naive soul that theatergoers were amused because Gene was just naturally funny.

Before long, the two men became friends, and Mel told him about *Springtime for Hitler*. Brooks confided that the screenplay had a perfect role for Wilder and that when the time came for the film to be made, the role was definitely Gene's. Wilder was thrilled at the opportunity. After *Mother Courage* ended its run, Gene heard nothing further from Mel. Thereafter, Wilder undertook more Broadway work and went to Hollywood for his first movie job, a supporting part in Warren Beatty's *Bonnie and Clyde*. After completing that period gangster film, Wilder went back to Manhattan and worked on the stage. One day, out of the blue, Mel appeared at Gene's dressing room and announced excitedly that he had the backing for *The Producers* and Wilder was now needed for the role. Gene quickly accepted the assignment.

One of the key supporting roles in *The Producers* was that of Franz Liebkind, the wacko Nazi zealot living in Greenwich Village who has written an awful play about Adolf Hitler. It is this play that Max and Leo acquire to be their hoped-for overnight Broadway flop. Originally, Mel thought that one of his neighbors on West 11th Street might be ideal for the offbeat part of Liebkind. He was Dustin Hoffman, then a struggling off-Broadway actor. Hoffman read for Brooks and agreed to play the odd-ball character. However, at the last minute Dustin was offered the young male lead in Mike Nichols's new screen project, *The Graduate*. (Coincidentally, Anne Bancroft had already accepted the role of Mrs. Robinson in that picture, which was to be shot in Hollywood.) With Hoffman now out of the running, Mel thought he might take on the role himself. Then he realized that such a chore would distract him from focusing his attentions on the consuming task of directing the movie. He held open auditions and chose Kenneth Mars, an intense young actor, to play the nutty German. Comedian Dick Shawn, whom Bancroft knew, agreed to appear as L.S.D., the drugged-out hippie singer who is cast as Der Führer in the musical within the movie.

Other auditions turned up Christopher Hewett (to play Roger De Bris, the untalented Broadway director who has a penchant for dressing in drag) and Lee Meredith (as Ulla, the shapely Swede who comes to work for Max and Leo). Anne Bancroft recommended Andréas Voutsinas, a fellow performer at the Actors Studio, for the role of the waspish Carmen Ghia, De Bris's swishy assistant and possessive lover. Joe Bologna, an actor acquaintance of Mel's, proposed that his stage actress girlfriend, Renee Taylor, would be just right for the small part of Eva Braun, Hitler's consort.

Filming on *The Producers* began on May 22, 1967, at the Production Center at 221 West 26th Street. The first day of the shoot Mel was so keyed up by his overwhelming responsibilities as director that when it came time for the first scene to be filmed he yelled "Cut" rather than "Action." The novice moviemaker had much more to learn about moviemaking.

According to Ralph Rosenblum, the movie's veteran film editor, who suffered a stormy working relationship with Brooks through much of this production, Mel seemed to be in well over his head on his debut directing assignment.

In his book, *When the Shooting Stops, the Cutting Begins: A Film Editor's Story*, Rosenblum remarked of Brooks, "Did he know that in the movies you could shoot only about five minutes of usable film in a day? . . . Brooks couldn't stand the waiting, and his impatience quickly extended to the cast. He soon found himself in a head-on conflict with the mountainous Mostel. The first time the star couldn't perform with just the inflection Brooks wanted, the entire project seemed to be slipping from the director's grasp. After several faulty takes, he started to shout, 'Goddamn it, why can't you . . .' but Mostel turned his head like a roving artillery gun and barked, 'One more tone like that and I'm leaving.'"

Soon it became a case of Mel Brooks asking assistants about his truculent star: "Is that fat pig ready yet?" with Zero Mostel remarking, "The director? What director? There's a director here?" (In fairness, part of Mostel's enormous bursts of temperament on the project could be attributed to the fact that some months before filming began he had been in a bus accident and suffered a severe leg injury. During the making of *The Producers*, the damaged limb was still causing Zero a great deal of pain and required him to limit the length of his workday. As for Brooks, he said later of Mostel, who died in 1977, "He could be wicked and cruel and he could be almost sweet, loving, kind, generous. The great thing about Zero was that he was uniquely gifted. He was really, truly talented, more talented than any actor except for Sid Caesar that I have ever worked with.")

• • •

Because Mel was a novice in helming a movie, his learning curve occurred on the actual shoot. The pressures of all the creative demands placed on Brooks made him out of sorts. The heavy organizational requirements thrust on this man—a person who thrived on spontaneity and found comfort in disorganization—made him frantic. Sometimes Mel hid his crushing concerns beneath a synthetic air of jauntiness in which he was overly solicitous to everyone in sight and put on an impromptu comedy routine to amuse and distract onlookers. At other times, he buried his mounting insecurities behind a bluster of authority. On several occasions, this caused problems on the set when a technician stepped in to suggest that what Brooks was demanding be done for a particular scene had hidden (negative) consequences. One day, cinematographer Joseph Coffey screamed at Mel, "You can't do that; it's even not cinematic!" This did not sit right with the fledgling filmmaker, and, typically, he became more insistent on having his way. Said Coffey, "That was the end of our romance."

One morning, at the end of screening the dailies on *The Producers*, Mel agitatedly rushed up to the front of the room and snarled at film editor Ralph Rosenblum, *"You just listen to me.* I don't want you to touch this fuckin' film again! You understand? I just finished with Coffey this afternoon—I told him I don't need his help, and I don't need your help either! I'll do it all myself. Don't you touch this film, you hear?! Don't *touch* it, until I finish shooting!" Such flare-ups led producer Sidney Glazier to shake his head in wonderment as he mumbled, "I don't know why Mel has to do this. Why does he have to make it so difficult?"

On a particularly unfortunate occasion, a harassed Brooks completely lost his cool with Joan Barthel, a reporter who had been invited onto the film set to write an important feature story on the making of this offbeat comedy. The director was in an especially foul mood that crucial day. He demanded of the visitor, "What the fuck do you want? . . . What do you want to know, honey? Want me to tell you the truth? Want me to give you the real dirt? Want me to tell you what's in my heart?" A near-apoplectic Glazier rushed over to make amends to the badly shaken Barthel. He told her, "They call me the producer. Pray for me." Barthel's *New York Times* article ran with an uncomplimentary photo of Mel Brooks in mid-tirade. It was captioned "A man losing his grip."

As Mel proceeded by trial and error, the production staggered toward completion. Often Brooks would leave the studio late at night and arrive home unable to fall asleep from the many tensions of the day. His face took on a gray, pallid look. The next morning the dailies from the previous day's shoot would be screened. With that out of the way, Brooks would launch into a short bit of shtick as he walked among the crew and cast preparing for the morning's shoot. Then it was back to the ultraserious Mel the film director.

At last, after an eight-week shoot, it came time, on July 15, 1967, to film the sequence set at the circular fountain at Lincoln Center. The footage of Leo, now a convert to Max's devious plan, running giddily around the edge of the fountain (as the water sprayed heavenward) took hours to execute properly. As dawn broke, the scene was finally completed. It was the end of principal photography on *The Producers*. Thereafter, an exhausted Brooks, Zero Mostel, Gene Wilder, and some of the others on hand repaired to the Brasserie for breakfast. For the next several months, Brooks and Ralph Rosenblum labored over the editing of the film. Brooks hated losing any of his precious footage but conceded that some bits were extraneous to the plot. In poring over the "Springtime for Hitler" number, he was unhappy with the way one of the performers sang his solo line. So Mel dubbed in the words "Don't be stupid, be a smarty. Come and join the Nazi Party." It was his contribution as an actor to the picture.

•   •   •

In late November 1967, Avco Embassy arranged for a test playdate of *The Producers* in Philadelphia at a small suburban theater, as well as one in Washington, D.C.—without giving the movie any real advertising support. (By this point, Levine and Avco Embassy were deeply involved in releasing *The Graduate*—which proved to be a tremendous critical and commercial hit—and had little time, interest, or spare funds to promote the unconventional *The Producers*.) Mel Brooks and his faithful helper, Alfa-Betty Olsen, as well as Joseph E. Levine and a few executives from the film company, attended the "opening" in Philadelphia. When the small contingent entered the huge theater, it was nearly empty. The picture started and the only one of the few attendees to respond with gales of laughter was a bag lady seated way down in front. When the film ended, Levine and his associates glumly marched up the aisle, said nothing to Brooks or Olsen, and departed in their limousine. Mel and Alfa-Betty returned to Manhattan by train convinced that Avco Embassy would now shelve *The Producers*. When he reached home, a grim Mel gave his wife the full account of that evening's disaster. He and Anne then began reading to each other passages from various books to help them get through what Brooks termed "the worst night of my life."

Then fate came to the rescue.

Peter Sellers came to Los Angeles in the late fall of 1967 to make a new picture, *I Love You, Alice B. Toklas!* Bored by life in Los Angeles, the star formed a weekly film screening club. Each member, in turn, was to suggest an interesting feature to be unspooled. The selected movie would be shown in a private screening room, and food and drink appropriate to the country of origin of that night's picture would be served. On January 13, 1968, Paul Mazursky, a writer on the *Toklas* film, was hosting for the group a showing of Federico Fellini's *I Vitelloni*. Paul's wife prepared a large pot of pasta for the occasion. A good wine, appetizers, and some marijuana-laced brownies completed the menu. When Sellers and the others were seated and ready for the evening's festivities to commence, it was suddenly discovered that no one had ordered a print of the Italian movie to be shipped to the screening room. Sellers became outraged. In the midst of the actor's storming, the projectionist inquired if the group might like to see a new picture that was sitting on the shelf. It was called *The Producers*.

The film ran and proved to be a big hit with its giddy audience, most of whom were already high from the marijuana-tainted brownies. (If Sellers had any memory that he had once been offered a key role *in The Producers*, he did not say so.) Peter was so enthralled by the comedy that he insisted upon immediately calling Joseph E. Levine in New York. He awoke the executive at home and told him that this Mel Brooks picture was the funniest movie he had ever seen. The next morning Sellers took out ads in the trade papers *Daily Variety* and the *Hollywood Reporter* in which he extolled the virtues of the forthcoming *The Producers*. (Sellers's testimonial, which was later reprinted in the *New York Times*, included, "Brilliantly written and directed by Mel Brooks it is the essence of all great comedy combined in a single motion picture. Without any doubt, Mel Brooks displays true genius in weaving together tragedy-comedy, comedy-tragedy, pity, fear, hysteria, schizophrenic-inspired madness and a largess of lunacy of sheer magic.")

Between this wonderful endorsement by Sellers and continued pressure by producer Sidney Glazier, Joseph E. Levine reluctantly released *The Producers* in New York City at the Fine Arts Theater. Many of the Manhattan-based reviewers did not respond favorably to the unorthodox movie. Renata Adler (of the *New York Times*) judged it "a violently mixed bag" and "shoddy and gross and cruel." She noted, "I never thought black comedy of this dilute order could be made with the word or idea of Hitler in it anywhere. . . . I suppose we will have cancer, Hiroshima, and malformity musicals next." Pauline Kael (of the *The New Yorker*) argued,

"*The Producers* isn't basically unconventional, it only seems so because it's so amateurishly crude, and because it revels in the kind of show business Jewish humor that used to be considered too specialized for movies." In contrast, a few critics were enthusiastic about the unconventional entry. Wanda Hale (of the *New York Daily News*) liked the picture's spirit: "Anyone, from whose head came this fantasy with profound undertones, can be forgiven for occasional looseness in direction." Gene Shalit (of *Look* magazine) also appreciated this celluloid laugh fest. He noted in his review: "No one will be seated in the last 88 minutes of *The Producers*, they'll all be rolling around on the floor."

Despite the mostly unfavorable critiques, positive word of mouth caught on, and *The Producers* ran for nearly a year in New York. In Los Angeles and Chicago the film enjoyed a similar long run. However, in smaller cities and especially in the hinterlands, the picture met with a mild response from perplexed and/or disinterested moviegoers. As a result, the movie was considered a box-office failure. (It required several years of reissues before the film registered a profit.)

Then, on February 24, 1969, the Academy Award nominations were announced. To most people's great amazement, *The Producers* received two Oscar bids: one for Mel Brooks's original screenplay and one for Gene Wilder as Best Supporting Actor. At the April 14, 1969, Oscar ceremonies, held at the Dorothy Chandler Pavilion in Los Angeles, Wilder lost out to Jack Albertson (in *The Subject Was Roses*). Later in the evening's proceedings, Frank Sinatra came to the podium to present the Oscar for Best Original Screenplay. (The other nominees included, among others, Arthur C. Clarke and Stanley Kubrick for *2001: A Space Odyssey* and John Cassavetes for *Faces*.) When the envelope was opened, it was Mel who had won the coveted prize. Appearing both astonished and extremely pleased, a suave-looking Brooks (garbed in a tuxedo) raced up on stage to accept his award. Rendered nearly speechless by his unexpected win, he thanked the Academy of Motion Picture Arts and Sciences and then added, "I'll just say what's in my heart: 'Ba-bump, ba-bump, ba-bump.'" Wearing a big grin, he then walked off the stage amid applause and laughter.

Later that momentous evening, Brooks and Anne Bancroft attended the Governor's Ball, the official post–award show party. During the evening, many celebrities came over to congratulate Mel, among them Buddy

Rich, the famous drummer who had once given young Melvin Kaminsky free drum lessons. Brooks described their reunion: "He hugs me, he says, 'Mel Brooks!' He puts on a big sad face, almost tearful. 'You know, you got an Academy Award, you're launched in films, it's so sad. You coulda been a really good drummer.'" According to Mel, "It was the greatest tribute I ever got about anything."

23

Jumping in Front
of the Cameras

Ninety percent of the reviews on *The Producers* called it disgusting, horrible, stupid, inept, etc. And if I took those reviews to heart, I never would have made another movie. So a good lesson is, when the critics sit you on their shoulders and say you're the greatest thing since cranberry juice, take it with a grain of salt; and when they crush you, go somewhere, suffer your pain in your little dark emotional cave, come out, and work again.

—Mel Brooks, 1983

While *The Producers* was struggling to find its audience outside of New York, Chicago, and Los Angeles, Mel Brooks was already mapping his next career step, hoping to strike his next deal while his name still had currency within the industry. He claimed that "from a few critics and respected friends, I got the message, 'Make more movies.'" As a result, he had two films in development, plus he was working on a stage play. The latter was *Have You Heard, Bronsky Is Dying*. It dealt with a New York City garment industry businessman who hoped to build a pyramid to himself in the suburbs. Brooks tailored the part for Zero Mostel, but the theater project never came to fruition.

In July 1968, Brooks elaborated grandly on his moviemaking plans to the *Los Angeles Times*: "I'm a wild amalgam of chutzpah (guts) and mazel (luck). . . . I'll do films for a couple of years and then, when I grow up, I'll decide what I want. That they should give me money for this make-believe is beyond me. I feel at the end of the day I should carry something or say 'Yes sir' for all the money I get."

In that statement he was being more than a little facetious. As director/writer of *The Producers* he had received a relatively modest $35,000 for all his toil. For his second picture, his salary improved. He was handed $50,000 to write, direct, coproduce (through his Crossbow Productions), and even take on an acting role in the new project. However, if this amount was amortized over the three years it took to make, and one deducted taxes on such proceeds, Brooks's income was actually around only $8,000 per annum.

One of Mel's planned cinema undertakings had been an untitled venture that concerned movie style and technique. That soon moved to the back burner in favor of the other more promising project, *The Twelve Chairs*. The new production was set up in the coming months by the loyal Sidney Glazier, Mel's benefactor on *The Producers*. Despite Brooks's latest Oscar (for Best Original Screenplay), the major Hollywood studios still did not consider this zany maverick a very bankable commodity. Thus, as a last resort, Glazier turned to UMC (Universal Marion Corporation) for a modest distribution deal.

The film was to be based on a 1928 satire by Russian journalists Ilya Faynzilberg and Yevgeny Katayev, who used the pen names of Ilya Ilf and Evgeny Petrov to disguise their true identities. Among the duo's several popular collaborations was a short novel called, in its English translation, *Diamonds to Sit On*. It was set in 1927 Russia and related the misfortunes of a trio of avaricious men seeking valuables secreted in one of a set of 12 dining room chairs. Brooks had heard the picaresque story as a child and remembered it fondly. In the 1950s, when Mel was reading a great deal of Russian literature—thanks to the influence of his TV comedy writer mentor, Mel Tolkin—Brooks had read the piece. Over the years, *Diamonds to Sit On* had been picturized on a few occasions, including as the 1937 British comedy *Keep Your Seats Please* and the 1945 Hollywood entry *It's in the Bag*, costarring Fred Allen and Jack Benny.

Mel was convinced that the Russian tale boasted strong universal themes: "It's the story of a quest for all that you're told you can have— luck, diamonds, riches. Not fame. I mean I wanted to be famous. But I'm talking about what I think every poor young boy thinks about—winning the sweepstakes, having somebody you never heard of die and leave you a lot of money."

With a budget of only $1.5 million, it would have been near impossible to re-create 1920s Russia on a Hollywood sound stage. However, shooting the story in the Soviet Union was also out of the question, due to the strained cold war relations at the time between Russia and the United States. Then, it was discovered that a deal could be made to lens the movie in Yugoslavia, in and around Belgrade. Production was set to start on August 25, 1969.

As Brooks lovingly polished the screenplay for his second feature, he analyzed the several production lessons he'd learned from making *The Producers*. Using multiple cameras to shoot each scene was beneficial because it provided sufficient coverage for the editing process and often avoided the necessity of reshooting sequences later on. Having survived the many challenges of his first directing assignment, Mel was now more confident in his filmmaking abilities, and, in turn, more flexible about heeding the advice of experienced coworkers. He had also learned that by choosing his cast carefully, he would need to spend far less valuable time on the set coaching particular actors and thus could focus more of his attention on the overall scenes.

In retrospect, Mel realized he had been wise on *The Producers* to have had his screenplay so carefully worked out before the start of filming and to ensure that the story line always focused on "What do the characters want?" While Brooks had given Zero Mostel, Gene Wilder, and other cast members the freedom to improvise bits of action (always subject to Mel's final approval) he had avoided a lot of potential production problems by insisting that everyone stick to the written dialogue. (An exception had been in the courtroom, in which Brooks allowed Wilder to provide much of Leo's touching speech concerning Bloom's friendship with Max Bialystock.)

In reexamining his feature film directorial debut as a guidepost for his future helming, Brooks wished he had had the wisdom at the time to make more severe edits in *The Producers*. (Belatedly, Mel felt the film "should end about four minutes after the 'Springtime for Hitler' number; all that stuff that comes after the number in the film should have come before.")

• • •

In casting *The Twelve Chairs*, Mel originally wanted three actors from the United Kingdom for his leads: Alastair Sim, Albert Finney, and Peter Sellers. Unfortunately, these choices all fell out. At this juncture, Anne Bancroft made a few casting suggestions. She had performed with Frank Langella in William Gibson's *A Cry of Players*, a drama that had closed after a relatively short Broadway run in February 1969. Bancroft thought the lanky Langella, then in his late 20s and yet to have made his movie debut, would be a perfect Ostap Bender, the slick con artist. It was also Anne who proposed that Dom DeLuise, whom she had seen on TV, would be appropriate to play Father Fyodor, the clergyman corrupted by grief. It was Langella who took Brooks to see the movie musical *Oliver!* and told Mel of the screen actor playing Fagin, "There's your Vorobyaninov." That player was Ron Moody, who had once been a top contender for the Broadway musical *All American*, for which Mel had provided the book adaptation. Moody was soon signed to play the aging nobleman who had been reduced to poverty and a near friendless existence in the wake of the Russian Revolution. Wanting to test his acting skills beyond his 2000 Year Old Man appearances and the brief bit he did as "Mr. Forget It" in Robert Downey Sr.'s 1969 feature film, *Putney Swope*, Brooks cast himself as Tikon, the often drunk janitor. Tikon was the nonsensical former servant to Vorobyaninov, who misses the good old bad days under the czar. He is continuously pining for those bygone times, when masters thoughtfully beat their domestics into proper submission.

By the late summer of 1969, Mel and his company were headquartered in Belgrade. Michael Hertzberg, the assistant director on *The Producers*, was the new film's producer. Like the supporting cast, many of the crew were recruited from England or Yugoslavia. Veteran cinematographer Djordje Nikolic proved to be a great boon to the production, giving the film its old-world, storybook look.

Brooks was thrilled to be able to bring this Eastern European story to the screen. "I'm a Russian Jew, and finally, I could bathe in everything Russian that's in me. . . . I can't tell you what it was like for me to make that picture in that country. I felt like I had come home. There are Russian textures of that in the film. Eating black bread. The shot of the borscht with the dollop of sour cream. I went there and said to myself, 'Ah, it's not Brooklyn: It's Kiev!' . . . That, and the emotionalism of being Russian."

Mel was pleased with the favorable production deal made with the Yugoslav government: "For $450,000, we got everything—cameras, soldiers, and extras. There was no time limit. They wanted to keep as many of their film people busy, so we had a crew of about 1,000 milling around. I felt like David Lean filming *Lawrence of Arabia*." The moviemaker related of his latest filmmaking experience, "The Yugoslav crew was very nice and helpful, but you had to be careful. One day in a fit of pique, I hurled my director's chair into the Adriatic. . . . On all sides, angry voices were heard and clenched fists were raised. 'The vokers,' I was informed, 'have announced to strike!' 'But why?' 'You have destroyed the People's chair!' 'But it's mine! It says Mel Brooks on it!' 'In Yugoslavia, everything is the property of the People.' So we had a meeting, poured a lot of vodka, got drunk, started to cry and sing and kiss each other. Wonderful people!"

Dom DeLuise, who became a lifelong friend of Brooks's on this shoot, said of Brooks, "Mel is not unenthusiastic about his work. If he saw a mountain, he'd say [for my character to], 'Climb it.' If he saw a brook, he would say, 'Jump across it.' If he saw a stone wall, he would say, 'Bang your head into it.'" Frank Langella had a similar recollection of Brooks's vitality on this celluloid project: "His energy was phenomenal. There was a tree in the way of a shot and he tried to pull the tree out of the ground. In one scene, I was supposed to row a boat through the moon's reflection on the water. But the arc kept moving, so it appeared the moonlight was following us. Once, we got so far out to sea that they couldn't find us. At 3 in the morning, Mel jumped into the water to swim out to find us." Ron Moody found it a rewarding experience to work with Brooks: "I think he's the only person living today who's a direct link—an active direct link—with the golden age of comedy."

Years later, Langella reminisced of this filmmaking experience in Yugoslavia, "Mel paid me about 45 cents to do the movie. It was a number so ridiculously low. We all lived in each other's pockets for seven to nine months. We lived in a hotel where everything was rewired. If you picked up a phone, the lights shut off. But we were all together the whole time. We were a very tight, happy family. That's an overused phrase, but it's true. . . . I was 20-some-odd years old, waking up every morning in the presence of Mel and Dom, two of the truly funniest men on Earth. I don't think I ever laughed as much on a film set, and I doubt

I ever will again. . . . Everyone called me kid on that film, and I remember [the producer] Michael Hertzberg saying to me, 'It ain't all going to be like this, kid.'"

Because Brooks would be busy overseas for so many months on *The Twelve Chairs*, Bancroft arranged her work schedule (including an upcoming TV special) so she could spend extended periods in Yugoslavia with Mel. Besides providing her husband with moral support during the shoot, Bancroft prodded him to write the song he felt the picture needed. The bouncy yet fitting number was the cynical "Hope for the Best, Expect the Worst." (As he had for *The Producers* and would for many pictures to come, the very talented John Morris provided the film's sound track, as well as an arrangement for Mel's number.) Reflecting Brooks's relatively lighthearted mood on *The Twelve Chairs* set, a playful Mel coaxed his wife to appear briefly as an extra in a take of one scene as a practical joke on the film's editor, Alan Heim.

By December 1969, principal photography on *The Twelve Chairs* had concluded. As was Mel's then habit, the editing on this picture extended for several months into the new year. (Brooks reasoned, "I can never let a picture go, I think I could work on *Twelve Chairs* for the rest of my life. I spent a year of my life making that picture, I thought it was going to be my masterpiece.") The resultant film was released in October 1970.

In comparing Brooks's new offering to his first feature film, several critics pointed out the parallel of male bonding between two dishonest souls. But reviewers also noted technical dissimilarities between the two pictures: *The Producers* had a crude, in-your-face look, boasted high-energy performances, and was extremely fast-paced (until the anticlimactic segment following the "Springtime for Hitler" production number). Conversely, the lovingly photographed *The Twelve Chairs*, despite its many chase sequences, was far too leisurely paced even in its slapstick scenes. With the exception of Mel's zesty misfit character, the figures in this Russian tale were not especially engaging or memorable (certainly in comparison to *The Producers*' Max Bialystock, Leo Bloom, Franz Liebkind, Roger De Bris, and even Ulla).

The serious comedy found a few boosters. Judith Crist (of NBC-TV) weighed in with: "*The Twelve Chairs* is a complete joy! A comedy to warm the heart and leave the ribs aching." *Playboy* magazine judged that the movie "obeys no rules except those governing the lost art of pure comedy . . . cast of superlative clowns, led by Ron Moody, the memorable

Fagin of *Oliver!*" Many critics suggested that Mel's supporting performance was the real highlight of the picture—and in many ways it was.
Sadly, his character appeared only briefly in the film.

The reaction of Pauline Kael (of the *New Yorker*) to *The Twelve Chairs*
was, "It's a bit forlorn, this attempt to make comedy out of old comedy
that has lost its satirical bite." *Variety* predicted that the new release had
"doubtful mass appeal." The trade paper's prediction proved correct. *The
Twelve Chairs* came and went rather quickly in distribution, leaving no
trail of box-office profits.

The overall failure of Brooks's second picture was especially bitter for
Mel, who had put so much of his heart and soul into the literate project.
(In years to come, Brooks rated *The Twelve Chairs*, *The Producers*, and
Life Stinks as "the films I'm most proud of.") He explained his strong
attachment to this 1970 release: "When I wrote *The Producers* it was really
a private story with universal features. Then I wrote *The Twelve Chairs*,
and it was very private. You had to know about the Russian sensibility, from
the muzhik to the czar, to appreciate *The Twelve Chairs*, even though the
human aspects were once again universal. Both pictures deal with love
and greed, but *The Producers* got a cult audience . . . and *The Twelve Chairs*
got an even smaller one. So if you were a Jewish intellectual whose parents had emigrated from Russia you could like my pictures, but there were
hardly any of those in Amarillo, Texas, where you gotta play in one of
their three or four theaters or else you're outa luck. . . . You gotta get into
one of the John Wayne houses or you ain't never gonna break out and
they ain't gonna play you in a John Wayne house if you're gonna do private ethnic stories, even though they do have ubiquitous human parallels."

Over time, as the deep wounds to his pride slowly healed to some
degree, he gained perspective from these two box-office misfires. "I was
so fed up with my movies and my failure. I thought I had given the best
of me, brilliantly, beautifully delivered, what I was exactly, the human
being that I was . . . the Jew that I am, in both pictures, and they were
not, to my mind, well received. I realized later why—because they were
too private. What do Americans know about a coupla Jews on Broadway?
What do they know about Russia?"

Now much less idealistic about his cinematic vision for future projects, Brooks vowed that if he ever gained the opportunity to make another
film, it would be far more mainstream in subject matter. Equally important, he decided that, if at all possible, he would avoid the ego-satisfying

temptation of writing any future screenplays alone. Thinking back to his salad days on *Your Show of Shows* and *Caesar's Hour*, Mel appreciated anew the overall value of being able to test all his creative ideas with script collaborators, who could, hopefully, keep him and his developing screenplay on a better commercial course. In making this essential decision that played such a strong role in his future, Brooks reasoned, "I didn't want to go back to the tables and risk another gambling session with my career."

24

Back in the Running—Again

Nothing good comes out of going for the money. If you do something
lovely from your heart, you might get lucky and make some money. But
if it doesn't come from your heart and soul, if you don't believe in it
from your fingertips to the tips of your toes, it's not going to be good.
You've got to do it because you love it.

—Mel Brooks, 2004

While Mel Brooks was filming *The Twelve Chairs* abroad and then editing his feature back in the United States, Anne Bancroft was preparing for a new television project. It was an hour-long special for CBS-TV,
set to air on February 18, 1970. The program was titled *Annie, the Women
in the Life of a Man,* and explored the many emotional facets of the contemporary female. It was directed by Martin Charnin and boasted the
services of nine writers, including Gary Belkin, Herbert Sargent, Jacque-
line Susann, Thomas Meehan, and Brooks. Jack Gould of the *New York
Times* rated the sophisticated offering "a tour de force of such a multi-
plicity of charms, humor and talent that it is almost hard to believe." As
for its star (Bancroft), the critic judged, "Rightfully, she should be the
toast of the country by tomorrow morning." (Brooks was referred to in the
Times's critique as "Mel Brooks, the husband of Miss Bancroft.") The
special went on to win two Emmy Awards: Outstanding Variety or Musical Program and Outstanding Writing Achievement in Comedy, Variety or
Music. Out of that TV pickup assignment Brooks became friendly with
Thomas Meehan, and later the two writers would collaborate on several
films (including *Spaceballs*) and stage projects (such as *The Producers*).

•   •   •

With his professional future largely in limbo, Brooks found himself faced with more than ample free time to indulge two of his major hobbies. To fill his many empty hours, he browsed through New York City bookstores in search of volumes of classical literature (especially Russian) to add to his growing library. Whenever he happened upon a knowledgeable sales-clerk in these shops, he stopped to have a long conversation with him or her, eager to share his growing knowledge of good books. Often, he would return to such stores, hoping to engage the same bright clerks in further literary discussions.

Another interest of Mel's (the former drummer) was expanding his collection of recordings. One day, Brooks had an encounter with a young customer at a basement shop on West 8th Street. Years later, the college student could still recall the incident vividly. "A short man appeared in the doorway above me, jacket thrown over his shoulders like a cape. . . . In a loud theatrical voice, he called out to the manager, asking if his records had come in. When he heard that they hadn't, he was about to leave, when he looked down, noticed scripts under my arm and asked if I was an actor. I told him I was only a student and he said: 'Would you like a quick lesson? I'll show you 10 ways to smoke a cigarette—give me one.'

"He then proceeded to act out a series of freeze frames that would have done justice to the most emotive of silent film stars. He announced 'anger' and proceeded to puff away, smoke billowing, eyes glaring, jaw tensed, fists gripped, and body poised to fight. . . . He went on to fear, love, sadness, lust, embarrassment, etc. and in much too short a time was finished. He wished me luck as an actor and with a flourish, Mel Brooks turned and made his exit."

•   •   •

In the midst of Mel's latest career stall, there was a joyful personal event. On May 22, 1972, the Brookses became parents of a baby boy, who was baptized Maximilian Michael Brooks in honor of each parent's father. Although neither Brooks nor Bancroft was especially religious, it was important to Anne to have her infant undergo a ritual celebrating his birth. The couple agreed that if Mel permitted Max to be baptized, then

Anne would go along with the youngster being bar mitzvahed when he turned 13.

Bancroft said of becoming a mother, "We tried and tried and suddenly had Max when I was 41, the last possible moment. We should have called him 'Nick' for 'in the nick of time.' I was at the peak of my career and my looks, but I pulled back. Wanted to be with him. One of the perks of show business, a reason we go into it, is we don't have to work every day—especially women. When you become a wife there are certain demands put on you. Work is important for a man's identity. It's not that important to women. They have a choice." Later, in describing her parental responsibilities, she said, "During the time of Maximilian's growing up, I did about one project a year. Before he went to school, he came with me wherever I went. Once he went to school, then I really had to cut it down to be available. You have to make those kinds of compromises. But that's who I am. Other people might not have to make those deals."

As for Brooks, now a father of four and already in his mid-40s, his elation at Max's birth must have been tempered by many pressing concerns. He had to be speculating how he could best be there for his newborn child while not overlooking the three children from his first marriage. Then too, this new addition to the household must have caused Mel great worries of how he was going to properly support his expanded family.

• • •

Just when everything seemed so bleak in Mel's career, along came Brooks's fortuitous 1973 encounter with the powerful talent agent David Begelman. Miraculously, the latter soon engineered an offer for Brooks to write and direct *Blazing Saddles*. The film's tremendous box-office reception not only thrust Mel back into prominence, but made the zany man far more of a household name than he had been, for example, when his 2000 Year Old Man albums were such a craze in the 1960s. By all standards, Mel had made a monumental professional comeback—one that brought him industry admiration and public adulation.

With his regained prominence, Mel found himself called upon by reporters to analyze the special appeal of his loony, trailblazing film. Brooks emphasized, "Clichés are just the ornaments. The tree has to be solid. The movie has got to be about something. Take *Blazing Saddles*. It was about whether a black could survive in the good old West. It may seem like a silly picture but, to me, it had a strong underpinning because it was really about love." He reasoned further, "But most audiences only remember the ornaments of a comedy—the jokes. They don't see the tree. It's dark. It's all bark. But what would all the ornaments be without the tree for support? They'd just be a pile of shiny baubles on the ground."

Thrilled by the enormous success of his latest picture, Brooks predicted, "I think in ten years, and I'm tooting my own horn now, *Blazing Saddles* will be recognized as the funniest film ever made. Just funny— I'm not talking about other faults or virtues, I'm just talking about the amount of laughter evoked. I think it's funnier than other movies, even Mae West and W. C. Fields, or Buster Keaton or the Marx Brothers, all of whom I love. The only thing that might compete with it for the amount of laughter are the Three Stooges shorts." It led him to ask rhetorically, "Should I be happy that I've spawned such insanity? Yes, I'm very proud and very ashamed at the same time." In his estimation, "*Blazing Saddles* allowed me to be the lovely Rabelaisian vulgarian that I am. I mean those cowboys farting around the campfire allowed me for the first time to really exercise my scatological muscles."

At the time, Brooks had no way of forecasting that his wild and wacky feature would have its greatest impact on the next generations of film-makers, who set about pushing the envelope even further throughout mainstream cinema. These would include such moviemakers as Terry Gilliam (in *Monty Python and the Holy Grail*), David Zucker, Jim Abraham, Jerry Zucker (of *Airplane!* fame), and the Farrelly brothers (with *There's Something About Mary*) and actor Jim Carrey (with his lowbrow comedy in *Ace Ventura: Pet Detective*).

• • •

Now that Brooks was riding so high in Hollywood, the industry watched with keen interest to see what the unorthodox Mel would do as a follow-up to the oddball success of *Blazing Saddles*.

25

A Monster Hit

It's very hard to break through in our business, because the public is murderous. They're envious and contemptuous of anybody who would stick their neck out. So very few people get through that skein of public ferocity. Most people think you don't make it because of apathy. It's not [the case].

—Mel Brooks, 1974

On one hand, Mel Brooks was jubilant that the megasuccess of *Blazing Saddles* allowed him to be taken seriously by the Hollywood establishment, which respected anyone who could create such a substantial box-office hit. On the other hand, the veteran talent still yearned to be taken seriously by film reviewers and the moviegoing public.

As to being called zany, Brooks argued, "It's a convenient pigeonhole for lazy minds. If they [i.e., the critics] really knew my work, you could not say zany Mel Brooks and seriously discuss *The Twelve Chairs*, *The Critic*, or certain aspects of the early *Show of Shows*, when tragedy and comedy met so beautifully. I object to it because I think you could call Picasso zany because he's not a naturalistic painter, or dull. Or you could call Dalí zany. But they're great artists and we've got to learn that abstract comedy or surrealistic comedy is not necessarily cheap."

Mel emphasized, "You start with a vision, and you just want it to come out that way. You do everything in your power short of a criminal act to make sure it comes out that way. You're the only one who has the vision. All these scenes, these tiles in the grand mosaic of your brain, you're the only one who has the whole vision. I suspect that's the trouble with a lot of films, that they're not writer-director made. They're director-made. And that the writer is the only one that has the true vision." Now that Brooks had the comforting reassurance of having turned out such a significant box-office hit, his self-confidence was restored—and then some. In this mode, he enthusiastically expounded to the press on the impetus behind his expanding activities in the filmmaking process: "I think I enjoy writing the most, because that's really the genesis. The explosion of a new idea in your brain is really the happiest moment. Directing is good, too, because you can mold and shape and sculpt. Acting is good, because it cuts out another middleman; it cuts out an actor who may not do it as well as you can, who may not understand it and get the nuances. I am very happy to be doing what I'm doing because a lot of people just work for wages. If the money wasn't good, I'd still be doing it. If they'd let me do it I'd still do it. I mean, essentially, it's just showing off."

●　●　●

Even before *Blazing Saddles* was released, in February 1974, Mel Brooks found himself working on a new Hollywood screen project. It stemmed from the fertile imagination of Gene Wilder. Perhaps inspired by Mel's ability to be a screenwriter, director, and actor, Gene had aspirations of one day following in that same career path. For now, however, Wilder focused on being a performer—and a very much in demand one at that. Back on the East Coast—before he became involved with *Blazing Saddles*—Gene had had an idea of adapting Mary Wollstonecraft Shelley's Gothic horror novel, *Frankenstein*, for the screen. Wilder recalled his creative process: "I took a yellow legal pad and a blue felt pen and I wrote *Young Frankenstein* on top. . . . And then for two pages, I thought what could happen to me if I suddenly found out that I was an heir to Beaufort von Frankenstein's whole estate in Transylvania. And I finished the two pages. I called Mel [Brooks]. I told him, Well, he says cute. Cute. That's all he said."

Later in the summer of 1972, Mike Medavoy, then Wilder's talent agent, asked Gene if he might have any ideas in mind that would be suitable for teaming Gene on camera with two new Medavoy clients. The personalities in question were Peter Boyle (a stocky character actor best known for such films as *Joe* and *The Candidate*) and Marty Feldman (a British performer—mainly in TV series—who had unusually angular features and bulging eyes, which often darted about wildly and out of sync with each other. It occurred to Wilder that he could incorporate roles for both Boyle and Feldman into his *Young Frankenstein* property.

Over the coming months, Gene, the film writing novice, wrote snatches of his screen treatment (and screenplay drafts) in between movie assignments—one of them being *Blazing Saddles*. Meanwhile, Medavoy showed Wilder's treatment to Michael Gruskoff, who had produced two films (*The Last Movie* and *Silent Running*) and was looking for a new venture. Gruskoff liked the *Young Frankenstein* concept and the package of Wilder-Boyle-Feldman. He suggested that adding Mel Brooks to the deal would make it an easier sale. Mel was just then finishing principal photography on *Blazing Saddles* and was again reluctant to work on a film that was not based on his own material. Eventually, it was agreed that Brooks and Wilder would work together on a new (fourth) draft of Gene's screenplay and that, if the property should sell, Mel would direct the picture.

While Brooks was engaged in postproduction activities on *Blazing Saddles*, he and Wilder met during evenings at the Bel Air Hotel (where Gene was staying) to reshape the *Young Frankenstein* script. Whatever the difference of personalities between the two men, and their varying viewpoints on this joint effort, the pair worked relatively fast and harmoniously on the screenwriting collaboration. (One of their few creative disagreements occurred when Gene insisted there must be a sequence within the film in which young Dr. Frankenstein reveals his creation to the public and the monster is dressed for the occasion in formal attire. This leads to the creature and his creator launching into song and dance to Irving Berlin's "Puttin' on the Ritz." Brooks thought this vaudeville-style number would be too frivolous and out of context within the rest of the story line. However, the usually meek Gene stood firm on this point and Mel acceded to his partner's wishes. The odd sequence proved to be one of the most memorable scenes in the entire picture.)

Brooks said of the teamwork with Wilder, "We really had fun, we were like a couple of kids. When I'm writing a script, I don't worry about plot as much as I do about people. I get to know the main characters— what they need, what they want, what they should do. That's what gets the story going. Like a child, I listen to the characters. . . . You can't just have actions, you've got to find out what the characters want. And then they must grow, they must go somewhere."

Later, Wilder acknowledged that in the long run, working with Brooks on this feature film had been tremendously beneficial to his own career growth. "Mel has all kinds of faults. Like his greed, his megalomania, his need to be the universal father and teacher, even to people far more experienced than he is. Why I'm close to him is not in spite of those faults but because of them. I need a leader, someone to tell me what to do. If he were more humble, modest, and considerate, he would probably have more friends, but I doubt whether he and I would be such good friends. He made me discover the *me* in Mel. He taught me never to be afraid of offending. It's when you worry about offending people that you get in trouble."

While Mel and Gene were refining their latest draft of *Young Franken-stein*, Mike Medavoy negotiated a potential deal for its filming at Columbia Pictures, where Peter Guber was then head of production. By the time Brooks and Wilder finished revamping the screenplay, the project was estimated to require a $2.3 million budget. However, Leo Jaffe, chairman of Columbia Pictures and part of the old guard who didn't "get" Brooks, insisted the studio would only fund the project to a maximum of $2 million.

Negotiations between Columbia and Brooks/Wilder had bogged down over the budget, but what really killed the prospective transaction was Brooks's insistence that *Young Frankenstein* be filmed in black and white rather than in color. Mel was not being arbitrary or old-fashioned in this "artsy" demand. He reasoned that since this picture would be a tribute to director James Whale's classic genre entries (*Frankenstein* and *The Bride of Frankenstein*), the new entry must recapture the look of those atmospheric 1930s productions, which had been filmed in black and white. On a more practical basis, Brooks's team had already done makeup tests for the monster and discovered that the appropriate skin look (i.e., a greenish tone) lost its proper effect when photographed in color.

Columbia refused to back down on the issues of the budget and their insistence that the movie be lensed in color. (In actuality, the studio was not that excited about the script.) This prompted producer Mike Gruskoff to shop the project elsewhere. Among others, he sent a script to his friend Alan Ladd Jr., a top production executive at Twentieth Century-Fox. Almost overnight, a deal was made with Fox.

• • •

During this period, Brooks had grown quite enthusiastic about making *Young Frankenstein*. Among the property's many virtues for Mel were that the film would deal with an individual who finds a way to sidestep death. This certainly appealed to Brooks, who had a lifelong concern with mortality. For another, Mel would be working in a genre that was close to his heart. "These [horror pictures] were the movies I loved most as a child. They burned images in my head: long shadows, backlighting, fog. I mean there was always fog in the rooms for no reason. Why fog? Crazy, but I loved it." Another intriguing aspect for the moviemaker was the story line's focus on medicine, long a topic of special interest to Mel.

In a mixture of facetiousness and utter seriousness, Brooks observed about the screenplay he and Wilder had fashioned, "In many ways we've gone back to the original thinking of Mary Shelley, if not her original story. I think she was the first person to discover womb envy. I think I'm the first person to call it that, but what it is, is that most men get even with women for being able to have children by saying 'I can paint, I can write,' and women say, 'You're full of shit. Look—a baby.' And of course, she's the winner. So here's this scientist and he says, 'All right, so can I make a baby. I'll put a few rods in his neck and plug him in somewhere and we'll make a life.' That's really it: to create life, like a woman."

Since Brooks was coscripting, directing, and coproducing the venture and was the pivotal force behind the success of *Blazing Saddles*, he met with little opposition when he stepped into the role of spokesman for the new project, which owed so much to Gene Wilder's idea and collaboration on the screenplay. Mel pointed out that *his* forthcoming picture dealt with "the ignorant vs. the intelligent. The mob vs. the intelligent people. . . . The story of Dr. Frankenstein addresses itself to the fear quotient. The monster is just symbolic of his mind, and the mob hates his mind, they hate his imagination." But Brooks also noted of this film, which tipped its hat to such horror genre satires as *Abbott and Costello Meet Frankenstein*: "If they [i.e., moviegoers] pay three dollars to forget about their problems and just want to laugh, that's fine too." In a rather disingenuous statement, Brooks (who always highly valued the importance of money) insisted, "You know, they could never pay me enough money to do what I do; it's a total joy, hearing people laugh. . . . it's wonderful, it's thrilling. That's the best."

• • •

By now, Brooks had developed a rationale for how he filled key roles in his movies. "I like people with big talents and small neuroses—not always an easy combination to find. I've discovered that if the neurosis is too big, it diminishes the talent and you wind up working too hard for what you get. I reserve the right to be the only psychotic on the set. I also try to surround myself with the people I love—make a family out of the company. So I tend to use the same people over and over."

The cast for *Young Frankenstein* was quickly assembled. Wilder was to be the finicky Dr. Frederick Frankenstein, a man who eventually learns to embrace his forebear's scientific accomplishments. Peter Boyle was to play the scary creation assembled from odd parts of stolen corpses, while Marty Feldman was to be Igor, the humpback servant at the eerie Frankenstein castle in Transylvania. Kenneth Mars (of *The Producers*) was handed the wacko role of the village's demented police inspector. Veteran actress Cloris Leachman, best known to the public for costarring on Mary Tyler Moore's TV sitcom, was hired as the loony housekeeper at the castle Frankenstein. (Leachman and Brooks had worked together on a few past TV shows. He wrote the role of the mysterious and sinister Frau Blücher especially for Cloris.)

Initially, Teri Garr, a dancer/singer with several (minor) credits on TV and in film, was tested to play Dr. Frankenstein's refined fiancée. How-ever, Brooks finally convinced Madeline Kahn to accept this featured role of the emotionally fickle young lady who develops an overwhelming yen for the physically well-endowed monster. Thereafter, Garr audi-tioned for and won the part of the German Inga, the scientist's buxom and very accommodating assistant. (Teri's mother had already been hired to do the women's wardrobe on this picture. During the production of *Young Frankenstein*, Teri and Gene Wilder embarked on a romance.)

Gene Hackman filled the last of the film's lead assignments. A sea-soned stage, TV, and film performer (and the winner of an Academy Award for *The French Connection*), Hackman thought it would be a lark to be part of the inspired insanity of a Mel Brooks movie. Preferring not to be billed (and thus give moviegoers a surprise), Gene took on the role of the Blind Hermit, who tries to befriend the inarticulate monster.

As for Brooks, in this feature, his performance contributions con-sisted of providing the noise of a screeching cat during the dart sequence, making the sounds of a werewolf in one of the Transylvania scenes, and doing a voiceover of the elder Frankenstein that is heard when his descendant explores the hidden lab. (It was also Brooks's handwriting seen in a close-up of a lab label that read, "Do NOT use this Brain—Abnormal.") To score this picture, Brooks signed on the faithful John Morris, with John C. Howard as film editor (as he had been for *Blazing Saddles*). Veteran cinematographer Gerald Hirschfeld joined the production team and, in years to come, would photograph several other Brooks projects.

• • •

Originally *Young Frankenstein* was scheduled to start shooting in November 1973, but it was not until February 26, 1974, that the cameras actually began to roll. During the 54-day shoot, the cast and crew went on location to the University of Southern California (for the Baltimore Medical School sequence) and to MGM's backlot. At Metro, the nighttime grave robbery sequence was shot in the yard of the church where Greer Garson was wed in *Mrs. Miniver*. The *Young Frankenstein* railroad station sequence was filmed at the site of Ronald Colman's arrival in *Random Harvest*. Part of the footage for the villagers storming the Frankenstein castle was accomplished on the central set of MGM's *The Brothers Grimm*. Brooks and company used the Mayfair Music Hall in Santa Monica to represent the Bucharest Hall of Science, where Dr. Frankenstein demonstrates his creation's lifelike capabilities.

Back at Twentieth Century-Fox, the Frankenstein castle—which covered 15,000 square feet and had battlements that rose to an impressive 35 feet—was erected by production designer Dale Hennesy at a cost of $350,000. Some of the atmospheric laboratory equipment utilized was supplied by Ken Strickfaden, who had saved many of the apparatuses he had created for the 1931 *Frankenstein* movie.

• • •

In a considerable change from his highly tense days as director of *The Producers*, Brooks felt one of his key jobs on the sets of *Young Frankenstein* was "to make everyone laugh." It was not unusual for Mel, in the midst of one of his impromptu performances for the cast and crew, to crumple to the floor and lie there clutching his sides with laughter. At other moments—between takes—he might engage one of his actors in an imaginary sword fight. A bit later, without warning, he might launch into his impersonation of Gene Kelly singing and dancing the title song of *Singin' in the Rain*. Completing his spur-of-the-moment exhibition, he might shout out to the onlookers, "[Federico] Fellini and Dick Lester are great directors, but are they tops in taps?"

Madeline Kahn enthused of her director on *Young Frankenstein*, "Mel is involved with controlled madness. I love that. I just love it. Mel is going for lunacy. He gets several takes on a scene and then he says 'Now do one more and go bananas!'—and often that's the one he likes. He is a courageous man. His humor is connected up to some main artery, like *Mad* magazine and the *National Lampoon*, and he's always on. I could never be that way: I've spent all my time and money to be re-spectable and dignified; to be a *lady*. I'd be afraid of just walking around and doing what I think is crazy. But Mel loves it!" (Years later, Kahn said regarding her several moviemaking adventures with Brooks, "They were fun, but there was also tension because everyone wanted to please him, so they felt they had to be funny.")

Sensing that one day Wilder would want to direct his own vehicles, Brooks made time during the *Young Frankenstein* shoot to give his friend pointers. Gene detailed, "Mel would say, 'Do you know the trouble I'm in because I didn't shoot that close-up? Don't do that.' I would say, 'To whom are you talking?' 'You, when you're directing.' 'Directing *what*?' Never mind,' he said." Meanwhile, Wilder gave his director/coscripter a few tips on their project, suggesting Brooks be less broad in his interpre-tation of their script.

As filming drew to a close, Gene got sentimental. He explained, "We've got only two more weeks of shooting. I don't want to leave Tran-sylvania. I've been so happy here." Brooks grew expansive about his latest screen project. He enthused, "What I wanted, was the truth behind the horror conventions, the way real people—crazy but real—would behave in that castle. And I wanted to do it with the greatest affection for those great old films. All the time we were shooting, I was sure the picture was going to be a failure. We were having too wonderful a time. Work should be painful, I thought. How can this be good if we're enjoying it so much?"

Brooks said of the tone he employed for *Young Frankenstein*, "It's not satire, it's a salute. It says, 'Mel Brooks Presents *Young Frankenstein*' so the audience will, of course, know that the comedy will go an inch or two further than one usually expects. But you can't keep winking because it diminishes the melodrama. The melodrama has to be there." He also pointed out, "Again I'm fooling around with the Germans. The only noticeable Jew is Dr. Frankenstein himself, who is played by Gene Wilder. We didn't play it Jewish, but I think it was there."

Above all, Mel highlighted with great fervor, "I don't want to make just another movie. I want to make trouble. I want to say in comic terms, 'J'accuse.' We dealt with bigotry in *Saddles* and with neo-Fascism in *Producers*. Underneath the comedy in *Frankenstein*, the doctor is undertaking the quest to defeat death—to challenge God. Our monster lives, therefore he wants love too. He's really very touching in his lonely misery."

Mel's primary criterion for judging if a scene worked was if it made him laugh. (He claimed he did not especially care what filmgoers at a showing might think of a particular sequence because, he reasoned, who knew if there ever would be an audience.) The next point was to please "the actors you're working with, and then it's the crew. You get a general sense of what's going on through the reactions of people on the set. You ask everybody. A sandwich girl comes by and you play a scene for her; she's totally uninterested, and if you get a laugh from her, you know you're doing well. Then the editing room and finally the screening. I believe in showing the rough cuts and reworking a film. I can change a picture right up until the end, I have that in my contract. And that means the sound track as well."

Unlike his past productions, Mel condensed the editing process on *Young Frankenstein*. Nevertheless, he remained true to his editing philosophy: "My principle of cutting is you start with a scalpel and end with a blunt axe. Everyone usually does it the other way around. You know, knocking out whole scenes and ending by refining. But I start by taking out an "and," an "if," or a "but." I play with a scene. Then when you have the rough cut, you start eliminating scenes. . . . In the final third of a picture you have to accelerate the pace; it has to gather speed and go over the top." (One film editor of a Brooks project noted, "The man is a demon. Nothing less than greatness will satisfy him. He has the lonely passion for perfection.") All told, Brooks edited *Young Frankenstein* 12 times—frame by frame. In the final week of postproduction work, the filmmaker spent many hours in a recording studio, providing grunts, snorts, groans, sighs, and so on to fill tiny gaps in the sound track.

• • •

As *Young Frankenstein* pushed toward its December 15, 1974, release date, Twentieth Century-Fox launched a strong promotional campaign. Brooks insisted upon actively participating in this crucial process. A facet of the studio's publicity onslaught was to have a huge billboard painted on the side of the Playboy Building on Hollywood's Sunset Strip. Soon thereafter, the Writers Guild of America West objected to the ad, which labeled *Young Frankenstein* a "Mel Brooks Film" without listing the picture's writing credits. Meanwhile, one of the studio ads was submitted to the guild, and this, too, was termed a contract violation, as was the film itself (which failed to repeat the writing credits at the end of the film along with the credits for the producer and the director). In the settlement, the guild received a $10,000 award—of which script collaborator Gene Wilder got $7,000.

Young Frankenstein premiered at the Avco Theater in Westwood, a community just west of Beverly Hills. Many critics noted that the film was far better structured than *Blazing Saddles* but—for better or worse—contained the usual array of lewd vulgarity, as well as Brooksian wordplay. (For example, arriving at the Frankenstein castle, Wilder's scientist notes, "What knockers," referring to the ornate fixtures on the massive front door. To which Teri Garr's shapely Inga responds proudly, "Thank you, doctor." There was also the inclusion of Mel's beloved gambit in which the odd servant opens the door and instructs Frankenstein, "Walk this way," and the doctor immediately duplicates the strange loping gait of the humpbacked Igor.)

The new release earned several enthusiastic reviews. Charles Champlin (of the *Los Angeles Times*) endorsed the picture as a "likable, unpredictable blending of slapstick and sentiment." Vincent Canby (of the *New York Times*) ranked it as "Mel Brooks's funniest, most cohesive comedy to date." Made at an estimated cost of $2.8 million, *Young Frankenstein* grossed well over $38 million dollars in domestic distribution and earned far more through its foreign release, reissues (promoted as "The Scariest Comedy of All Time"), and ancillary income. (By the late 1990s, Mel had earned well over $5 million from his involvement with *Young Frankenstein*, as he did similarly with *Blazing Saddles*. Over the decades, *Young Frankenstein* remained for many in the legion of fans of Brooks the filmmaker's ultimate creation: a well-crafted satire bursting with zany performances, loony plot twists, wonderful atmospheric set pieces, and amusing satirical spins on the horror film genre.

Thanks to *Young Frankenstein* and *Blazing Saddles* being back-to-back hits, Brooks was Hollywood's new King of Comedy. It was a lofty position once held by Jerry Lewis and, earlier, by Charles Chaplin. However, the always wary Brooks remained suspicious of his latest run of good luck. Of his enviable industry standing he insisted, "I'll believe it when I'm dead. Five years from now, I could be back in the shit."

26

On the Hollywood Treadmill

Now it's emotional. I don't buy too much, but I can say no to jobs.
I can say no! A great relief. My throat doesn't click with anxiety when
I pick up the check. I drive the only Buick around here. That's a Jewish
car. . . . but money means to me, walking by a sporting-goods shop, I
see a nice pair of sneakers, I buy it.

—Mel Brooks, 1975

While Mel Brooks was absorbed in the making of *Blazing Saddles* and
Young Frankenstein, Anne Bancroft focused her primary attention on
raising their toddler, Max. Nevertheless, she found time to headline a
1974 ABC-TV special, *Annie & the Hoods* (for which Mel was one of the
guest performers), and to costar in two 1975 theatrical film releases, Neil
Simon's *The Prisoner of Second Avenue* and the period thriller *The Hin-
denburg*.

By now, Mel was weighing his career options under his recent multi-
film production deal with Twentieth Century-Fox Pictures. (Brooks's Crossbow Production Company had its headquarters on the studio lot.) There
were rumors that Brooks and Gene Wilder would follow up *Young
Frankenstein* with a spoof of *Dr. Jekyll and Mr. Hyde*. However, the rosy
success of Wilder's latest film allowed Gene to negotiate his own production agreement with Twentieth Century-Fox. In turn, this led to Wilder's
writing, directing, and starring in 1975's *The Adventures of Sherlock
Holmes's Younger Brother*, a project that utilized some of Mel Brooks's
"stock company" of actors and technical talent. As a result of this and
subsequent other Wilder showcases, Gene and Mel went in different

career directions and were unable to continue their successful working relationship, although they remained friends over the years.

When Brooks did return to work, he rather surprisingly chose to revisit his earlier stomping ground: television. (Mel reasoned, "I'm not turning my back on television just because I can write my own ticket in movies. After all, for a long time TV paid all my bills.") ABC-TV persuaded Brooks to quickly package a new half-hour TV series. His choice of projects was *When Things Were Rotten*, a wacky satire on the Robin Hood legend (a topic that Mel already had teased briefly in one of his 2000 Year Old Man recordings). The sitcom had been brought to Mel by comedy writer Normal Stiles, who had worked on the property with John Bonny. Brooks and others reshaped the entry, and Mel exerted his industry clout to launch the program.

When Mel was asked why he had selected this particular vehicle, he offered, "All my life, I am after dangerous comedy. . . . Dangerous comedy—that's the kind where you hit the ground, you want to stop laughing and you can't. With *Rotten* I have this effervescent, 'Meshuginah,' dangerous comedy." In touting his fall 1975 small-screen fare, Mel emphasized, "It was fun that roped me in. I couldn't resist the fun of somebody saying 'Hold Your tongue' and everybody holding their tongues." According to Brooks, the comedy expert, "With Robin Hood and Sherwood Forest, I thought I'd make the series kind of a blazing forest rather than *Blazing Saddles*—lots of people falling off horses and plenty of sets and locations. I love physical comedy."

Unlike the latitude that feature films allowed Brooks for his display of vulgar puns, sexual situations, and so forth, the television industry's censorship rules were, by comparison, far stricter. Another roadblock for Brooks in mounting *When Things Were Rotten* was finding a way to pack his typical humor into the 24 or so minutes allotted for each episode and then having to deal with home viewers being distracted by the program's rash of commercials. On the plus side, Brooks bubbled, "With costume comedy what we have is the chance to juxtapose medieval clichés against modern knowledge." He bragged, "We're giving viewers big, brave, visual comedy. We're taking them outdoors. They'll love it. We're handsomer, we're cuter, we're taller, and we're better than those other shows. We have six different, complicated sets, plus Sherwood Forest, plus a large, first-rate company of players. I honestly think we'll be one of the top 10 shows in just a little while."

For his cast of regulars, Brooks relied on two veterans of the old *Get Smart* series: Dick Gautier (cast in the title role) and Bernie Kopell (as sidekick Alan-a-Dale). Dick Van Patten (who became a regular in several of Mel's later projects) was recruited for the series (as Friar Tuck) after the veteran actor and Mel met on the tennis courts at the estate of TV talk show host Merv Griffin and quickly became great pals. (By now, Brooks had developed a passion for playing tennis, a favorite sport of his wife's). The attractive Misty Rowe was cast as the heroine, Maid Marian. Filming took place largely at Paramount Pictures (where an entire sound stage was devoted to Sherwood Forest and the Sheriff of Nottingham's offices). Location work was done in a forest near Thousand Oaks, California, as well as in Malibu and at other outdoor sites.

According to the show's star, Dick Gautier, "Mel was actively involved in the pilot episode. Although Jerry Paris was the titular director, Mel had a lot of input and rewrites on the spur of the moment and he was open to ad-libs and bits of business from the actors many of which had backgrounds in improv and comedy."

A few days before the debut of *When Things Were Rotten* on September 10, 1975, the Dope Sheet column of the *New York Times* reported, "Once again, the network schedules reflect the fact that Wednesday is the least-watched television night. The only item of interest is a new show conceived in the fevered mind of Mel Brooks for ABC: *When Things Were Rotten* to be seen at 8 P.M. The Robin Hood spoof was greeted with explosive laughter at the ABC convention, but whether it can generate enough stories for a weekly series remains to be seen."

Many critics applauded Brooks's series for being innovative compared to the formula shows then peppering the networks' lineup. However, a few weeks after the debut of *When Things Were Rotten*, critic John Leonard was writing in the *New York Times* about "The Worst Television Season Ever, Ever, Ever." He noted, "So far, we haven't even discussed quality, unless it's the quality of panic. Watching *When Things Were Rotten* is like being locked inside a package of bubblegum where the only card is Alvin Dark [a veteran major league baseball player]. I think Mel Brooks should turn himself off, but the nine-year-olds of America apparently disagree."

Initially, Mel's small-screen outing, with its cornucopia of sight gags, received high national ratings from home viewers. This solid response was partially due to Brooks's moviegoing fan base tuning in to the show to see if the same entertaining degree of irreverence and lunacy would be carried over to the television series. However, when they saw that—alas!—it was not, they quickly lost interest. Meanwhile, regular TV viewers proved to be more attracted to watching the competition during that Wednesday evening time slot: CBS's *Tony Orlando & Dawn* variety hour, and NBC's *Little House on the Prairie* family drama.

By December 24, 1975, after airing the already filmed 13 episodes, the network dropped *When Things Were Rotten* from its schedule. Per Dick Gautier, there were behind-the-scenes reasons for the program's sudden cancellation. He told this author, "This may not be gospel but from what I understand Fred Silverman was head of CBS and was pitched the Robin Hood concept and turned it down. They then went to ABC, made a deal for a pilot and we got on the air. Pretty good reviews, we didn't do badly in the ratings, *but*— and this is where politics rears its head—Fred Silverman then switched from CBS to ABC and there on the schedule and doing fairly well was *Rotten* which he had turned down. We were summarily axed. Politics, ego, or pragmatism? You tell me." Dick Van Patten recalls that Mel was extremely angry when his show suffered an inglorious demise.

• • •

It was through Will Jordan—with whom Brooks had worked back in the late 1940s at the little theater in Red Bank, New Jersey—that Ron Clark first popped into Mel's life. Clark was already an established TV writer (on *The Danny Kaye Show* and telefeatures) and playwright. Jordan arranged for Ron and Mel to have a lunch meeting, during which Clark proposed the idea of a new screen comedy, whose gimmick would be that for nearly the entire film no words would be spoken. (The characters' conversations would be conveyed to the audience in traditional silent cinema fashion through title cards containing dialogue and via the actors' pantomime.) One can only imagine how Brooks, the lifelong verbal pundit who thrived on exploiting on-camera vulgar dialogue and crude sounds, responded to such an audacious suggestion. At first blush, Mel seemed the very last filmmaker in Hollywood to be amused by such an apparently uncommercial conceit. Then, slowly, the challenge of making such a gimmick work artistically and commercially appealed to Brooks's sensibilities and ego. Mel was soon envisioning the great pleasure he would derive from demonstrating to Hollywood bigwigs that he could both resurrect silent screen comedy and maintain audience interest among 1970s filmgoers. The more enthusiastic Brooks became about the off-the-wall concept, the more determined he became to convince Twentieth Century-Fox to approve this seemingly unviable screen idea. Over several months, he and Clark worked in tandem with two other TV comedy writers (Rudy DeLuca and Barry Levinson) to whip together a screenplay. (In devising their story line, the four authors riffed on many of the roadblocks they were encountering in persuading Twentieth Century-Fox to green-light their vehicle.)

According to Brooks, "The studio bosses at 20th Century were thinking about some kind of light noise, a buzz maybe [on the movie's sound track]. Because they were afraid there would be just deadly silence, and it can get very uncomfortable sitting in a silent theater. . . . But I said, 'No! There won't be any silence! The people will be laughing. The sound track will be the audience itself! Laughter! Laughter will be the sound track. We don't have to worry about silence!' But I put in 90 minutes of music, like a rug from beginning to end, just to be on the safe side."

As it evolved, *Silent Movie* became Brooks's tribute to the glorious silent screen comedies he had so enjoyed watching as a child back in Coney Island. It was also a forum for barbed attacks on the growing trend in 1970s Hollywood of "multinational companies and conglomerates getting into the movie business. They're moving into an art form and I [Brooks] hate them for it." In casting the feature—set in the mid-1970s—Mel handed himself his first leading role in movies. He also utilized the talents of such past teammates as Marty Feldman and Dom DeLuise as the hero's daffy sidekicks in order to create a contemporary counterpart to the Three Stooges. (For Brooks, the Feldman and DeLuise characters also served as surrogates for his three real-life brothers, with whom he had been so close during his childhood.) Brooks also found a role for his longtime pal Sid Caesar, whose career had never rebounded after his heyday with *Your Show of Shows* and *Caesar's Hour*.

During the filming of *Silent Movie*, which began production on January 5, 1976, and shot for 12 weeks, Brooks claimed to have dealt with a great obstacle on the set—getting an audible reaction from the crew. "We could not get the crew to laugh! There we were, knocking ourselves out to be funny, and behind the camera, not a snicker. This was a veteran crew. After 50 years of making sound movies, they were afraid if they made a noise it would spoil the shot. Fer chrissakes, fellas, I said, there's not even a microphone. Laugh a little! Yuk it up!"

Within the extremely episodic narrative, Brooks is seen as accomplished filmmaker Mel Funn, whose career has fallen apart because of his alcoholism. Now recovering from substance abuse, Funn suggests to the beleaguered head of Big Picture Studios (played by Caesar) that he can save the company from corporate raiders by making a contemporary comedy that can't miss at the box office. Its gimmick will be that it is a silent picture that, in all other respects, utilizes the latest movie technology.

Mel Funn is joined on his quest by his two goofy, juvenile-acting pals. The happy-go-lucky trio sets out to recruit major stars for its proposed movie so the studio will approve the project for filming. In time, the daffy threesome persuade Burt Reynolds, Liza Minnelli, James Caan, Paul Newman, and Anne Bancroft to appear in their offbeat venture. (Their one failure is trying to woo the French mime Marcel Marceau to appear in the picture.) Meanwhile, Funn and his cohorts combat the dastardly corporate forces of Engulf & Devour. In the process, the well-meaning, dapper Mel so charms the enemy's sexy spy (played by Bernadette Peters) that she falls in love with him.

One of the two biggest pluses of *Silent Movie* was Brooks's performance as the nattily dressed, personable hero. The other was the extended cameo provided by Anne Bancroft. She deliciously hammed it up as the regal movie star whose night on the town includes a stopover at the Rio Bomba Club. She soon finds herself ensnared in a wild tango with Mel and his two bumbling cronies. During the madcap dance, the agile Anne is tossed wildly about by the goofy trio, has her head smashed into a wall, and survives other indignities. In executing this highly athletic number, the real-life husband and wife proved a dexterous on-camera team. While they might not have been the logical successors to the elegant Fred Astaire and the graceful Ginger Rogers, Brooks and Bancroft admirably proved they were game performers and a duo very much in synch with each other. Bancroft, so long associated with heavily dramatic roles, exuded great joy at kidding her serious professional image, even mugging and crossing her eyes on camera.

In making *Silent Movie*, Mel discovered, "Making a silent, believe me, is more difficult than a talkie. That's why my respect for the old silent stars has grown." Concerning guiding himself on camera, Brooks allowed, "Directing myself relieves some of the frustration from impulse to reaction. . . . But I'm not going to tell myself how much I like me or I'll ask for more money." Mel the director also had to ride herd on Brooks the cowriter of the film. There was one sequence in the picture that as much as Mel the scenarist liked it, Brooks the director knew had to be excised from the release print. The scene in question was set at the Chez Lobster restaurant. There, a huge lobster is the tuxedo-garbed maitre d'. He greets two well-dressed lobsters and leads them to a vacant table. Brooks recalled, "Already, we thought this was hysterical. Then a waiter lobster in a white jacket shows them a menu that says 'Flown in Fresh from New York.' They get up and follow the waiter lobster to an enormous tank, where a lot of little human beings in bathing suits are swimming nervously around. The lobster patrons point to a tasty-looking middle-aged man. The waiter's claw reaches into the tank. It picks up the man, who is going bananas, and that was the end of the scene. We loved it; we thought it was sensational. Every time we saw it, there was not enough Kleenex to stuff into our mouths." But, alas, the filmmaker admitted, "It died at sneak previews."

Brooks and his creative team maneuvered through the postproduction process of *Silent Movie* in a surprisingly short period (for Mel) to have it ready for its scheduled debut on June 16, 1976. The critics had reservations about the final results, noting, in particular, that the film's pacing was far slower and the energy far less manic than, for example, Brooks's *The Producers*, and this made the viewer all too aware of the picture's hit-or-miss quality. Vincent Canby (of the *New York Times*) argued, "The lack of spoken dialogue doesn't disable the character. It's the concept. When you have a Mel Brooks who doesn't allow himself to be rude, testy and master of the low leer, you don't have a funny man. You have an affable floorwalker. He's a surprise and sort of pleasant but not what you were expecting." Canby concluded, "*Silent Movie* is not the greatest movie Mr. Brooks has made, but if you adjust your expectations, it could be one of the nicest things you'll see all summer." John Simon wrote in *New York* magazine, "The scenario is basically no sillier than those of the old silent comedies, but the innocence is gone. Some gags are too . . . esoteric; others are takeoffs on the old ones, and seem to kid something that depended on its deadpan dedication. Brooks is not an eloquent mime." Stanley Kauffmann (of the *New Republic*) judged, "None of the picture made me double up with laughter . . . still there are some good sight gags."

Silent Movie was made for about $4.5 million (with another $5 million devoted to release promotion) and generated $21.24 million in domestic theater rentals. While the picture was certainly profitable, it was not in the same league as *Young Frankenstein* (which owed so much to Gene Wilder's input) and thus not the anticipated financial bonanza Twentieth Century-Fox had counted on so heavily to rescue the studio during a particularly bad fiscal quarter.

Mel Brooks, Ron Clark, Rudy DeLuca, and Barry Levinson were nominated for a Writers Guild of America Award in the Best Comedy Written Directly for the Screen category, but lost to Bill Lancaster (for *The Bad News Bears*). On a more positive note, the National Association of Theater Owners (made up of 8,000 film exhibitors) named Mel Brooks director of the year for his work on *Silent Movie, Young Frankenstein*, and the upcoming *High Anxiety*. Said Brooks: "I was delighted, especially so since the N.A.T.O. convention is going to be held in Miami and it'll give me a chance to see my little Jewish mother, who lives there."

In this same period, U.S. film exhibitors ranked Mel Brooks fifth on their annual list of the 25 stars who demonstrated the greatest box-office appeal. (Interestingly, Brooks's only starring appearance to this time was in *Silent Movie*, in which he did not speak.) Mel, the one-time bumbling tummler at Catskill Mountain resorts, was enthralled that he should now have such wide appeal as a performer with the moviegoing public. Giddy with success, Brooks could not resist ribbing Burt Reynolds, Mel's box-office "rival," who was then ranked sixth in box-office popularity. Whenever Mel phoned Burt, Brooks would start each conversation with: "Hello, Six, this is Five speaking."

• • •

In 1971, Avery Corman wrote *Oh, God!* a comedic novel that was later adapted into a screenplay by Larry Gelbart, once part of the impressive writing team on *Caesar's Hour*. Carl Reiner, another veteran of that vintage TV series, agreed to direct the big-screen project. At one point en route to production, it was rumored that Mel Brooks would take on the title role of the Lord, with Woody Allen (who had worked with Brooks on Sid Caesar's TV specials in the late 1950s) projected to play the young grocery man who is recruited by God to help spread the gospel. That intriguing casting did not happen and the resultant film teamed George

Burns with singer-turned-actor John Denver. It became an enormous box-office success.

Instead, Brooks, delighting in his power to generate his own career decisions, chose to focus on another of his own vehicles. He reteamed with his *Silent Movie* collaborators (Ron Clark, Rudy DeLuca, and Barry Levinson) to create *High Anxiety*. The thrust of the new project was to spoof "two things I love desperately: Alfred Hitchcock and psychiatry. Ever since I was a little boy watching *The 39 Steps* and *The Lady Vanishes* wash over me in a dark movie house, I was lost in that world of Robert Donat, Madeleine Carroll, English accents, railway instead of railroad, windows on both sides of the compartment. I just couldn't get over it."

Also of key importance to Mel in seizing on this property was the fact that this film would showcase Brooks in a dream role: as a Cary Grant–type hero. "I've always wanted to be the character I'm playing: Prof. Richard H. Thorndyke. I mean I like a hat that comes down on both sides. I like a Phi Beta Kappa key. I like a gray suit. I mean there it is a dream come true: I'm a Nobel Prize–winning psychiatrist in an Alfred Hitchcock picture. That's a kid's fantasy." As a bonus, Brooks also had a cameo as the hero's look-alike, an actual killer.

As the project revved up at Twentieth Century-Fox, Mel expounded to the media on his personal guidelines for creating a commercially successful feature. "You don't want to make a picture just for the smarties. That's no good. You want all the people. You want a potato salad picture. You know what I mean by a potato salad picture. You're in the deli and there's this guy with a little piece of potato salad stuck in the corner of his mouth, and he's talking about your picture to his cronies. He's saying, all the time with the potato salad hanging, 'You gotta see this Mel Brooks pitcha, you'll laugh so hard you'll pish yourself.'"

Mel's ambition in his new venture was to create a narrative that would be understood by anyone—including those not familiar with Alfred Hitchcock's oeuvre. However, for aficionados of Hitchcock there would be an extra layer of fun in witnessing Brooks's farcical twists on famous sequences and setups from various of the master's classic screen thrillers, including *Spellbound, Vertigo, Psycho, The Birds,* and *North by Northwest.* Fearful of possibly offending the great Sir Alfred, Brooks visited Hitchcock at his Los Angeles home to gain his seal of approval for *High Anxiety*. Mel relished detailing his meeting with Hitchcock: "He's a very emotional man.

I told him that where other people take saunas to relax, I run *The Lady Vanishes* for the sheer pleasure of it. He had tears in his eyes. I think he understood that I wasn't going to make fun of him. If the picture is a send up, it's also an act of homage to a great artist. I'm glad I met him, because I love him."

• • •

In devising his "dapper" alter ego for *High Anxiety*, Brooks allowed his flight of fancy to run loose. Here was an opportunity for a short, average-looking man to transform himself into a romantic leading man. At least in the make-believe of this cinema excursion, he could compensate for the many years of being the mug who envied the handsome men who made easy conquests of the opposite sex. "In my heart of hearts, I always wanted to be Errol Flynn. . . . Yeah, I was heartbroken. And I always wanted the most beautiful, long-waisted, long-legged women in the world to fall on their knees and pray to me. But as life and God would have it, it was the other way around. Every time I see a tall, beautiful woman, I just crash to my knees and I pray to her. I say, 'Please, just give me a slap in the face, something. Show me that you know I'm alive, too.'"

Another impetus for Brooks to make *High Anxiety* was to provide an on-screen forum in which he could imitate Frank Sinatra singing in a club. (For years, Mel had been doing his impersonation of the crooner at parties and on TV.) To that end, Mel wrote the song "High Anxiety," which John Morris scored for the new movie.

In assembling his cast, Mel chose Howard Morris to play his mentor, Professor Vicktor Lilloman. It was the first time Brooks and Morris had worked together in a decade, and the first movie ever in which the two old friends acted together. The occasion prompted Mel to say, "I look into Howie's eyes and I see my life there! We hug each other and laugh and cry a lot. . . . He's as funny as you want him to be and yet he's very moving and warm." In turn, Howard said of Mel, "He has always had the ability to cut through the shit. The way he has changed is that when you are eighteen or nineteen and you have that instinct, people think you're crazy. You think you're crazy. Now he has the confidence, having proven himself economically."

Brooks again asked Cloris Leachman to take on the role of another celluloid villain. (Mel enthused about her, "Cloris' genius is that she never plays comedy for laughs. She's deadly serious as the character.") To make her new screen character (Nurse Charlotte Diesel) unique, Leachman chose not to reprise the ridiculous Eastern European accent and stern countenance she had used to play Frau Blücher in *Young Frankenstein*. To heighten her sinister portrayal, she took the initiative to pencil in a light mustache, add additional shoulder padding to her outfits, and raise the costume's torpedo-shaped breasts to just below her chin, and she decided to talk out of the side of the mouth. Her exaggerated appearance gave even the notoriously screwball Brooks pause. However, she stood her ground, saying, "My intention is not to do something I've done before." Mel finally went along with Leachman's suggestions for her character.

Madeline Kahn returned to Brooks's fold for the third time, this go-round cast as the very blond, glamorous heroine, Victoria Brisbane, whose father is being forcibly detained at the Psycho-Neurotic Institute for the Very, Very Nervous. Harvey Korman came aboard as the murderous Dr. Charles Montague, who is putty in the hands of his sadomasochistic lover, Nurse Diesel. Ron Carey, who had had a small role as a corporate miscreant in *Silent Movie*, had a far more vocal role in *High Anxiety*, as the hero's hyperactive chauffeur/helper. Dick Van Patten, another member of Mel's stock company, joined the ensemble as a nervous clinic staffer who knows far too many dastardly secrets to remain alive. Since Brooks made a policy of having his collaborators on the set during filming, he decided to give each of them (Ron Clark, Rudy DeLuca, and Barry Levinson) a small role in the proceedings. Even Mel's lawyer, Alan Schwartz, had a bit role (as a psychiatrist).

Filming on *High Anxiety* began on April 25, 1977, on location in San Francisco, with scenes lensed at the ultramodern Hyatt Regency Hotel (which boasted futuristic glass cylinder elevators that were a critical plot point in the picture), Fisherman's Wharf, and historic Fort Point (the latter under the Golden Gate Bridge on the exact spot where Hitchcock had shot an important sequence for *Vertigo*). Back in Los Angeles, the production shot at Fox and at such area locales as Mount St. Mary's College, the Bonaventure Hotel, and Los Angeles International Airport. The shoot ended on July 14, 1977, four days ahead of schedule. The final sequence, in which the leading man is seen fleeing from a flock of attacking pigeons, was shot in a park in Pasadena, California.

Later, Brooks acknowledged that in *High Anxiety*, "One of the clichés I nearly used was, I was going to open with a small Swiss village and you see a train that is obviously a toy train. And I was going to have a big foot crush the village and say, 'Oops I'm sorry.' But I thought that was a little too exquisite and a little too subtle and I never did it." In the same picture, Mel also had a notion of having his hero come out of George Washington's nose on Mount Rushmore wearing a green jumpsuit. His script collaborators talked him out of it. (On the other hand, Brooks couldn't resist the prankish gimmick of having the movie camera shooting the movie crash through a set wall as it dollied in and out of the action.)

In contrast to his earlier films (*The Producers* and *The Twelve Chairs*), Brooks now worked quite rapidly on the sound stages. (By this point, Mel kept graphs in his office, delineating "dialogue, dialogue . . . laugh.") Typically, Brooks maintained an open set on his productions so friends (and even studio executives) could drop by to say hello and watch the progress of the shoot. It was Mel's goal to have a happy and silly ambiance during the shoot so the cast and crew would feel relaxed and be comfortable about offering suggestions.

Having deliberately chosen "self-starters who don't have to have every nuance of behavior explained," Brooks encouraged them to improvise on their physical movements but *not* to vary from the dialogue of the final script. (Mel had also come to realize, "You can't make up the movie as you go along. It's too expensive.") An example of giving cast members freedom to devise funny bits was the clinic sequence in which Mel's character is making his rounds of the facilities. One of the more deranged patients (played by Charles Callas), who thinks he is a cocker spaniel, comes up on all fours to the hero, begins sniffing the newcomer, and then starts to hump the man's leg. As Callas told this author, he thought up much of his business for this sequence.

When it came to interacting with the extras, the filmmaker was very much in his element, thriving on having a large audience eager to do his bidding. During a medical convention scene, he briefed the banquet hall full of extras: "You are all supposed to be psychiatrists at a convention so you're allowed to have a lot of nervous ticks. You can mumble a lot, but don't laugh till you get home." When a tourist mistakenly barged into the room, Brooks quipped, "Lady, you're in a shot! If you can act, stick around."

On the other hand, the hyperactive, highly focused Brooks could, on occasion, be a bit too much for his cast. Madeline Kahn said, "Sometimes he gets very high-powered." Harvey Korman observed, "You must be very careful he doesn't engulf you." And Howard Morris noted, "He has a hysterical kind of energy that causes some people to call him the Monkey because he sometimes appears to be climbing the walls."

By August 31, 1977, Mel was screening a work print of *High Anxiety* for a gathering of 200 executives and workers at Twentieth Century-Fox. Before the showing, the convivial host said, "My beloved, you are guinea pigs." Mel ended his welcoming speech with: "Finally, let me say that I wish you well, but I wish myself better." Further on in postproduction, Brooks invited Hitchcock to a prerelease screening of the picture. When it was over, the master of suspense walked out without saying a word. Brooks thought, "Oh, boy, he hates it." However, soon thereafter, Sir Alfred, knowing Mel was a wine connoisseur, sent Brooks a case of 1961 Haut-Brion (an expensive vintage) with a note that read, "A small token of my pleasure, have no anxiety about this."

High Anxiety premiered in New York City on Christmas Day, 1977. Vincent Canby (of the *New York Times*) weighed in that it was "as witty and as disciplined as *Young Frankenstein*, though it has one built-in problem: Hitchcock himself is a very funny man. His films, even at their most terrifying and most suspenseful, are full of jokes shared with the audience. Being so self-aware, Hitchcock's films deny an easy purchase to the parodist, especially one who admires his subject the way Mr. Brooks does." Canby pointed out, "As the afflicted Dr. Thorndyke, Mr. Brooks plays it so very, very straight that just the memory of one of his famous leers is funny." *Variety* applauded Brooks as a "chance taker" who reveled here in "toying with the technical references" to Hitchcock's canon of classic films and decided that "nearly all of these gags . . . score." However, the trade paper alerted, "Where the film becomes uneven is the individual scenes which sway from the movie's larger design."

Roger Ebert (of the *Chicago Sun-Times*), long a fan of Brooks's, had many reservations about Mel's newest movie release and gave it a rating of only two and a half stars (out of a possible four). "Almost all of Hitchcock's fifty-three or so films have their great moments of wit. And wit — the ability to share a sense of subtle fun with an audience — is not exactly Mel Brooks's strong point. He takes such key Hitchcock moments as the shower scene from *Psycho*, the climbing scene from *Vertigo*, and the shooting in *North by Northwest* and he clobbers them. It's not satire; it's overkill." Ebert observed that, in the process of affectionately spoofing

Hitchcock, Brooks almost buries "his own comic talent in the attempt to fit things into his satirical formula. The best moments in *High Anxiety* come not when Brooks is being assaulted in the shower with a rolled-up newspaper, but when Brooks leaves Hitchcock altogether and does his own crazy, brilliant stuff."

The film's finest moments of inspired lunacy include scenes depicting the hero coping with his fear of heights aboard an airplane and in the hotel's glass-enclosed outdoor elevators, which scale the heights of the skyscraper; the sequence in which the would-be cool and sophisticated psychiatrist croons a song in the hotel saloon; and the broadly played episode in which the fleeing hero and heroine escape police detection by passing through an airport security station dressed as an elderly Jewish couple engaged in a loud screaming match.

Made at an estimated cost of $3.4 million, *High Anxiety* earned $19.16 million in domestic theater rentals. Once again, while the picture enjoyed relatively healthy profits from its U.S. and foreign distribution and subsequent ancillary sales, it represented a growing trend with Brooks's pictures since *Young Frankenstein*: moviegoers were *not* making Mel's movies such a must-see event as just a few years ago and, thus, the number of tickets sold to Brooks's latest theatrical entries was slackening off.

Adding to the filmmaker's concern about his industry status and future, *High Anxiety* failed to win any nominations from either the Academy of Motion Picture Arts and Sciences or the Writers Guild of America. (The picture was up for two Golden Globes but lost out in both instances.) When *High Anxiety* did not receive any nomination from the academy or from the Writers Guild, Mel Brooks fell into great despair. According to Anne Bancroft, he was "as low as I've ever known him." Despite—or because of—the disappointment that tore at his self-confidence, Mel vowed, "I went into show business to make a noise, to pronounce myself. I want to go on making the loudest noise to the most people. If I can't do that, I'm not going to make a quiet, exquisite noise for a cabal of cognoscenti."

27

Stretching His Career Horizons

Sometimes, if people are staring at me; they see it's Mel Brooks, and I'm at a traffic light. I will pretend to have a heart attack and fall over my steering wheel. The horn will blow very loudly for a long time, and everybody will get out of their cars and start to run over—and then I'll drive away. Sometimes I'm really Meshuginah. Once, I was on a bus with a friend of mine and I put a lot of hard, white candies in my mouth. I just kept spitting them out. And I said: "I can't go on like this. My teeth are literally falling out of my mouth." And I kept spitting out these candies that looked like teeth as I talked. Hysterical. I just loved doing it.

—Mel Brooks, 1978

In a relatively short period in the mid-1970s, Mel Brooks had turned out four Hollywood feature films and a TV series. Each venture had demanded a good deal of his energy, creative input, and time, as Brooks wore so many hats on each project. In 1978, Mel had no new film project ready for release because he couldn't decide which project under consideration might be the best one to bolster his faltering box-office standing.

Now in his early 50s, he was still a man of youthful vitality and many enthusiasms. These interests—which helped to distract him from career pressures—included being a wine connoisseur with a well-stocked wine cellar, an avid tennis player, a book collector, a real estate investor, and a man who loved to host gatherings of friends. Most of all, after 14 years of marriage to Anne Bancroft, Brooks was still a devoted husband and continued to remain in awe of her. (Brooks commented of his spouse, "She is a remarkable woman. Every year I see her grow more as a person and as an artist. I really like her, you know? As well as love her. . . . I think that that's really what a good relationship is based on—liking each other. If someone tried to pin me down on what makes a relationship work—'Is it having enough money?' 'Is it sex?'—I would say, 'It's good company.'")

The Brooks family now resided in Beverly Hills at 915 North Foothill Road. The expansive estate boasted a swimming pool and a guesthouse. One visitor to the house during that time recalled recently, "The interior was very classy: decorated by Anne in shades of beige and brown; natural-colors. I found the furniture magnificent and perfectly matching the colors. I remember well a huge 'early American' cupboard in the living room. It looked great."

Mel remained in contact with his three children from his first marriage. He saw them when he was on the East Coast promoting his latest projects or when vacationing at Fire Island, or sometimes they visited him in Los Angeles. His eldest, Stefanie, now 23, had attended Brandeis University and, thereafter, for a time, was a production assistant within the film industry working on such features as *Going in Style*, *The First Deadly Sin*, *The Cotton Club*, and *84 Charing Cross Road*. However, most of Mel's quality time was spent with his and Anne's child, Max, now six.

In 2003, when Max Brooks was promoting the publication of the first book (*The Zombie Survival Guide*) he had written, he recalled his childhood spent in Southern California. "I was always an outsider. The kids I went to school with were far richer than we were, but I was singled out as the rich kid because everybody knew who my dad was. . . . We lived in the hills, so for me it meant trees and wild shrubbery and every Sunday walking the dog to the top of the hill with my dad and looking out over LA. Dad didn't like living there, though—I think it offended his sense of morality. He was always uncomfortable with being flashy. . . . He used to drive me to school every day and his car was a 1982 Honda Accord, which I thought was the coolest car in the world.

"In his mind, money is not a status symbol—it's a defense against medication. When he was a kid, his four back teeth were rotting, and they said to his immigrant Russian Jewish mother, 'We can pull them for 50 cents or we can fill them for a dollar.' She thought, 'What a bargain—

pull them!' So for him, money is something to protect you from the dangers of the world."

Mel had his own recollection of his last-born's formative years: "Max was such a terrific kid. He was like one of those science-fiction children who know more than their parents. He was very bright and very good-natured. When he was only about nine, we went traveling around Europe with friends and we ended up in Venice. There were these rows of cabanas on the beach and we were next to a French couple. The woman was saying, 'You are paying for the sun—why isn't your child on the beach?' So I decided to find out, and had a look in the changing area in the back, and there he was . . . writing his first story. I never encouraged it, though. I don't know where he got it from. I guess life was hard, living with his mother and me, and he liked make-believe a lot better."

Brooks also noted of his son, "He couldn't understand why a stranger would come over to our table in a restaurant and tell us how much they adored us and wanted a picture or an autograph. . . . I think I was a bad father in that way too; I was always kind to fans at his expense. Not spending enough precious moments with him. . . . I was afraid to go to a lot of places. I never took him to a lot of baseball games because . . . you can get surrounded by a lot of crazy people. There's a brush stroke of paranoia there, which kept me from a normal father and son thing."

• • •

By the late 1970s, Mel Brooks was still riding the crest of his *Blazing Saddles* and *Young Frankenstein* successes. Based on their box-office returns, and to a lesser degree his next two pictures, he enjoyed real power within the Hollywood film industry and liked to talk about his enviable position in the community. (If some of Brooks's statements at the time smacked of self-serving remarks geared to bolster his ego and to remind the business of how important he was, so be it. Tinseltown was used to such pronouncements and took them with a grain of salt.) Mel allowed, "It's an achievement of a kind to know that I can walk into any studio—any one in town—and just say my name, and the president will fly out from behind his desk and open his door. It's terrific, it's a great feeling. My worst critic is my wife. She keeps me straight. She says, 'Are you pleasing that mythical public of yours again, or is this really funny and heartfelt?'"

Despite his string of recent successes, Brooks remained very much a product of his childhood. "I'm a Brooklyn boy who was brought up in a materialistic society. And I know that money makes right. Not might but money. Money is everything."

The successful entertainer acknowledged, "All kinds of things make me laugh. I like 'life' things better than I like made-up things. People don't know how wonderfully funny they are. . . . I like to really see characters like that [e.g., a fat woman in a bakery arguing over calories]. . . . And I miss that in Los Angeles. In New York you see a lot more of it—a lot more crazies on the street, a lot more action in the little retail stores, and a lot more give and take 'twixt and 'tween the public. . . . And it's hard for me to observe life now, because even if I try, say in a restaurant, a place where people congregate, they're looking at me. So being famous is not a good idea for being a writer."

When Mel was asked to reveal his upcoming career plans, he somewhat dodged the question with his response: "I'll wait to be thoroughly moved, rocked by an idea. Just remarkably insane, I hope, and a joy to work on. You have to surround the insanity with a great deal of logic and sense. Let me get a great, insane idea and then house it in a good, logical structure and I'm very happy. I'll write it for a year, and then if it's no good, I'll tear it up and go on to another one. But if it's good, we'll make it. Usually we know when it's going well. When it writes itself, we know it's good."

One of the topics Brooks was increasingly being asked to comment on were the career parallels and dissimilarities between him and the nearly 10-years-younger Woody Allen, his chief rival as the contemporary king of American film comedy. (At the time, Allen was riding his own crest, having won two Oscars, for directing and coscripting 1977's *Annie Hall,* and was soon to release *Manhattan.*) Mel noted of his competitor and himself, "Woody will feel something and then disguise it skillfully and issue it. I know what I do best and I am theatrical. Woody is not theatrical. He's shy and very private, almost academic. . . . I chose not to be philosophical or intellectual. I choose to tap dance as much as I can. I think of it as a job, not a mission and not an artistic endeavor."

•   •   •

In 1979, Mel's only big-screen output was a cameo appearance in Jim Henson's *The Muppet Movie*. He was on camera briefly as the mad Professor Max Krassman, one of the live characters who encounters Kermit the Frog when the latter is convinced by his talent agent (played by Dom DeLuise) to try his luck in Hollywood. The family-fare entry was a huge commercial success.

Meanwhile, Brooks had been quietly laying the groundwork for new show business ventures of his own. He had formed a new production company, Brooksfilms, to take the place of Crossbow Productions (whose final project was *High Anxiety*). Mel intended for the new entity to produce serious films beyond his own comedic projects. In forming the organization, he was motivated by the conviction that "somewhere in the Talmud, it tells you that you must return a portion of your gain in this world. You must give back." In addition, he had been prompted into this new business venture because he had thought, "I'm just becoming a crowd-pleaser. What have I got to say? . . . I couldn't use my art just to make a living." (There also must have been a part of Brooks that sensed he should cover his options in the film business, in case his screen comedies continued to dip in popularity at the box office.)

According to the moviemaker, "I very skillfully hid my name when I created Brooksfilms. I very assiduously kept the name Mel Brooks away from [these projects]." Brooks understood that if the public at large associated his brand of humor with the output of Brooksfilms it would set up wrong expectations for the company's releases.

It was Mel's belief that he could best express his decades-old love of the (international) cinema by encouraging new filmmakers to make creative and ambitious projects. (There was also a practical reason to Brooks's giving a helping hand to relatively new talent: "I'm not really that benevolent, loving and giving a human being. I'm really being much more selfish. I think that first-time people doing a big first-time job in any field will give you 110 percent. If you find the right people and you give them an opportunity, you know the bread you cast upon the water will not come back soggy. You're going to get something good there.")

One of the first individuals to benefit from Mel's new production banner was his wife, Anne. She had been coping with the longtime film industry problem of diminishing career opportunities available to leading ladies once they passed the age of 40. Recently, Bancroft had suffered through a thankless role in the 1976 potboiler *Lipstick*, while giving an Oscar-nominated performance in the next year's *The Turning Point*. Thereafter, challenging movie role offers had dried up for her, and she turned to TV (playing Mary Magdalene in the miniseries *Jesus of Nazareth*) and returned to the Broadway stage (in William Gibson's *Golda*, a short-lived drama about Israel's premier, Golda Meir).

Meanwhile, Bancroft had attended the American Film Institute's Directing Workshop for Women in Los Angeles. There, she directed two shorts, *The August* (starring Hope Lange, which was never released) and *Fatso*. Both were shot in black and white in a video format. She chose not to ask Brooks for advice. When asked why she made this decision, she told an associate, "I don't want to direct a Mel Brooks film. I want to direct an Anne Bancroft film! This is a matter of identity! And Mel agrees with this!"

Nevertheless, Mel did provide his spouse with the encouragement to turn *Fatso* into a full-length feature. It was to be released by Brooksfilms through Twentieth Century-Fox. Stuart Cornfeld, who had been an assistant to the producer on *High Anxiety*, served as producer of the new venture, for which Anne was the costar, director, and scenarist. Dom DeLuise, Candy Azzara, and Estelle Reiner (the wife of Carl Reiner) repeated their roles from the short subject in this drama about an Italian American man (DeLuise) who is seriously overweight, causing his concerned sister (Bancroft) great stress. The hefty, good-natured hero only abandons his devotion to food when he falls in love with an attractive lady (Azzara) from the neighborhood.

While *Fatso* was officially Bancroft's screen project, Brooks did make his presence felt on the production. Years later, in Mollie Gregory's 2002 book, *Women Who Run the Show*, Brianne Murphy (the cinematographer on *Fatso*) recalled, "I was never allowed to go to dailies. Nobody went to dailies except Anne and Mel, so I'd see the film at the lab before I came to work in the morning. Usually at dailies, the DP [the director of photography] goes with the director and the director tells the DP what she likes and doesn't like. The editor usually goes, too. But in this case only Mel went with Anne. I guess he told her what he liked. Word had gotten around that he was very controlling.

"But on the set everybody loved Anne and we had a wonderful camaraderie. Around four or five in the afternoon, Mel would come to pick her up. We never knew when he'd arrive and it seemed to be at his convenience rather than hers because whenever he did appear, she'd start wanting to complete a shot. One day, he came on the set, not introduced to anyone and not saying hello to anyone. . . . Mel goes over to the video assist to look at it and in the middle of the shot he says, 'Cut, cut, that's no good, that won't work, cut it.'

"My camera operator, Bob Lavar, a big man, took his eye away from the camera, looked down at Mel, looked over at me, and said 'Who the fuck is that little guy?' All hell broke loose. Very upset Anne picked up her stuff and left. It was a wrap. . . . No one ever says 'Cut' except the director. Ever.

"The next day, I came in to the set and we're all lit and ready to go. No Anne. After an hour or so, the assistant director came to me and said, 'Bri, Anne wants to see you in her dressing room.' I went in. Her eyes were all red and she said that she'd been crying all night. 'This is just terrible what happened yesterday,' she said, 'and I hate to tell you this, but Mel says you have to fire Bob, the operator.'

'What on earth for?'

'Mel says he's potentially dangerous.'"

According to Murphy, for the next day there was a battle of wills over whether the camera operator would or would not be fired. Finally, the matter was dropped and "we all got back to work." In summing up her experience on the film, the director of photography noted, "Anne Bancroft is a very talented person. I always thought she could have been a great director."

Fatso was released on February 1, 1980, to mildly positive reviews and generated a relatively modest $7.65 million in domestic distribution. After that experience, Bancroft never again directed another feature. She reasoned, "I think to be a director you have to have a certain kind of personality which I don't have. I do not like manipulating people. My greatest philosophy is to let everybody just be who they want to be, but it isn't workable. Somebody has to have a very dominating hand, and I just don't have that kind of hand."

• • •

At the time of *Fatso*'s pending release, Mel was persuaded by the press to comment on his wife's new picture. He remarked, "The title is funny, yes—but it says so much about the hurt inflicted on fat people. And the movie is funny, but it also condemns society for making outcasts of fat people, and examines the psychology that makes these superfat people want to throw their lives away. Because, really, that's what they're doing."

His observations reflected a theme that would course through many of the projects brought to the screen by Brooksfilms in the coming years: that of individuals who are different from society's norm and how these outsiders react to and deal with the world. (Such outcasts were certainly close to the heart of Mel Brooks, who, from childhood on, had been both a victim and a product of being "different" from the average man.) This attitude was particularly evident with Brooksfilms's next major film offering, 1980's *The Elephant Man*.

The idea was brought to Mel by his babysitter's boyfriend. The evolving screenplay was based on various nonfiction accounts of John Merrick, who lived in nineteenth-century England and who suffered from a physically disfiguring disability called neurofibromatosis. For much of his short life he existed as a carnival sideshow freak gawked at by paying audiences. He spent his last four years at London Hospital, cared for by a sympathetic surgeon. The quite bright and polite man died in 1894 at age 27.

This insightful, sensitively told story was certainly a far cry from such Brooksian mirthfests as *Blazing Saddles* and *Young Frankenstein*. However, because the venture resonated so deeply with Mel, he worked extremely diligently over a long period with the project's young scriptwriters (Christopher De Vore and Eric Bergren) as well as with David Lynch, the film's director (and cowriter on the final screenplay). Brooks said later, "I have a lot of pride in ownership of that film." He also acknowledged, "I knew the critics would take offense if there was a property they felt was sacred and the bean-farting wacko from *Blazing Saddles* was going to put his grimy paws on it." For this reason, Mel served as the uncredited executive producer on *The Elephant Man*, while the film was produced by Jonathan Sanger (already established as part of Mel's production team from past projects).

Keeping to the spirit of David Lynch's concept for this unusual case study, Brooks agreed the picture should be filmed in black and white. It was shot economically in England and boasted a strong cast, including John Hurt in the title role, Anthony Hopkins as the caring physician, and Anne Bancroft as the stage actress who befriends the human oddity. The well-crafted feature was released by Paramount Pictures in the fall of 1980 and received high critical praise. Made for an estimated $5 million, it earned several times that amount at the box office, drawing in a lifetime gross of over $26 million. *The Elephant Man* received eight Academy Award nominations, including in the categories of Best Film, Best Director, Best Screenplay (adapted from another medium), and Best Actor (John Hurt).

The Elephant Man was an amazingly prestigious and rather profitable undertaking for the fledgling Brooksfilms. It added enormously to the regard with which Mel was held in the movie industry. When the public realized that the film was a product of the zany Brooks, it caused many detractors of the self-acknowledged vulgarian to perceive the successful filmmaker and highly complex individual in a new light.

This Brooksfilms release paved the way for the company's several other pictures in the 1980s. As on *The Elephant Man*, Mel's primary function was always to remain behind the scenes in order to package the property and get it made as effectively and efficiently as possible. (Having learned the hard way about the rampant creative accounting procedures in the film business, Brooks became a shrewd negotiator. As a part of his education in the financial ins and outs of moviemaking, Mel hired the highly experienced and adept Emile Buyse—who supervised Twentieth Century-Fox's overseas sales—to do the same for Brooksfilms. Brooks worked closely with Buyse on Brooksfilms' releases, often making extended public appearance tours abroad, where Mel—like Jerry Lewis before him—was even more highly regarded than back in the United States.)

In 1982, Brooksfilms was responsible for two releases: *My Favorite Year* and *Frances*. The first was a nostalgic comedy set in early 1950s New York City and concerned zany happenings at a *Your Show of Shows*–type of TV program. It featured Joseph Bologna as a Sid Caesar–like star of the small screen and Mark Linn-Baker as a young TV staff writer (a part that had many parallels to Mel Brooks's own life). Actor Richard Benjamin made his feature film directing debut with this project, which contained vivid performances by the Oscar-nominated Peter O'Toole (cast as an Errol Flynn–like swashbuckling movie star) and Lainie Kazan as Baker's colorful mama. The popular comedy, released by MGM, went on to gross over $20 million.

This was followed by the Universal Pictures release of *Frances*, a strong drama based on the tormented life of the beautiful actress Frances Farmer. She had defied the Hollywood studio system in the late 1930s and early 1940s, became an alcoholic, spent long periods in the hell of mental institutions, and finally emerged a shell of her former rebellious self. Both Jessica Lange as the beleaguered Frances and Kim Stanley as her overly possessive mother were Oscar nominated. The controversial feature, which was meticulously directed by Australian-born filmmaker Graeme Clifford, was not a financial success, but like *The Elephant Man*, it enhanced the prestige of Brooksfilms within the Hollywood community.

Thereafter, the once very promising production company seemed to lose its professional way, turning out 1985's *The Doctor and the Devils*. Lensed in England, it dealt with grave robbers who supply a physician with corpses for his medical experiments. (Some of its plot points recalled fragments of *Young Frankenstein* and certainly had an appeal for Mel, who never stopped being intrigued with the subject of man's mortality.) The horror drama was much in the vein of the 1950s and 1960s Hammer Film thriller releases. (It was directed by Freddie Francis, a veteran of that U.K. studio's creative team.) The picture was based on a 1940s screenplay by Welsh poet Dylan Thomas and revamped later by veteran screenwriter Roland Harwood. Despite an interesting cast (including Timothy Dalton, Jonathan Pryce, Twiggy, and Patrick Stewart), the Twentieth Century-Fox release received scant American distribution and grossed only $147,000.

This was followed by 1986's *Solarbabies*, a different type of science-fiction picture set in the distant future. It focused on a group of orphans escaping oppressive government forces. Directed by Alan Johnson (who had choreographed a few of Brooks's past features), it proved to be both a critical and commercial loser for Brooksfilms and MGM. (In his review in the *Washington Post*, writer Paul Attanasio assessed, "*Solarbabies* is a hilariously bad movie that doesn't make much sense and isn't much good when it does. Director Alan Johnson has stolen most of his visual ideas from Ridley Scott [*Blade Runner*] and George Miller [*The Road Warrior*], and he hasn't the slightest idea how to direct actors. That said, the movie has its campy pleasures, particularly in the godawful dialogue.") It was another box-office flop, grossing a mere $1.58 million in distribution.

Far more successful was Brooksfilms's remake of the 1950s hit *The Fly*. With a relatively lavish $15 million budget, this 1986 Twentieth Century-Fox release was directed by David Cronenberg and costarred Jeff Goldblum and Geena Davis. It revolved around an eccentric, brilliant scientist who has successfully delved into matter transportation. However, his experiment to transport himself goes awry when a fly accidentally enters one of the transportation booths. Using the slogan "Be Afraid. Be Very

Afraid," the feature had a worldwide gross of $60.63 million. (It led to a far less impressive sequel, 1989's *The Fly II*.)

Then there was Brooksfilms's 1987 release, *84 Charing Cross Road*, based on a best-selling book by Helene Hanff (which had become a BBC teleplay and a hit in its stage adaptation). One day, while the Brookses were relaxing at the beach at Fire Island, a man had come up to Anne and given her a copy of the novel. She fell in love with its story. Mel purchased the screen rights to the property as an anniversary gift for his spouse. The resultant picture was helmed by Britisher David Jones. The intimate drama focused on a single woman (a New York–based script reader) with a thirst for great literature. She begins a correspondence of many years with a London bookseller, a married man, who supplies her with used copies of wonderful editions of books she wants. This feature proved to be an impressive showcase for Anne Bancroft and Anthony Hopkins as the two letter writers who nurtured each other, via the mail, for decades. Unfortunately, this delicate Columbia Pictures release only grossed $1.08 million in distribution.

Despite its limited commercial appeal, such picturemaking as *84 Charing Cross Road* exemplified the finer artistic qualities within Mel. He also found it reassuring that these films struck a responsive chord with his public.

One day in winter 1987, Brooks attended the funeral of an entertainment industry notable in Los Angeles. There was quite a celebrity turnout, including Barbra Streisand, Bette Midler, and Shirley MacLaine. At the service, Mel was seated next to Jeanette Etheridge, who owned a hip café in San Francisco and who mingled with the show business crowd. Etheridge recalled her conversation with Brooks at the event. "And I lean over to him and say, 'You know I think you're wonderful, and I just love your movies.' And he looks at me with an absolutely straight face and says, 'We're at a funeral.' And I think, Oh my god, what have I done? Because he's right. We are at a funeral. And then he leans over and says, 'Which one did you like the best?'"

28

A Mighty Monarch at Last

I was the baby and I always expected to be the king of France because
I was treated like the king of France. I'm still waiting for my crown.

—Mel Brooks, 1971

While Mel Brooks was launching Brooksfilms in the late 1970s, he had
not forgotten his obligations to his fan base nor to his distributor,
Twentieth Century-Fox, to prepare a new personal screen project for
release—one in the same vein as his past film genre satires. In searching
for a fresh subject to lampoon, it occurred to Brooks that since his alter
ego, the 2000 Year Old Man, intimately knew so much about history and
its many notable figures, why not a Brooksian excursion that romped
madly through several eras of civilization? The filmmaker reasoned that
there would be many delicious targets to skewer as the episodic celluloid
chronicle dipped in and out of various eras of mankind's progress through
the ages. (If Mel had any reservations about this concept being overly
ambitious—and more than a bit unadventurous in its dependence on a
satirical formula that, admittedly, had been so successful for him in the
past—he kept them to himself.)

This essentially unwieldy notion led Mel to ponder, "Where do you
start? Well, I guess you start where history starts—somewhere back in pre-
historic times. Who lived there then? What did they say to each other?
What did they eat? Whom did they kiss? When did the first artist appear?"
He then questioned, "What part of history should I do? Would the audience go for a film that had many stories rather than one? I needed mortar

and glue to put the whole thing together. Something big. Orson Welles, I thought. He's big! He'll be the mortar—the narrator."

Thus was born 1981's *History of the World: Part I*. In preproduction, Brooks, the consummate self-promoter, touted that this vehicle would be "the height of my vulgarity." He reasoned, "The worst thing you can be accused of is good taste." On this particular cinema showcase he avoided utilizing a writing group, choosing to go it alone as scriptwriter. (Mel's violation of his early 1970s decision always to create film projects in tandem with others may have been inspired by a wish to save on the production budget. He could also just have wanted to give himself more artistic freedom to indulge his own scriptwriting ideas unadulterated by anyone else's thoughts, and, if the results were successful, then to enjoy the attendant glory all on his own.)

Mel explained his gestation process in preparing a screenplay: "I write for a long time before I get around to shooting. I pass my stuff around for reaction. I pass each chapter around. My wife sees it first. Then my friend Joe Heller. Then the girl that works in the candy shop." He pointed out, "You've got to let the chips fall where they may. You've got to be guileless. You can't do it for critics. I fought for an R rating for *History of the World*. [His last R-rated feature had been 1974's *Blazing Saddles*.] The kids want you to go all the way. They're not middle-aged people who sit home and watch television all the time. They want bravery, honesty, no compromise."

Brooks assembled several members of his moviemaking stock company: Sid Caesar (as the chief caveman), Madeline Kahn (as Empress Nympho), Dom DeLuise (as Emperor Caesar), Cloris Leachman (as Madame DeFarge), Harvey Korman (as Count de Monet), Howard Morris (as the Court spokesman), Ron Carey (as Swiftus, the agent), and Andréas Voutsinas (as Bernaise); Brooks's frequent writing team (Ron Clark, Rudy DeLuca, and Barry Levinson) provided cameos. Brooks also brought together several veteran comedic talents (including Shecky Greene, Jackie Mason, Jack Carter, Jan Murray, Bea Arthur, Sammy Shore, and Charles Callas) for choice on-camera bits in this costume comedy. Mel even recruited *Playboy* empire founder Hugh Hefner (and several of his *Playboy* Bunnies) to make brief on-camera appearances.

Originally, Brooks had intended the key role of Josephus, the black slave, to be played by Richard Pryor. However, Pryor had recently been severely injured when he accidentally set himself ablaze while freebasing cocaine. Richard was replaced in *History of the World: Part I* by the skilled tap dancer Gregory Hines, who made his feature film acting debut in this picture. For good measure, Brooks allotted himself five (!) major roles in the big-screen proceedings: Moses, Comicus (the Roman comedian), Torquemada (the Grand Inquisitor of the 15th-century Spanish Inquisition), Jacques (the *pissoir* boy in the French Revolution sequence), and France's randy and self-absorbed King Louis XVI (who'd rather seduce tempting courtesans than heed the needs and demands of his oppressed subjects).

History of the World: Part I began its 16-week production schedule on May 5, 1980, with some of the film being lensed in England at the Shepperton Studio. Said Brooks of his directing chores: "It's a lot of fun. But I won't say it's not a lot of grueling hard work—getting up at 4:30 A.M., then working a 12-hour day, then staying until 9 P.M. rehearsing with the actors or plotting the next day's moves. It's very physically demanding." He acknowledged, "Your temperament is very critical. The director that sulks destroys the mood of the entire set. So no matter what horror I run into, I try never to be petulant. I'm up. I'm positive. When things are going badly, when you're stuck in the rain on a location and the mud is getting up to your knees and you haven't shot for four hours and it's getting colder and you know that you may have to start lighting and shoot into the night and everyday is miserable, that's when I do my '2000-year-old man' routine or I do some improvisation with the cast and get them all in a good mood."

One of Brooks's inspirations for his diverse acting assignments in this frolic through history came from the screen comedy *Roman Scandals*. That 1933 musical had starred Mel's lifelong show business idol, Eddie Cantor. According to Brooks, "When I played 'Comicus' in the Roman scenes of my film *History of the World: Part I*, I thought of myself as Eddie Cantor. I wore the short little toga and I made my eyes pop out in reactions, like he did. My 'Comicus' was a tribute to Eddie Cantor. He was my timing, my excitement."

The most costly sequence within *History of the World: Part I* was the Spanish Inquisition segment. The elaborate set for this section of the episodic movie cost close to $1 million. The footage focused on Jews being tortured in all sorts of gruesome ways in order to make them convert to Christianity. When all else fails, the cruel Torquemada (played by an ebullient Brooks) summons a throng of seemingly virtuous nuns to deal with the thorny situation. In short order, the young women strip off their religious habits, revealing that they are wearing bathing suits underneath. They then begin an elaborate exhibit of synchronized swimming, during which the Jewish victims are tossed in the waters and subjected to the sadistic whims of the tormenting nuns. (Alan Johnson choreographed this intricate production extravaganza in the manner of 1930s movie director Busby Berkeley.)

As the ballast for this major section of the film, Mel collaborated with his longtime friend and coworker Ronny Graham on the music and lyrics for "The Inquisition," to which Brooks and his chorus of monks perform a song and dance. However shocking, unsavory, and over-the-top the tasteless showpiece might have been, the controversial ensemble piece was a memorable showstopper.

If Mel's Moses gave no competition to Charlton Heston (the star of the 1956 *The Ten Commandments* movie epic), Brooks was far more entertaining on camera than Heston as the revered Biblical figure. In Mel's account of the Hebrew leader, Moses is the bungler who accidentally drops 5 of the 15 commandments that God had provided on stone tablets and has to make do with the remaining 10. Brooks also shone as the hyperactive Comicus, the Las Vegas–style stand-up comic of ancient Rome who is ordered to give a command performance for the Emperor at Caesar's palace.

In the well-mounted French Revolution sequence, Mel borrowed from his *Blazing Saddles* characterization of the leering Governor William J. LePetomane. Brooks proved to be an exceptionally bawdy French monarch, a lustful despot who finds great delight in ogling the tantalizing cleavage of his lovely female subjects. For this supremely self-centered ruler, there is ample evidence for him to constantly repeat, "It is good to be the king." (This bit of dialogue from *History of the World: Part I* became very closely associated with Brooks, especially after he recorded a rap record titled "It's Good to Be the King." The single, with its comical couplets written by composer Peter Wingfield, rose to the #67 position on the *Billboard* music charts.) Also in this extended 18th-century segment, Brooks was able to indulge his penchant for playing screen heroes by portraying the king's look-alike, Jacques the lowly servant, who is willing to bravely sacrifice all for a lovely damsel in distress (played by Pamela Stephenson).

Brooks described his editing process on this feature: "After I finish shooting, I take all the secretaries at the studio to a sneak preview. I showed them a two-hour, 20-minute rough cut of the picture. I had 11 of these screenings. I let them cut the picture for me. I note the places where they smile or laugh and where they smoke or start chattering. . . . Then I screen the picture for the audience it's designed for, which is about 90 percent kids between the ages of 14 and 19. It's kids 15 years old that are keeping the movie business alive, kids that if they like a picture like *Star Wars* they'll go see it six times. It's all repeat business. . . . I'm not interested in people over 40. They never go to the movies. When they do go, they complain about the parking lot, the driving, things like that. Kids go to see the picture. They don't worry about the setting."

Released in June 1981, *History of the World: Part I* did not win many endorsements from the reviewers. Janet Maslin (of the *New York Times*) assessed, "Part of the problem with *History of the World: Part I* is that it's tired, so tired that the cheerful outrageousness of Mr. Brooks's earlier films has become waxen. The jokes often recall *The Producers* and particularly *Blazing Saddles*, but never are they as bold as they were the first time around." For Maslin, the coming attractions for the picture and a commercial for *Part II* that closed the current movie were far more hilarious. "That's because many of Mr. Brooks's comic ideas here are better glimpsed as snippets than as 20-minute routines." (The trailer tacked onto the end of *History of the World: Part I* was a satire on film industry practices of making endless sequels to a hit picture. The footage contained bits of the supposed planned follow-up to Brooks's epic. It included scenes from "Hitler on Ice," which allowed Mel, once again, to lampoon der Führer and reduce him to a comic skating figure. There was also a burlesque of outer galaxy movies and their intricate, mammoth spacecraft. For this sequence, "Jews in Space," Brooks wrote the music and lyrics for its title song.)

Roger Ebert (of the *Chicago Sun-Times*) complained that Brooks's new release was "a rambling, undisciplined, sometimes embarrassing failure from one of the most gifted comic filmmakers around. What went wrong? Brooks never seems to have a clear idea of the rationale of his movie. So there's no confident narrative impetus to carry it along. His 'history' framework doesn't have an approach or point of view; it's basically just a laundry-line for whatever gags he can hang on it."

Compounding the poor critical reception to *History of the World: Part I*, Twentieth Century-Fox had previously undergone a change of regimes, and Mel's industry pal Alan Ladd Jr. was no longer in charge on the film lot. The new administration did not have great faith in the way Brooks's new picture had shaped up and allotted it a particularly unspectacular ad campaign. Even worse, the movie opened in only 484 theaters domestically (which reinforced what the studio thought of the film's chances to succeed with 1980s moviegoers). With such hurdles to overcome, the expensively produced *History of the World: Part I* grossed only $20 million domestically (a far lesser amount than *Young Frankenstein*, which had cost far less to make). However, Brooks still managed to emerge from the thorny situation a financial winner.

Before this picture had gone into production, Brooks had met with Alan J. Hirschfield, the new head of production at Twentieth Century-Fox. Mel made the executive an offer. He told Hirschfield, "You are going to give me $10 million to make *History of the World: Part I*. I am not going to take any fees. But you are going to give me all the foreign rights." When Hirschfield said no, it prompted Mel to take more creative steps. "I said I was going to call the *Wall Street Journal* and tell them I was selling all my stock in 20th Century-Fox because I had no faith in the current management." (At the time, Brooks insisted later, he did not have one share of studio stock.) The Fox boss then agreed to the deal, which included giving Mel TV and home entertainment rights abroad to this feature. As a result, even though the picture had disappointed critics and moviegoers alike, the filmmaker made more money from *History of the World: Part I* than from any other picture he had done to that date. The movie grossed about $35 million abroad, leaving Mel's Brooksfilms with a $7 million profit.

· · ·

Following the release of *History of the World: Part I*, it was rumored anew that Brooks and Gene Wilder might reunite for a new picture. That reteaming never took place, nor did Mel's participation as a producer for a projected musical (*One of the Boys at the Globe Is a Girl*) by Brooks's longtime pal Ronny Graham. Meanwhile, in late 1981, Anne Bancroft costarred with Max Von Sydow on the Broadway stage in *Duet for One*. That drama closed after a mere 20 performances.

Together again in Los Angeles, Mel and Anne thrived on spending time with their son, Max. (Bancroft noted, "The best time of the day is when the family comes together at about 7 o'clock. We sit down to dinner and Max comes in and eats with us and we sit and talk and are a family from 7 on. . . . Coming together as a family is one of the great rewards of life and of having a family.") For recreation, the Brookses (especially Mel) enjoyed playing tennis. Occasionally, the couple had a night out on the town, such as going to the Tail o' the Cock restaurant in Studio City to hear Johnny Guarnieri perform at the piano. When Brooks's friend Joseph Heller was diagnosed as suffering from Guillain-Barré syndrome, Mel made trips back to New York to give emotional support (and his medical opinions on the writer's serious ailment).

Mel's Brooksfilms had two pictures (*My Favorite Year* and *Frances*) in distribution in 1982, and Brooks hoped to have his production company make a screen version of Toni Morrison's novel *Tar Baby*. He was also negotiating with South African playwright Athol Fugard to write an epic film about apartheid. Although this project did not happen, it reflected Brooks's point of view in selecting serious subjects for his firm to undertake. "Any time we see a flag about the human condition that appeals to us, we're going to see if we can't surround it with the right help and nourishment." To Brooks's way of thinking, "One of the purposes of art is to make things right that are eternally wrong. And the job of the artist is to paint a picture of life as truly and honestly as he sees it and add that extra dimension of hope, and of fantasy, and of dream."

• • •

Back in 1942, Ernst Lubitsch had produced/directed *To Be or Not to Be,* a very dark comedy about Adolf Hitler's occupation of Poland during World War II and how a troupe of actors in Warsaw join with the underground to outwit the Nazis. The well-mounted feature costarred Jack Benny and Carole Lombard. Weeks before the picture was released, Lombard died in a plane crash while returning to Los Angeles following a hugely successful war bond sale tour. That tragedy dampened moviegoers' enthusiasm for seeing *To Be or Not to Be.* The lack of audience interest in the "comedy" was heightened by the film's highly controversial subject matter—lampooning the German dictator and his reign of terror. Most American moviegoers were focused on winning

World War II and did not find the picture's story line anything to laugh about.

Over subsequent decades, *To Be or Not to Be*—through frequent TV showings and art house revivals—became a cult favorite, appreciated for its comedic approach and the famous Lubitsch style. In 1974, the classic film was screened to great success at a Los Angeles film festival. By late the next year, industry publications were reporting that Mel Brooks and Anne Bancroft were considering teaming on camera for a remake of *To Be or Not to Be.*

With other projects intervening, it took until the fall of 1982 for the new *To Be or Not to Be* to move into actual production. Many months before, Mel had hired Ronny Graham to collaborate with Thomas Meehan on updating the 1942 script. (Meehan was the writer who had worked with Brooks and Bancroft on her 1970 TV special. Since then, he had won a Tony Award for writing the book of the hit Broadway musical *Annie.*) Brooks looked forward to the challenge of taking on the screen role in which Jack Benny, another of Mel's great show business inspirations, had made such a lasting impression. The project also provided Brooks with yet another opportunity to take creative potshots at Hitler (including portraying the German leader in a comedic song-and-dance number in the play within the movie).

Casting the new *To Be or Not to Be* proved to be something of a family affair. When Bancroft was asked how she came to join the project, she said, "I didn't decide. My husband said, 'You're going to do this part.' I said, 'All right, darling.'" When asked if she had wanted to work with her spouse before, Anne responded, "Not particularly. When we'd go to parties, we'd sometimes sing a couple of songs together, but that's it." Also hired (for a small role as Rifka's boy) was the Brookses' son, Max. Anne described what brought that about: "He has been begging us for a part, so we gave him one line in this movie, because I thought he should know what it's like. After about three days, he decided that he would wait until he was older to be an actor. I don't blame him. I mean, there was so much work to it that he didn't expect, like just being there. When you're needed, you have to be there. You can't be off reading a book or playing. So he was very disenchanted by the whole thing, which made me very happy."

Others signed for the picture were Tim Matheson as the handsome young Polish pilot who has a mad crush on Anne's flirtatious character, the queen of the Warsaw stage. The villainous Nazi undercover agent was played by José Ferrer, with Charles Durning and Christopher Lloyd as two bungling German officers. Ronny Graham was cast as Sondheim, a backstage worker at the theater, and James Saake played Bancroft's gay dressing room helper/confidant.

Almost from the start of packaging this project, Mel had decided against directing or writing this film. (Brooks's decision might have been influenced by the critical roasting he had received for his scripting/ helming of *History of the World: Part I*.) For the record, Mel reasoned, "I was making a little bit of a move toward a more complicated character, the most complicated I've ever played. I wanted a director's eye on me, watching my excesses as an actor, helping me to strive for the more subtle moments so that I didn't play everything 'over the top.'" Alan Johnson, who had choreographed several of Mel's past movies, made his feature film directorial debut with *To Be or Not to Be*, which was a Brooksfilms production.

Later, Brooks acknowledged that both he and Anne had great concerns about working together in such a major capacity. He said, "We wondered if we'd get on each other's nerves. But we became closer. You know, when I'm working on a movie, I eat lunch with nobody. I go to my trailer. I learn my lines. I eat a little cottage cheese. I rest. I have to be alone. But during this film, at lunchtime, I found myself knocking on Anne's door and saying, 'What are you doing, dear?'" He also admitted of his spouse: "My wife is more than a good friend. She's my ultimate [filmmaking consultant]. . . . If she says, 'I'm not moved'—a movie has to be moving, no matter how brilliant it may be intellectually—I don't do the movie. I trust her judgment about emotions more than anybody else's on earth."

During the filming of this black comedy at Twentieth Century-Fox, veteran character actor Charles Durning had an opportunity to see all sides of Mel the star/producer at work. Durning said, "He's a brutally honest man, Mel. After I'd done one scene, he said, right in front of everyone, 'Garbage you give me.' That absolutely rocked me." Later, an apologetic Durning spelled out what he had "really" meant by his remarks concerning the filmmaker's directional methods on the sound stage. The actor said, "I would like to stress that the words do not reflect the zany, set-side atmosphere of the film. Mel and I are the best of friends.

Sometimes his outrageous humor, when used to break the tension that exists on some sets, might be misconstrued."

In the revamp of Lubitsch's version of *To Be or Not to Be* for Brooks's edition, only 50 to 75 lines of dialogue from the original were retained for the new picture. (This worked out to be about one key line per film scene.) When the picture was completed and screened, industry sources noted that the original film received no mention in the opening title cards. (Only in the closing titles were the source materials and its creators identified.) This led to a controversy with the Writers Guild. Brooks remembered, "We spent three months trying to get the Writers Guild to let us give credit [to the original]. . . . We wanted a card in the main title saying, 'Based on the Ernst Lubitsch film written by Edwin Mayer from a story by Melchior Lengyel.'" According to Mel, the guild refused this suggestion because its rules were geared to provide its members with full credit for their work. In contrast, guild officials said the problem was that Mel Brooks wanted to use a single title card to acknowledge both Lubitsch and the film's writer. Always seeking to put a humorous spin on even the most ticklish situation, Brooks noted that he was even prohibited from using a gag credit title card on the film that would have read, "Additional Dialogue by William Shakespeare"—this was a reference to a performance within the film of "Highlights from Hamlet" by Mel Brooks's character.

Fox chose to release this still very dark comedy during the Christmas season of 1983, a marketing decision that seemed ill advised. Most reviewers found little to cheer about in this holiday entry. Harry Haun (of the *New York Daily News*) argued that Brooks's film "slavishly reproduced" the original, which only pointed up the flaws of the remake. Kevin Thomas (of the *Los Angeles Times*) gave a cogent assessment of why Mel's new film so badly missed the mark: "This reworking of a classic was probably doomed from the start on two formidable counts. First, Brooks and his associates could never be accused of having anything remotely resembling a Lubitsch touch: that celebrated, indefinable combination of wit, subtlety and sophistication that allowed the legendary Berlin-born director to get away with implying just about anything, although even he was accused of bad taste in making his *To Be or Not to Be*." Thomas continued, "Second, we know far more than was known in 1942 of the full extent of the Nazi evil, especially in regard to the fate of the Jews. In *The Producers* Brooks carried off his 'Springtime for Hitler' number . . . Somehow an entire movie that depicts Nazis as the buffoons of fantasy, while we know full well that the peril of Brooks' largely Jewish acting company is all too real, isn't very funny but instead is merely crass. (Ironically, for all its sparkle, the original actually took the Nazis far more seriously than this remake does.)" As to the coleads, Thomas judged that they "can't be said to rise above their material, despite occasional winning moments."

To Be or Not to Be suffered an unremarkable reception at the box office. It grossed only $13 million in domestic distribution. Brooks made known his distress at the lack of filmgoer enthusiasm for his new showcase. He lay part of the blame on the studio for opening it during the Christmas period, when family-oriented fluff was the traditional fare. He added, "It was also mismarketed. It was billed as a Mel Brooks romp when it wasn't. It was a very different cup of tea. It's an exquisite, subtle, very compelling, very touching movie." (However justified Mel's complaints may have been, the bottom line was that *To Be or Not to Be* had widely missed its mark in judging audience tastes. It was another indicator to industry observers that Brooks was losing his Midas touch with picturemaking.)

. . .

While Brooks and Bancroft were abroad promoting *To Be or Not to Be*, Mel hosted *An Evening with Mel Brooks* in London, which aired in the United Kingdom. Here, Mel was truly in his element. He told jokes, chatted amiably with the studio audience, sang a few numbers, and even submitted to a humorous competition with the British actor Jonathan Pryce as to who could provide a better rendition of Hamlet's "To Be or Not to Be" soliloquy. (Pryce did his performance live, while Brooks's was a film clip from the new picture.) Anne was in the audience that evening and came up on stage to re-create with Mel one of the (few) highlights from *To Be or Not to Be*: their duet—in Polish—of "Sweet Georgia Brown." This delightful TV special documented just how varied an entertainer Brooks could be when given the proper forum.

Also while he was publicizing *To Be or Not to Be* in Europe, Mel's musical video ("The Hitler Rap") was released, and this novelty song, derived from the stage burlesque within the movie, became a popular item on the music industry charts.

In the wake of *To Be or Not to Be*, Brooks was asked if he and Bancroft would consider working again together. He quipped, "We're not the Lunts. If we find something that we really want to do together, maybe we will." (At one point in the late 1980s, there were plans for the couple to reunite for *I Love You to Death*, with Mel directing his wife and Kevin Kline. However, when that black comedy was made in 1990, it was Lawrence Kasdan who helmed the movie, and Tracey Ullman was Kline's costar.)

The media also inquired whether Brooks had any interest in starring in a full version of Shakespeare's *Hamlet*. He said definitely, "No!" According to Mel, "I think I can use all the forms of comedy to say what I want to say about the human condition. If you can make 'em laugh, it's your duty to do so."

29

Next Stop, Outer Space

The image of a wacko is important to me, even though it's not really me. It's a comforting image for people who want to see a happy, wacko movie. And the real me takes refuge in it. If people think I'm a wacko, I don't have to reveal anything. I can keep whatever is truly me private. Every celebrity fights for anonymity. My anonymity is the serious Mel Brooks.

—Mel Brooks, 1987

In the 1980s, Mel Brooks often found himself diverted from preparing new screen vehicles for himself because of his overriding fascination and concerns with supervising Brooksfilms. The project that gave him and his film production company the most problems was their 1986 movie *Solarbabies*, directed by Alan Johnson.

Brooks had arranged private financing for this sci-fi entry so that he would have more flexibility in choosing a distributor for the finished product. Before Mel had completed the fund-raising process, he was forced to dip into his own bank accounts in order to start filming in Spain before the rainy season hit. "Then, when I was into it for something like $5 million or $6 million, the financing collapsed." Ideally, Mel would have called off the picture. However, he was advised that he couldn't exploit such a loss as a tax deduction because "I had no income." Caught in a pinch, he had to negotiate a bank loan, which proved to be a stressful ordeal. ("It was scary. I couldn't sleep. I actually had a kind of nervous breakdown.") Ultimately, Mel sold the picture to MGM, which allowed him to pay back his bank loans and recoup his investment. (The picture itself proved to be an artistic and box-office flop.) After that nightmarish experience, Brooks vowed not to again permit himself to indulge in such risky enterprises.

• • •

Perhaps as early as conceiving the madcap "Jews in Space" sequence for the trailer at the end of 1981's *History of the World: Part I*, Mel was toying with the idea of doing a full-length spoof of science-fiction movies. By 1983, the concept was listed on the slate of upcoming projects for Brooksfilms. Soon Mel was chortling to the media, "I have in mind a picture called *The Planet Moron*. It'll be the first really rich satire of all the science-fiction movies. 'Don't fire your lasers: they may be friendly.' That sort of dialogue. When they invade, I want to be able to say, 'We're surrounded by Morons.'"

Nearly six years had passed since Brooks had directed his last screen entry, *History of the World: Part I*. He enunciated some of his reasons: "I only direct things I write. I'd rather write the Ninth Symphony than conduct it. And these days, it takes three years to do the script and set up the deal and—well—I just won't direct a picture I haven't written."

The show business veteran, now nearly 60 years old, had mixed feelings about helming a new big-budget movie (and, in turn, the youth-focused film industry was beginning to wonder if Mel had grown seriously out of touch with the new crop of moviegoers). Sometimes, he expressed his concerns in a serious tone: "Frankly, I hate directing. I only direct in self-defense [of protecting my screenplays]. It's like building a building and having someone else paint it and furnish it. They're going to get it wrong!" On other occasions, he masked his beliefs on the subject behind a veil of glib amusement. "There's nothing worse than being on the set. All the excitement and the merriment and celebration. You know, all the sociability—what are we going to eat today? Where are you going for the weekend? . . . But all I can think about is what happens afterwards. I know that all those people are going to leave me and go on to another picture, while I'm stuck in the editing room for months, slaving over the film."

As the new Brooks project got under way, Mel and his collaborators (Thomas Meehan and Ronny Graham) decided that a primary set of references to be spoofed in *The Planet Moron* would be George Lucas's enormously successful *Star Wars* trilogy (released in 1977, 1980, and 1983). But, rightly so, Brooks questioned whether he was on the right commercial/artistic track. "It's a paradoxically risky venture; on the one hand, to parody a film genre, the genre has to have been around long enough to become a genre, and yet in the case of the space films, although there certainly is much to parody, interest in the genre seems to be on the wane. Even George Lucas has stopped making them." (Later, Anne Bancroft would comment on her husband's preproduction concerns: "Mel is always so unsure when he starts out. When he began . . . [*The Planet Moron*] he was filled with self-doubt. Anxiety feeds on that, and when he's not happy, I'm not happy. But that's when you must do something— be there for each other."

Actually, at the time that Mel put his sci-fi spoof at the top of his production list, he was scripting another movie project, *Scared to Death*, a satire of the mystery genre. However, he shelved that screenplay because he came to believe that its commercial appeal might be too narrow. By now, the projected *The Planet Moron* had undergone a name change to *Spaceballs*. (The title switch was done to avoid confusion with a 1985 sci-fi comedy from the United Kingdom titled *Morons from Outer Space*.) As Brooks, Meehan, and Graham began writing, Mel contacted George Lucas—as he had Alfred Hitchcock when making *High Anxiety*—to gain the filmmaker's seal of approval on the planned big-screen spoof. Lucas's one request to Brooks was that if Mel went ahead with the satire of the *Star Wars* movies, Brooksfilms would refrain from merchandizing anything from *Spaceballs* (which could interfere with Lucas's ongoing *Star Wars* merchandizing bonanza).

Over many, many months, Brooks and his writing team whittled down their script from 315 pages to, finally, a 126-page version. Meehan acknowledged of the results, "Unlike *To Be or Not to Be*, we were going for everything. It's much more of a vulgar picture, full of wild, low comedy." Ronny Graham commented on the long development period of getting the property to the actual filming stage, "Of course, we have our disagreements. After a while, cabin fever sets in and we start to shout at each other." He went on, "Mel's very vehement. If he doesn't like a line you write, he'll shout and stomp and holler. He'll bellow, 'You're totally wrong. You don't know anything about comedy!' . . . But here's what really happens. He'll fight ferociously against something Ezra [Swerdlow, the producer] or I suggest, but all the while he'll be rolling that idea around in his head. And if the idea has any merit at all, he won't necessarily admit it. But he'll find a way to use it in the scene."

The filming of *Spaceballs* began on October 28, 1986. A production deal had been set up at MGM, where Brooks's friend Alan Ladd Jr. was then chairman and chief executive officer. The budget allocated for this genre spoof was a substantial $22.7 million, a good deal of which was devoted to utilizing the latest high-tech special effects and to creating the impressive sets. For the shoot, Brooksfilms took over the giant Stage 30, one of the three biggest stages on the MGM lot. Much of the outdoor filming was accomplished in the desert around Yuma, Arizona, as well as at assorted southern California sites: a church in Pacific Palisades, locales near San Diego, and sections of Imperial County (home of the Salton Sea and the Imperial Sand Dunes).

To play the picture's hero, Brooks chose Bill Pullman. (Said Brooks, "The studio fought me on that choice. They wanted Tom Cruise or Tom Hanks—anybody named Tom who cost $2 million. . . . That's what wrong with this business. If you make it a 'Tom' movie, it's no longer a parody, it's a 'Tom' movie, and you have to build scenes around him.") The heavy-set comedian John Candy claimed the role of the hero's half dog, half man sidekick, Barfolemew. Daphne Zuniga was contracted to portray the spoiled princess, comic Rick Moranis was assigned the role of the villainous Dark Helmet, and Joan Rivers was hired to provide the voice of Dot Matrix, Zuniga's robotic helper. George Wyner, an excellent second banana character actor who had been in *To Be or Not to Be*, was on tap as Colonel Sandurz, while Dick Van Patten returned to the Mel Brooks camp as the daffy king. In comparison to his several parts in *History of the World: Part I,* Brooks cut back on the number of roles he assigned to himself in *Spaceballs*. In this slapstick intergalactic odyssey, Mel cavorts as the dapper, sinister President Skroob (whose motto is "Skroob the People") and as the pint-sized Yoghurt (the wise old soul whose favorite saying is "May the Schwartz be with you").

Spaceballs was released in June 1987. Gene Shalit (of TV's *Today* show) ranked the picture "eight trillion on the laugh meter" and the *Wall Street Journal*'s reviewer rated it "extremely funny—buoyantly tasteless." However, more on target was Richard Schickel (of *Time*) who wrote, "It's not that Mel Brooks has lost his cunning, though he does need a freedom of speech not to be found under a PG rating. What's missing is that zany old gang of his, ranging in size from Zero Mostel to Marty Feld-man, in shape from Madeline Kahn to Dom DeLuise (who does deliver the voice of Pizza the Hutt in *Spaceballs*). With their living-caricature presences, they could have proved and improved Brooks' comic points. And when comic invention failed him, they could have earned laughs just by standing there, making faces. There is simply nobody like them on this trip."

Hal Hinson (of the *Washington Post*) decided, "What you're conscious of throughout this movie is that you're sitting in your seat, not laughing at performers who desperately want you to laugh." Roger Ebert (of the *Chicago Sun-Times*) carped, "Brooks's intelligence and taste seem to switch off when he makes his own films, and he aims for broad, dumb comedy: Jokes about names with dirty double meanings are his big spe-cialty. Maybe the reason *Spaceballs* isn't better is that he was deliberately aiming low, going for the no-brainer satire. What does he really think about *Star Wars*, or anything else, for that matter?"

Spaceballs brought in a relatively low gross of $38.11 million in domestic distribution. (This was in sharp comparison to the grosses of the year's five top Hollywood productions: *Three Men and a Baby* [$167.78 million], *Fatal Attraction* [$156.64 million], *Beverly Hills Cop II* [$153.55 million], *Good Morning, Vietnam* [$123.92 million]), and *Moonstruck* [$80.64 million]). Fortunately for Brooksfilms and MGM, *Spaceballs* did well in its later home entertainment versions, and Brooks counts this entry as one of his most successful releases on VHS and DVD. This, in turn, led to recurrent talk of Brooks's making a sequel to the feature, something that would not occur for nearly two decades.

• • •

In 1987, the year that *Spaceballs* debuted, the Brookses moved to a fresh Los Angeles address—a hugely spacious 12,000-square-foot house on La Mesa Drive in Pacific Palisades, close to the Riviera Country Club. Their new residence towered over the others in the exclusive neighborhood, with their Spanish-style house boasting an indoor swimming pool. The family also had a getaway home in the expensive community of Malibu. The family's other real estate holdings included a co-op apartment on Man-hattan's East 89th Street, beachfront condos on Fisher Island off Miami, and, over the years, various residences in Long Island's Southampton.

Despite his growing material riches, Mel had not abandoned his concerns for the world at large. "I still rail at all the injustices that rear their head in this world. I get angry about our President's polices, about Jell-O TV, about the crap that passes for culture and society's wholesale neglect of whole segments of our population."

Brooks also had learned to insulate himself against the fickleness of critics and the public, who were always finding new, and usually younger, favorites to adore. "Listen, I know that everybody has worn out their welcome—[Charles] Chaplin, [Buster] Keaton—everyone has. I've had waves of anxiety after a picture hasn't done so well. I say, 'It's over, it's over, I've been replaced by [filmmaker] Ivan Reitman!' . . . When the critics kill you, it hurts, at least at the time. But the feeling doesn't last. I learned a long time ago that it's the process that counts, not just the result." However, he admitted, "It does bother you when someone doesn't like your work. It confirms your worst fears. You try not to get caught up in it. But sometimes I feel like writing these critics a letter, saying, 'Why so angry? What was there to hate so much?' I want to tell them, 'I mean no harm. I only wanted to entertain you.'"

On one subject, Brooks had no equivocation—his luck in finding Anne Bancroft and keeping her love over the decades. He said of his wife, "I'm very, very lucky that we're still lovers as well as good friends. Besides, she saves me a couple of hundred a week that I'd be spending on psychoanalysts. I tell her everything, and she tells me what to do." Brooks enthused, "Anne is simply terrific. She's beautiful, she has great shoulders, and she makes me laugh."

In response, the revered actress said of her zany spouse, "I do make him laugh, that's true. Mel's sort of jaded about funny things, because he knows almost everything, but I guess I'm spontaneous. Things pop out, and that makes him laugh. That's why our marriage works so well." She elaborated, "When you strip away who we are as Mel Brooks and Anne Bancroft, and you think of us as children, you can see we would have been in love as kids. We have the same values. We think alike about what's important and what makes us happy. It's the simple things—our son, my garden, making other people happy. Our life revolves around our family and friends." She admitted of Mel, "He is not that easy to get to know. He is often 'on' in public. He's funny, he's fast, and he talks a lot. But that's a façade. Mel is much more private than I am. He's enormously sensitive, and he's twenty times as funny in private and a thousand times more lovable."

Anne explained the special dynamics in the Brooks household: "[Mel's] energy fills the house—and so does my son's. Sometimes there's not much room for mine. So whatever I need, I ask for, and if I don't get it, I scream. Then I get it." She detailed, "We have a motto in our family: inch by inch, life's a cinch. Yard by yard, it's very hard. I say it to my husband at the start of every film. I say it to my son before every test. Now, I wish someone would say it to me."

She also revealed one of the greatest pleasures in her daily life: "Learning. I didn't always know that, but just the fact that I can still learn is thrilling to me. It doesn't have to be anything earthshaking. Listen, I bought a book on pruning the other day and just read the first few sentences. I learned something, and it made me happy all day. I was going to be able to prune these trees in my garden, and it lifted me up to the ceiling!" (Eventually, Bancroft, the devoted gardener, became a proud member of the California Fruit Growers Association.)

• • •

In the spring of 1987, Brooks was among those who received Life Achievement Awards from the newly formed American Comedy Awards. (The others were Steve Allen, Woody Allen, Sid Caesar, Jonathan Winters, Lucille Ball, Carol Burnett, Bette Midler, Mary Tyler Moore, and Lily Tomlin.) However, Brooks regarded public acclaim for his latest show business venture as the best prize he could receive and, therefore, was anxious to find a new vehicle that could accomplish that goal. After launching *Spaceballs* in the United States and abroad, he found himself with too much time on his hands and no appealing film deal in the works. Wanting to keep active in show business, he returned to the world of television, which many industry observers regarded as a comedown for the filmmaker.

Mel's new TV project actually owed its impetus to the 1988 movie comedy *Big Business*, costarring Bette Midler and Lily Tomlin. When the makers of that Touchstone/Disney Studio feature were unable to negotiate permission to film sequences of the comedy at Manhattan's Plaza Hotel, they chose to build a huge hotel set on the studio's sound stages in Burbank, California. That set was still standing, and Disney executives decided to initiate a TV sitcom that would make use of the costly structure.

The studio turned to Mel Brooks to come up with a property. In turn, Brooks chose to work with the much-younger Alan Spencer (as producer) on the project. As an adolescent, the star-struck Spencer had snuck onto the set of *Young Frankenstein* and, once there, had become friendly with actor Marty Feldman. In the process, the young man pursued his idol, Mel Brooks, and, eventually, the intruder and Brooks developed a father-son type of friendship. Subsequently, Spencer developed a career in television. Most recently, he had created, written, and produced *Sledge Hammer*, an off-the-wall detective series that ran on ABC-TV from 1986 to 1988. (Spencer had written in his high school yearbook that his dream was one day to work for Brooks. Said Alan: "When my dream came true, I used to drive to work with him and he'd be doing these non-stop routines. I thought I'd died and gone to heaven.")

Brooks's new offering, *The Nutt House*, revolved around a once elegant Manhattan hotel that had fallen on hard times, largely due to mismanagement by its staff of insanely incompetent workers. Disney greenlighted the project, and Brooks and Spencer began pitching their show to the networks. According to Spencer, he and Mel had a meeting with NBC. "We went in and winged it." Before the meeting with the "suits," Brooks had advised his less-experienced associate: "Talk a lot and make 'em laugh, then leave. You're on the air."

The network bought the half-hour program and set its debut for fall 1989. In casting the venture, Brooks turned to some old reliables: Cloris Leachman (in a dual role as the eccentric elderly owner of the hotel and the starchy, oversexed head housekeeper), Harvey Korman (as the pompous hotel manager), and Ronny Graham (as the befuddled doorman). Mark Blankfield, who had been in Spencer's *Sledge Hammer* and would be in later Mel Brooks productions, appeared as the myopic elevator operator.

There was much hype regarding *Nutt House*'s premiere on September 20, 1989. However, the show's high profile was short-lived. Howard Rosenberg (of the *Los Angeles Times*) reported, "There are moments . . . that are knee-slapping funny. Nevertheless, the script by executive producers Mel Brooks and Alan Spencer is an example of a few great jokes going a short way." Rosenberg observed, "Korman and Leachman are a riot. In their hands, absurdity was never better. . . . Yet even they can't sustain lumpy material that ranges from exquisite nastiness to excruciating slapstick, with much more of the latter."

By its second week on the air, *Nutt House* had slipped badly in the home viewers ratings. By October 25, 1989, the expensive-to-conceive sitcom had been canceled and aired its last episode. It left Brooks angry and humiliated and wondering, once again, where to find his next show business options.

• • •

The 1970s and 1980s had been an especially bullish period for independent film production companies in Hollywood. In this era, there always seemed to be a plentitude of investors—both in the United States and abroad—to back such firms even on the more chancy ventures. (This was still the time of enticing tax shelters, a situation that ended when the U.S. government finally plugged the legal loopholes for most such lucrative tax write-offs.) By the end of the eighties, investors were generally far more cautious about funding "glamorous" movie production companies. As a result, many of the smaller firms were hard-pressed to finance new projects privately. One such operation was Mel's decade-old Brooksfilms Ltd.

In late 1989, Brooks was persuaded to undertake a public offering to raise $13 to $16 million for upcoming movie/TV projects at Brooksfilms. (Unfortunately, Brooksfilms had earned only $323,000 in fiscal year 1989, and Wall Street analysts predicted that the company might register a loss in 1990.) Mel's planned stock offering prompted *Time* magazine to report, "Comedy is hot today, but Brooks may be running out of gas. He has had no major hit since *Blazing Saddles* and *Young Frankenstein* in 1974, which reaped a total of more than $86 million in North America alone." The publication also alerted, "Hollywood insiders say dealmakers have been weary of Brooks. 'He's not hot enough that he can make any film he wants [with a top studio],' says the president of a major studio."

In the past, Mel the comedian and raconteur who loved to entertain most any type of audience at any given moment had undertaken extensive tours to promote his latest movie and television vehicles. Now he took his dog-and-pony show on the road on behalf of Brooksfilms' bid to go public. He visited Oppenheimer & Co. brokerage houses in both the United States and Europe. Looking quite distinguished in his conservative suit, Brooks typically opened Q&A sessions with a joke and a few Hollywood anecdotes. Then he got down to serious business, explaining that this offering was not a vanity situation. "I want to make movies. I'm an energetic guy." This said, the showman had to field blunt queries from the brokers as to why Brooksfilms thought it could sell its stock at many times higher than its current market price. He was also asked to explain such Brooksfilms overheads as his approximately $4 million annual salary from the company. His response was, "Taxes! Why the hell should I produce revenues and pay taxes on them when I own the company? I took the money and paid it to Mel Brooks to avoid double taxation. By going public, I'm taking a 1,000 percent drop in salary. How can I ask the public to invest in a company that produces annual revenues of only $323,000. I mean, that's ridiculous!" (Following Brooks's stopover at Oppenheimer's Seattle office, one broker at the session admitted, "My attitude changed over the course of the meeting, coming to believe that Brooks was interested not just in being entertaining, but in making a buck."

However, by February 1990 the much-touted financing package had been shelved after Oppenheimer & Co. was only able to place about $6 million (or 40%) of the planned offering. The brokerage firm attributed the unsatisfactory response to "general market skittishness."

The unsuccessful stock offering was another staggering blow to Mel, who was already suffering the ignominy of living down his trio of disappointing 1980s films and the quick rejection by home viewers of his *The Nutt House* series. It must have seemed to Brooks that all his many decades in show business counted for little with audiences, reviewers, and industry decision makers. With so many overwhelming career misfires in so many forums of show business, Mel somehow had to come to terms with the growing industry belief that he was a relic—having been passed by a new breed of comedic talents who had taken his vulgar brand of satiric comedy to new levels of crudeness in order to spark audience interest. His whole professional world seemed to be crashing before his eyes, with little to no potential of pulling out a new miracle from his hat to recharge his dwindling career and reputation.

It was little wonder that Mel Brooks titled his next picture *Life Stinks*.

30

Back to Work

In a strange way, I don't think I could make a serious movie. I'm too private to do it. What I really feel is nobody's business. I need a comedy proscenium to disguise it in. . . . I like filmmakers who are storytellers, not psychologists. I just don't like to interpret my work that much. For example, sometimes I think my pictures are ripe with blatant sexuality, only so I can hide things I really feel—affection, love and desire. Maybe by being really blatant about the sex . . . I can disguise the more subtle feeling.

—Mel Brooks, 1987

Typically, when an individual reaches the age of 65, he or she retires from the work world or, at least, thinks about cutting back on the daily grind. However, Mel Brooks was far from the usual person. His zest for entertaining the world and his inner need to do both that and maintain his status as a comedy-world giant had neither dissipated with time nor shrunk from the adverse public reaction to his string of increasingly less profitable show business projects in the 1980s. He remained committed to perpetuating his career. Without professional activity, Brooks would be a man without real identity or purpose, and that was not an option for him.

• • •

One might have thought that for Brooks's first new directorial/starring vehicle since 1987's *Spaceballs*, he would have reverted to another of his wild and wacky genre satires—something to evoke his zany and highly successful screen comedies of past decades. However, in recent years,

Brooks had been undertaking a reevaluation of his life and his work—a lot of it the result of his career's floundering in the ever-changing world of show business.

Back in 1978, he said, "Why should I waste my good time making a straight dramatic film? Sydney Pollack can do that. The people who can't make you laugh can do that." However, by the mid-1980s Mel was saying, "I hide the serious Mel Brooks from the public and the critics. You can't show them that—it's confusing. . . . My comedies are probably the most serious thing that I have to offer the world. They say the deepest things about human behavior. A lot more than *The Elephant Man* or *My Favorite Year* or *Frances*. If you really get into *Young Frankenstein* or *Blazing Saddles* or *The Producers*, you will find the external varieties of human behavior are greater, with a lot more care and respect than most dramas."

By the start of the 1990s, Brooks was ready to come out to the world as a purveyor of films about serious topics. (Moving into new arenas of filmmaking would also be a way to curtail the penchant of reviewers and moviegoers for comparing a new Mel Brooks picture with his comedic successes of the 1970s.) Thus, his new vehicle of choice was *Life Stinks*.

Brooks claimed the spark for creating his new screen showcase occurred one day when he was driving on a southern California freeway and the water pump in his car broke. He exited near downtown Los Angeles to find a garage to handle the repairs. Mel remembered, "I looked around and said to the guy pumping gas, 'Where is this, Calcutta?' There were tramps everywhere. Beggars, homeless, what have you. Mendicants. It was shocking." This set Brooks to cogitating about the social inequities surrounding him. This, in turn, led him to thinking he would like to explore the conflicting and contrasting strata of society, just as filmmaker Frank Capra had done in his classic 1930s and 1940s feature films (such as *Mr. Deeds Goes to Town* and *Meet John Doe*). Later, Brooks happened to attend a screening of Preston Sturges's 1941 *Sullivan's Travels*, a classic comedy that explored the very social issues that were percolating in Mel's mind. Thus inspired, Brooks began to map out a comedy (to be filmed in black and white) that would address just such concerns. However, eventually, he realized that the script was "heavy, much too heavy, preachy." He decided he needed fresh input, and linked up with Rudy DeLuca, a veteran writer of several past Brooks vehicles, along with the much younger Steve Haberman, a University of California graduate who had worked in production capacities on such films as 1987's *Return to Horror High*.

The three men "funnied up" the screenplay and agreed it should be made in color.

By early June 1990, the project (initially titled *Life Sucks* but changed to the less pessimistic and less idiomatic *Life Stinks* during preproduction) was under way. Mel cast himself as Goddard "Pepto" Bolt, the crass Los Angeles real estate tycoon who has always been too busy making a fortune to appreciate life. Lesley Ann Warren took on the role of Molly, the eccentric, feisty bag lady who helps Bolt survive on the city's mean streets. Jeffrey Tambor appeared as Bolt's unconscionable business rival. Mel's old friend Howard Morris was signed as Sailor, one of the Skid Row denizens whom Bolt befriends.

The film was made for Alan Ladd Jr.'s regime at MGM. By the time the feature was in postproduction, there was a serious question as to whether the studio (recoiling from yet another painful corporate ownership changeover) might soon go out of business. It left in question the fate of such current studio productions as *Thelma & Louise* and *Life Stinks*. Finally, after months of speculation about whether Brooks would have to find another distributor, MGM released the PG-13–rated feature in mid-July 1991. In an era when most mainstream features received saturation bookings in over 2,000 theaters, *Life Stinks* debuted on only 865 screens. It was a strong indicator that the studio's powers had already concluded that the picture would have limited success in the marketplace.

Reviewers found occasional moments of Brooksian delirium in *Life Stinks*, such as the extended slapping scene between the "hero" and a delusional bum (played smartly by Rudy DeLuca) or the dance interlude (to Cole Porter's "Easy to Love") between Brooks and Warren. However, many agreed with Jack Matthews (of the *Los Angeles Times*), who asked rhetorically, "Is there anyone out there in Ronald Reagan's mortgaged America who wants to spend two laugh-filled hours on Los Angeles' Skid Row?" (Matthews did acknowledge of the new release, "It is a remarkably effective blend of slapstick and pathos, a story about a morally stunted industrialist forced to live among the homeless and to learn from them. Combining laughter and pain is never easy, but Brooks—fighting his own bad instincts, as well as the gag-huckster image he now calls 'the bane of my existence'—managed to inhabit this world without a note of condescension.")

Hal Hinton (of the *Washington Post*) was far less charitable toward Brooks's modest new showcase: "Once upon a time he was hilarious.

And can still be, in interview, which is his true art form. But for some time now, his movies have not even cruised near the neighborhood of funny. And this one is the bottom of the barrel."

In contrast, Roger Ebert (of the *Chicago Sun-Times*) championed Mel's latest picture as "warm and poignant." He judged, "Brooks, as usual, is his own best asset. As an actor, he brings a certain heedless courage to his roles. His characters never seem to pause for thought; they're cocky, headstrong, confident. They charge ahead into the business at hand. There is a certain tension in *Life Stinks* between the bull-headed optimism of the Brooks character, and the hopeless reality of the streets, and that's what the movie is about."

However, despite such boosts from Ebert and a few other critics, after a few weeks in domestic distribution, *Life Stinks* disappeared from view. Made at an estimated cost of $13 million, it only grossed $4.1 million in the United States and Canada. It fared better abroad but not sufficiently well to recoup its costs.

Brooks was crushed anew by the failure of his pet project and had a hard time coming to grips with its unfavorable reception. In 1993, two years after the fiasco, a still smarting Mel told Larry King on the latter's cable TV talk show, "I tried to do a story of what was happening in America and blend it with insane physical comedy, and it worked—it worked in Europe. It didn't work here. I mean, I think I was too close." A decade later, the filmmaker was still proclaiming the injustice of the picture's failure. "The best movie I made in a long time was a movie called *Life Stinks*. I was crucified. 'Don't annoy us, please.' It was that 'go away' phenomenon, so *Life Stinks* quickly went away. It'll be discovered, I'm probably dead 100 years, they'll say [it's] the best movie this little Jew ever made."

• • •

By 1992, Brooks was considering his next option as a moviemaker. With son Max soon old enough to be out on his own and wife Anne Bancroft back at work (on the Los Angeles stage, on TV, and in a rash of character leads in major movies), Mel needed to keep busy with his career, even if he seemed to be spinning his wheels. For one thing, there was Brooksfilms' latest effort, *The Vagrant*. However, this low-budget horror thriller starring Bill Paxton got a near nonexistent release (shown in only eight theaters!) by MGM before the very mild offering was relegated to the home entertainment market. Then, out of nowhere, a new movie project fell into Brooks's lap.

Evan Chandler, a Beverly Hills dentist, mentioned to a patient (J. David Shapiro), a fledgling scenarist recently arrived in Los Angeles from New Jersey, an idea suggested by Chandler's 11-year-old son. The concept was based on the boy's remark that Kevin Costner's recent box-office hit (*Robin Hood: Prince of Thieves*) "sucked." Thereafter, Chandler and Shapiro collaborated on a screenplay that, eventually, they pitched to Mel Brooks, who already had dealt satirically with the bandit king of Sherwood Forest in his 1975 TV series *When Things Were Rotten*.

A deal was made for Brooks to work with the duo to give their screen project the special Brooksian touch and his imprimatur, which would help to position the movie in the marketplace. Giving a typical industry spin to explain his attachment to the project, Mel said, "I think you must have affection for whatever you tease. I love Westerns. I love monster movies. And I love the story of Robin Hood." That interest went back to when Brooks was a child and "everybody wanted to be Errol Flynn." The imaginative boy had often warded off the forces of evil in his neighborhood with a wooden stick/sword (and adorned his makeshift hat with a feather taken from the local poultry store). Now he was ready to provide anew his comedic slant to the Robin Hood legend, using *Robin Hood: Prince of Thieves* as the "stepping-stone" for his burlesque. As he said, "Once I have something to chin on, I'm all set."

Brooksfilms Ltd. made a deal with Columbia Pictures to produce Mel's latest genre spoof. (Twentieth Century-Fox handled the domestic distribution while Brooksfilms was in charge of foreign distribution.) The cast was comprised of mostly new faces to the Brooks stock company: Britisher Cary Elwes as a prissy Robin Hood; stand-up comic/TV star Richard Lewis as the evil, leering Prince John; British comedian/TV star Tracey Ullman as the witchy Latrine; comic Dave Chappelle and singer/actor Isaac Hayes as two of Robin's men; Amy Yasbeck as the saccharine Maid Marian; and Roger Rees as the dastardly Sheriff of Rottingham. Mark Blankfield, who had been in Brooks's TV series *The Nutt House*, was given the role of blind Blinkin. Dom DeLuise added his presence in a cameo as a medieval gangster.

To complement—and bolster—the lineup of talent, Brooks cast himself as Friar Tuckman, a peddler of sorts who is better at distributing sacramental wine than in practicing the art of circumcision. (At one point in the casting process, Sean Connery, who had played King Richard in Kevin Costner's version of the Robin Hood legend, suggested to Brooks that he would repeat his role of the monarch—but this time in drag. However, as intriguing as this comic prospect was, he wanted a $1 million salary, which he planned to donate to Scottish charities. Connery's offer was turned down due to budgetary constraints. Instead, Patrick Stewart played the British ruler in a more conventional manner in the climax of *Robin Hood: Men in Tights*.)

Robin Hood: Men in Tights was shot on sound stages in Hollywood and on location in Canyon Country, about 30 miles northwest of Tinseltown. The picture boasted new songs by Brooks. With music provided by Hummie Mann (who had taken over for John Morris in scoring Mel's pictures), Brooks wrote the lyrics to "Marian" and "Sherwood Forest Rap." On his own, Brooks created the playful title song.

The PG-13–rated swashbuckling satire debuted in late July 1993. Vincent Canby (of the *New York Times*) was not impressed with the results. "The movie takes a long time to get off the ground, and then it wobbles. It hits a couple of ecstatically funny high points, only to plummet into a bog of second-rate gags, emerging a long time later to engage the audience by the sheer, unstoppable force of the Brooks chutzpah." For Canby, "The most damaging thing to be said about *Men in Tights* is that in spite of the references to *Prince of Thieves* and other comparatively recent films, it seems embedded in a movie world that's far more ancient. It's a shock when Mr. Brooks brings on Dom DeLuise to do his parody of Marlon Brando in his *Godfather* performance."

Rita Kempley (of the *Washington Post*) bluntly labeled Brooks an "increasingly creaky spoofmeister." She vivisected the film: "A predictable onslaught of bad taste and worse jokes, it mostly targets not the conventions of action-adventures but the sexual preferences of the merry men, who are variously referred to as 'pansies,' 'fagalas' and 'fruits.' Brooks fills in the spaces with broadsides derogatory to women and the one interest group you can readily afford to offend on film—blind folks."

The 104-minute *Robin Hood: Men in Tights* grossed $35.74 million in domestic distribution, but that was weak given its over $10 million production costs, plus additional marketing/distribution fees. (The source of the spoof, *Robin Hood: Prince of Thieves*, had grossed $165.5 million in the United States and Canada.) Following this release, Brooks severed his last ties with Twentieth Century-Fox, where he had headquartered his Brooksfilms since the late 1970s. He now took offices on a film lot in Culver City.

• • •

During 1993, a new Mel Brooks film effort went afoul. It was *Les Visiteurs*, a French-made fantasy comedy starring Jean Reno. The picture had been a box-office hit abroad, and Miramax Film decided to release the time-travel comedy in the United States in a dubbed version that was to be supervised by Mel Brooks. (Even taking this assignment showed just how anxious Brooks was to get back in the swing of the industry mainstream.) Following test screenings in Los Angeles, Miramax scrapped Mel's efforts. Instead, they gave *Les Visiteurs* a limited release in a subtitled version. A chagrined Brooks insisted, "I did the absolute best job I could. I felt the audience was really with it, but the guys at Miramax didn't see it that way. I don't know what they expected, but they didn't seem to understand that the words of the 'gospel' are dictated by the movement of the mouth."

• • •

In late November 1993, Neil Simon's *Laughter on the 23rd Floor* opened on Broadway. It was Simon's nostalgic recounting of life working for Sid Caesar on *Caesar's Hour*. Nathan Lane played the manic Sid-like central figure, Max Prince, with Ron Orbach as Ira Stone (a counterpart to the actual Mel Brooks). The comedy was a sizable hit and drew attention to the real-life alumni of Caesar's TV variety show. Brooks, Carl Reiner, and the other originals were the subject of many media interviews about the good old Caesar days and what each participant had been up to since then. (In 2001, the Showtime cable network aired a revised version of the stage hit, with Lane re-creating his part of Max Prince and with Saul Rubinek now cast as Ira Stone).

There were many tributes to the talented Sid Caesar in the 1990s, all of which brought the star's legendary writing squad (back) into the limelight. Perhaps the most high-profile occasion was a conclave held at the Writers Guild Theater in Beverly Hills in January 1996. Hosted by Billy Crystal, the evening was a free-for-all of wisecracking kibitzers (including

Brooks, Larry Gelbert, Neil Simon, Mel Tolkin, and Carl Reiner) paying homage to the great Sid. The classic outing of veteran jokesters was video-taped and aired on PBS in August of that year. Mel proved to be one of the most enthusiastic and vocal participants in the event, relishing the opportunity to reminisce and wisecrack about the golden old days, when his best creative years still lay ahead.

• • •

In 1994, Anne Bancroft announced, "I have the perfect dream—to live four months in LA, four in New York, and four in the Caribbean or Miami. I'd like my husband to come along, so I'll wait until he decides what he's going to do with his life. Actually, I don't think he'll decide. Life will decide for him. It always takes care of itself."

By then, the irrepressible if not always so indefatigable Mel, age 69, was at work on yet another feature film. (That Brooks found backing for a new screen venture after the less than stellar box-office and critical results of his recent offerings was a testament to the residue of industry esteem remaining from his early screen triumphs.) *Dracula: Dead and Loving It* harkened back to *Young Frankenstein* and the golden age of Brooks's film fare. The new project was set up at Castle Rock Entertainment (a production company cofounded by Carl Reiner's director/actor son Rob) for distribution by Columbia Pictures. (Ironically, Columbia was the same movie lot that had refused to make *Young Frankenstein* two decades earlier because Brooks had insisted it be filmed in black and white. *Dracula: Dead and Loving It* was to be shot in color.) Brooks collaborated on the screenplay with Rudy DeLuca and Steve Haberman.

Mel proclaimed that he was excited at returning to a horror spoof, a genre that was enjoying a new vogue with such recent releases and upcoming products as Francis Ford Coppola's *Dracula*, Peter Fonda's *Nadja*, and Eddie Murphy's *Vampire in Brooklyn*. Brooks pointed out, "Terror and comedy work very well together. There is a need to exorcise these devils, these demons, from our system, so that we don't have these nightmares." He noted, "In a way Dracula is even more insidious. Especially for women. They have this weird—I don't know if it's sexual . . . I think it is sexual—reaction to the whole legend. Frankenstein scares little boys, while Dracula scares and magnetizes grown women." It was Mel's intent to spoof the 1931 Bela Lugosi (camp) classic, not such celluloid riffs as George Hamilton's 1979 *Love at First Bite*.

More anxious than ever to seem hip and up-to-date, Brooks agreed that filmmaking techniques certainly had changed in recent times. "Everything has become quicker and more violent, even comedy. We're in the *Ace Ventura* school of funny. Trip, fall, scream, jump, bang—some of it very funny, some of it just noisy. And the young kids, 15 down to 9, are programmed to laugh on rhythm, on sounds. Dink! Dink! Dink! Bonk! They'll give you a laugh. It's like Beethoven, we'd get a laugh on his fifth—Bump-bump-bump-bah! It's perfect for the kids today. . . . It makes it more difficult to weave in information. It's all pay-offs. And I work a long time on these lush, green verdant valleys of information before I try for a peak of comedy. But I still do that, because it still works. And because I have to see the movie later, after we open and get our first week's grosses. Yesterday, after a good preview, they said, 'You could take this out, you could take that out . . .' And I said, 'Those are for me. Those are for after we open, so I can smile when I watch it!' And hopefully, there's a little triangle of people somewhere that'll like those jokes too."

In casting *Dracula: Dead and Loving It*, Mel recalled having seen some of the *Naked Gun* film comedies and being impressed by Leslie Nielsen's tongue-in-cheek performance as the clumsy "hero." He assigned the Canadian-born actor (who, like Brooks, was born in 1926) the lead role of Count Dracula from Transylvania. Harvey Korman once again returned to Mel's fold, this time as Dr. Jack Steward, the perplexed medico in charge of a loony bin of mad patients. Amy Yasbeck (from *Robin Hood: Men in Tights*) was contracted to play the beautiful heroine, while Lysette Anthony was chosen as the tempting ward who falls prey to the vampire. In an inspired piece of casting, the underrated Peter MacNicol (best known for playing the highly eccentric attorney on TV's *Ally McBeal*) played an English solicitor who falls under the count's deadly spell. Steven Weber (costar of TV's *Wings*) was made the picture's courteous but dense hero. Billy Crystal's daughter Jennifer had a small part as a nurse, while Anne Bancroft did a campy version of a gypsy woman, lampooning the bizarre performance of Russian character actress Maria Ouspenskaya in 1941's *The Wolf Man*.

Not to be left out of the fun, Brooks allotted himself the part of Dr. Abraham Van Helsing, the intense, thickly accented vampire hunter.

Later, Mel explained how he evolved his distinctive inflection for his interpretation of Van Helsing. "If you want to be a purist, he's Dutch. But everybody that's played him, including Edward Van Sloan right from the beginning, plays him with a Germanic haircut and accent. So I patterned myself after Van Sloan, cause I liked his haircut. I did that kind of Prussian crew-cut wig, and then I did this accent, which I love to do. Somebody said, What exactly is your accent, your German accent. And I said, Well, if you're a student of German actors, I'm about 90 percent [character actor] Albert Bassermann. . . . so I did 90 percent Albert Bassermann and 10 percent Hitler."

Filming began on May 5, 1995, on Los Angeles sound stages. Those who had worked with Brooks before were well acquainted with his concerted efforts to make his sets a center of joviality. But for newcomers to the Brooksian world, it all took getting used to. According to Ben Livingston, cast in the picnic scene, "I didn't know what to think." He described Mel being "bombastic and almost playing the part of a 1930s maniacal director." He remembered everyone laughing a good deal between shots and that "every day on the set was a comedy show." (Nielsen, a great prankster, got into the act by bringing a battery-operated fart machine to the set and had great fun watching people's reactions to the sudden barrage of crude noises the gadget made.) Livingston also recalled for this author that Brooks worked very quickly (especially on those days when he wanted to finish as early as possible to get to the horse racetrack, as watching the races had become one of his favorite pastimes) and that Mel's staff seemed to be on top of all production matters.

By now Brooks was adept at directing himself on camera. He was thankful for such aids as the video equipment used to film alongside the big cameras. Thanks to such technology he could immediately check how a scene had looked on camera. "Right after you do a take, you rush over to the monitor, you take a look, and you say, Let's do it again. Or you say, Don't touch it! Move on. Thank you, God!"

Then too, the veteran filmmaker was an old hand at the postproduction process and how the movie's final shape was essentially *not* determined by the director. "As soon as the rough cut is done my take on the movie is gone. From there on in, in a dark movie house, there's five hundred people who cut my film." One of the prerelease screenings was held in Pasadena. Brooks recalled, "So this bloodbath screening knocked out about 40 percent of the movie totally—this joke, this concept. And told us, More of this character! Peter MacNicol, they love him, stick more in! Steve Weber, oh they liked him! More Steve Weber! So we took our cue from the first screening, then we went to Burbank, and they [i.e., the marketing department] skewed [the invited guests to be] kind of young. . . . In a way, it was better, we got more laughs. It wasn't a very good screening, we got too many laughs. Because 12 year olds are very sweet, they're very generous. And if they think it should be funny, they laugh. And so it didn't tell us too much, it wasn't a good cutting screening. Then we went to Glendale, and we said, no 12 years old, 16 and up. And they were more severe. And yet we got laughs on nuances that we never got with 12 year olds."

As Brooks prepared for the film's debut on December 22, 1995 (a strange marketing choice; Halloween would have been a better time), he admitted to having concerns about the public's response. "I just hope that they [i.e., audiences] don't think that I'm aping the Zuckers [filmmakers Jerry and David, who made such screen spoofs as *Airplane!* and the Naked Gun series] now when I come out with a Leslie Nielsen movie. . . . I hope [they recall how far back I go]. That they wouldn't say, Who is this Mel Brooks, and why is he stealing the Zuckers' star and their type of comedy? That would certainly be ironic."

The critics gave *Dracula: Dead and Loving It* a very mixed reception. Georgia Brown (of the *Village Voice*) reported, "A bloodless Brooks supplies very few of his trademark taste-defying gags. Instead, he relies much too heavily on the stumbling and bumbling of his star, Leslie Nielsen, and the frantic mugging of Peter MacNicol." Janet Maslin (of the *New York Times*) labeled the picture "Mel Brooks's slight but amusing new parody." She noted, "Mr. Brooks may no longer be at the forefront of silly comedy, but he's still laying on the genre gags, horrible puns and enema references with dependable good cheer."

When the film was released abroad, Simon Rose (of the *London Sunday Mirror*) criticized, "Great title, shame about the movie. . . . Even Nielsen's mad mugging can't save things. Dracula moves window bolts with his mind, but he can't make the corners of our mouths turn up. . . . The only good thing to be said is that it's better than *Robin Hood: Men in Tights*. But so is everything." Adina Hoffman (of the *Jerusalem Post*) said, "The real belly laughs never come in *Dracula*, a film whose timing is comic but whose punchlines are strangely not. . . . Brooks's directing style has always been sloppy and rather haphazard. This was forgivable, however, when the jokes were sharp and numerous. The problem in *Dracula* is that the script . . . simply isn't amusing. The shticks range from passable (like the slurping-through-a-straw sound that Dracula makes when he drinks the blood of a beautiful young maiden) to really leaden. What's worse, some of the better lines are rehashed three or four times, till every last giggle has been drained away."

Dracula: Dead and Loving It accumulated a paltry $10.77 million in domestic distribution. Clearly, Mel Brooks was still out of favor with 1990s moviegoers, having failed to establish a new connection with his core audience. However, he had not lost his way with words when he was riled. Mel loved to tell people of the time he encountered film critic Roger Ebert, who had once been a great Brooks supporter. Brooks described, "I ran into Roger Ebert. He didn't like *Dracula*. He made no bones about it—thumbs, pinkies, every digit that he had. And I said to him: 'Listen, you, I made 21 movies. I'm very talented. I'll live in history. I have a body of work. You only have a body.'"

31

Comedy—Tonight!

A musical comedy is like a cinnamon bun. You keep moving it toward the center, getting ever sweeter and even more intensely satisfying. As you get closer to the core, it gets wetter and more gorgeous. With a musical, picaresque scenes are death. And you don't want to introduce a lot of new characters. Audiences want the people they've come to know and love to start going somewhere. A lot of writers try to solve their problems by introducing a fresh new character. They don't realize a bunch of new characters thins out the batter and the pancake gets flat.

—Mel Brooks, 2003

As Mel Brooks's filmmaking career continued to ebb in the late 1980s, he became increasingly active in other people's show business projects. It gave him something to do, brought in income, and kept his name alive with a new generation of audiences.

Mel provided the voice of Mr. Toilet for the 1990 comedy *Look Who's Talking Too*. For his friend Ezio Greggio (the Italian actor, director, screenwriter, and TV host), Brooks did a bit as the motel checkout guest in the 1994 movie spoof *The Silence of the Hams*. That same year, Mel had an extended cameo in the feature film version of *The Little Rascals*, in which he played Mr. Welling, the banker. In 1995, Mel made an audio guest appearance on the cartoon series *The Simpsons*. In 1998, Mel and Anne Bancroft were among those who helped to fund the making of *The Life and Times of Hank Greenberg*. (The well-regarded documentary dealt with the famous Detroit Tigers first baseman, who coped with anti-Semitism in the major leagues.)

In the 1998 animated feature *The Prince of Egypt*, Brooks utilized his distinctive, raspy voice to provide a small bit. For 1999's *Screw Loose*, produced and directed by Ezio Greggio, Mel had a lead assignment as a World War II veteran who has landed in a mental institution. He is "rescued" by the son of a combat buddy and enjoys outrageous adventures en route to being reunited with his long-ago pal. The Italian-made feature went almost immediately to home video/DVD in the United States. In the Swedish-made *Sex, lögner & videovåld*, made in 1992 but not released until 2000, Brooks had a bit part as a stressed old man.

However, it was Brooks's participation on the popular TV sitcom *Mad About You* that generated marvelous new acclaim for him. On September 24, 1996, he made his first appearance on the program, cast as Uncle Phil, a daffy old Jewish man who lives in Brooklyn. Mel was at his comedic best as the lovable relative of the series' lead character, Paul Buchman (played by Paul Reiser, who was a great fan of Brooks's). Mel brought zaniness, pathos, and dimension to his interpretation of the eccentric elderly soul with a thick old-country accent and a hairstyle that was always in wild disarray. Uncle Phil's favorite gambit was to thrust out his arms toward a loved one and order, "A firm embrace." Brooks's zesty performance was so endearing that he returned to the popular sitcom three additional times before the show ended its long run in 1999. For *each* of these guest-starring return appearances, Brooks won an Emmy Award.

Meanwhile, Mel, along with Carl Reiner, went back to the recording studios in mid-1997 to turn out a new comedy CD. *The 2000 Year Old Man in the Year 2000* was released on the Rhino label. It was for this fifth entry about the philosophical old soul that Brooks and Reiner won a 1998 Grammy Award in the category of Best Spoken Comedy Album. This revival of the 2000 Year Old Man led to Mel and Carl's doing guest shots on TV and at charity events around the country. Their book version of the new CD landed on the nonfiction bestseller list of the *Los Angeles Times*.

Despite these distractions, Brooks dearly wanted to return to filmmaking—to prove he still had the wherewithal to succeed in the business. He was working on a script titled *S.N.A.F.U*, a comedy based on Mel's misadventures as a combat engineer during World War II. To his great disappointment, he could not raise film studio interest in this or other potential screen projects (such as *Backwards to Forward*, his spin on Hollywood musicals).

• • •

If Brooks's career had spiraled downward, his marriage to Anne Bancroft remained rock solid. The media continued to be fascinated by the union of two such seemingly unlikely companions. However, there was no mystery for Bancroft about why she and her spouse had stayed together for so many years. "There is just nobody sexier than Mel Brooks. He has the most brilliant, unique brain. He keeps me excited from the moment I wake up in the morning to the moment I go to bed. There's nothing more exciting than interesting and unique ways of thinking." The veteran star also confided, "No, we don't discuss my work. We hardly discuss each other's work with each other. It's not one of our conversations. There's so much to discuss about life and so much to do, so many things that take up our time. And we very rarely discuss that. I don't think there's more than one sentence out of the week that's about show business." Mel's summary of his marriage to Anne was, "So we made a crazy child together and we have a pretty happy life. We like each other. We like Chinese food. We like foreign films. We like the beach. We really appreciate each other. So, I mean, it's been a great, great thing being married to Anne Bancroft."

There was also much speculation as to how Brooks had invested the profits from his lucrative decades in show business. In his trademark antic way, Mel explained his philosophy: "Real estate is a conservative and wise investment as long as you use it. Especially a house at the beach. You can put your feet on the sand. You can put your toe in the water. And you can always rent it." Besides his diverse real estate holdings on the West and East coasts, Brooks had invested in California state bonds, but had generally stayed away from stock market speculation. He especially had no interest in risking his hard-earned money on speculative commodities or futures. As he said, "You always have your house. It is hard to live in pork bellies—just the odor alone would chase you out."

Having reached the status of an elder statesman of comedy, Brooks was being compared and contrasted with new generations of funsters. In April 1997, *Entertainment Weekly* listed America's 50 top comedians. Robin Williams came in at number 1, Jerry Seinfeld at number 2, Roseanne at number 3, Jim Carrey at number 4, Albert Brooks at number 5, and Mel Brooks at number 20. The publication described Brooks as an individual who "has struck sparks with fellow comic giants Neil Simon,

Woody Allen, Carl Reiner, Sid Caesar, and Gene Wilder, injecting his jovial wackiness into an anarchic assortment of vulgar, gleeful parodies on both small and big screen. . . . In recent years, Brooks has seen his role as filmdom's premier satirizer pass into the hands of [others] . . . and his particular style of broad humor has come to seem mildly antiquated, but his occasional movies (*Robin Hood: Men in Tights*) and TV appearances (*Mad About You*) remind us that he's still here, comedy's big mocker."

When asked in the late 1990s to comment on the current state of comedy, Brooks responded, "You can't go too far if you're intelligent and your heart is in the right place. You can only go too far if you're stupid and you have nothing to say."

• • •

Since its 1968 release, *The Producers* had been a mixed blessing for Mel Brooks. On the positive side, it was his first feature film and had won him an Academy Award for Best Screenplay. However, in subsequent decades, critics insisted that *The Producers* represented the best of Mel Brooks's talents. They reasoned that from this creative high everything thereafter had gone downhill as Brooks became seduced into appealing to the public on a far more crass commercial level (e.g., *Blazing Saddles*). Many observers thought it was too bad that Mel had abandoned his more serious filmmaking (e.g., *The Twelve Chairs*) for the likes of *History of the World: Part I* or—even worse—*Robin Hood: Men in Tights.*

During these up-and-down career years, Mel had continued to write songs for his movies. However, that did not satisfy his longtime dream of one day creating a hit Broadway musical (to make up for the long-ago failures of *Shinbone Alley* and *All American*). Occasionally, Brooks considered converting *The Producers* into a song-and-dance extravaganza for the New York stage. Yet he always found reasons to put aside the idea as a pipe dream. Sometimes he reasoned aloud that it was better to leave the property as a cult film hit rather than to chance adapting it for Broadway and having it flop. On other occasions, he snapped, "That's my insurance policy. I'm saving it for my old age."

If Brooks's passing thoughts of converting *The Producers* into a stage musical remained unrealized, others saw bona fide commercial potential in such an adaptation. However, whenever someone approached Mel with this idea, he politely thanked the person and firmly said no. Then, in the late 1990s, music industry mogul David Geffen contacted Mel about turning *The Producers* into a Broadway show. Brooks courteously brushed off Geffen's notion. However, unlike others, Geffen refused to take no for an answer and doggedly kept after Brooks to move forward with the suggestion.

Geffen caught Brooks's attention at a particularly vulnerable time. Mel's career was in an awful decline, many of his longtime pals were seriously ill or dying, and he was feeling—more so than ever before—that the world and fate had turned against him. No one was more acutely aware of Brooks's depression than his wife. Hoping that *The Producers* project might renew Mel's zest for life and work, Bancroft joined Geffen's concerted effort to get Brooks to do the adaptation. (Anne even sent her spouse to see a psychiatrist, hoping the therapist could help Mel overcome his fear of tackling the project.) Finally, Brooks gave in to the ongoing pressure and said yes to Geffen's suggestion. (Thereafter, Mel referred to his wife as his Obi-Wan Kenobi for her wise counsel in pushing forward with adapting *The Producers* to the musical theater format.)

Brooks discussed this brewing project with his old pal and coworker Ronny Graham, who, among his many talents, was also a songwriter. The duo were soon joined by another friend and screen collaborator, Thomas Meehan. Since the latter was a Tony Award–winning writer of librettos for Broadway musicals, he seemed the perfect match for Mel. For a great many months he and Meehan worked on the book of *The Producers* at Brooks's Culver Studio offices. In retrospect, Meehan wondered to himself about the audacity of their task: "'My God, you've taken this perfectly classic movie and destroyed it. Where's Zero? Where's Gene Wilder?' . . . People suggest ideas for musicals all the time and most of them just don't, ahem, sing." (In July 1999, Graham passed away, leaving Mel and Tom to go it alone.)

At one point, David Geffen, who had agreed to back and supervise bringing *The Producers* to Broadway, suggested that Mel meet with Jerry Herman. Geffen believed that the composer/lyricist of such Broadway shows as *Hello, Dolly!* and *Mame* might be the right one to write the songs for *The Producers*. When Brooks visited with Herman at his Beverly Hills home, Herman sat down at the piano and announced, "I'll play you a couple of songs from the guy who I think should write the music for this." The songs were by Mel Brooks from his movies. Herman said "You're a very good songwriter. . . . What's more, you'd be crazy to do a Broadway musical of *The Producers* without including 'Springtime for

Hitler' and 'Prisoners of Love.' So you've already got two major songs written. All you have to do is write a dozen or so more and you've got yourself a Broadway score. Go with my blessings, do it!"

Sparked by Herman's encouragement, Mel set about composing the necessary complement of songs for the show. As in years past, he continued his routine of writing down lyrics on a pad of paper and envisioning a melody in his mind. When he had the germ of an idea, he hummed it/ sang it into a tape recorder, knowing that he would use a music arranger to score the song. (Eventually, it was Glen Kelly who served as Brooks's musical amanuensis.)

Anne Bancroft was witness to Brooks's long and often painful struggle with the song numbers. She recalled, "I admired his courage. He was putting his heart and soul into it. Sometimes, I'd come home from a very tiring day and say, 'Acting is so hard.' Then he'd put a blank piece of paper in front of me and say, 'That's how hard writing is!'" Finally, however, the score began to fall into place, and a pleased Mel was saying, "Only God knows why it took me so long to return to music. I've always wanted to write a musical. Music draws the dust off my soul."

As the book for *The Producers* took shape, Mel and Tom worked on one of the major flaws in the screenplay of the movie original: the plot letdown following the "Springtime for Hitler" showstopper. The collaborators fleshed out a new finale (which included having Leo Bloom run off to Rio de Janeiro with Ulla, but then return to New York to be a character witness at the trial of his friend Max Bialystock). Meanwhile, the writers dropped one of Mel's favorite characters from the Broadway original—L.S.D.—as being too quaint a figure for contemporary audiences. They added in the twist of director Roger De Bris stepping in at the last minute to play der Führer in the musical within the story. (Said Brooks: "A gay Hitler! Let us thank God.") In the process of punching up the original concept of spoofing Adolf Hitler, Brooks and Meehan expanded the lampooning of the story's outrageous gay characters.

Throughout this lengthy creative process, Brooks kept one goal firmly in mind: "If things are politically correct, it usually makes for a wonderfully dull show. When you try to hit home runs, you're gonna strike out a lot. So when you want to do a great, daring . . . musical, you're going to offend a lot of people. Otherwise, you're going to do something safe and nice, and you're going to have a banana on the stage instead of a devastatingly funny comedy."

It was Tom Meehan who suggested that London-born Mike Ockrent (the director of such Broadway hits as *Me and My Gal* and *Crazy for You*) would be ideal to helm *The Producers*. Moreover, Ockrent's American wife, Susan Stroman, was a much-in-demand choreographer with a string of important credits. Mel agreed to meet with Ockrent and Stroman and see if they all saw eye to eye on the show. Mel arrived at the couple's Manhattan apartment and rang the front doorbell. In a typical Brooksian moment when they opened the door, there was Brooks already singing one of the show's projected numbers. As Mel belted out the lyrics, he scampered and slid down a long hallway, veered off into the living room, and ended his number perched on the Ockrents' sofa with a smile on his face and his uplifted arms spread apart. Then, and only then, did he say, "Hello, I'm Mel Brooks!"

It was soon settled that Ockrent and Stroman would come aboard the venture. This led to many creative sessions with the Ockrents over the coming months. Then Mike suffered a relapse of his leukemia and died in December 1999. His devastated wife insisted that she would have to drop out of *The Producers*. Because Mel believed that work would be the best medicine for Stroman—and he had come to believe in her talents greatly—he begged her not to abandon their project. Eventually, she agreed to go on with the show, not only as choreographer, but also as director. (Brooks later said of Susan's participation in *The Producers*, "She took out all the vulgar stuff, cleaned me up and made me look pretty.")

Throughout this long gestation period, David Geffen had become increasingly busy with his duties at DreamWorks, a film production company he had cofounded, and with his music industry responsibilities. Geffen finally realized he would not have the necessary time to devote to *The Producers* as it headed to Broadway and dropped out of the project. This led to a crucial backers' audition held on April 9, 2000, at the Nola Rehearsal Studio on West 54th Street. To Brooks's great relief, the invited money people were enthralled with the pending show and the backing fell quickly in place. (Mel traded his underlying rights in *The Producers* for a percentage share as one of the producers. Later, after the show became a gigantic hit, he sighed, "I wish I would have put a million bucks into it. I mean, I would have gone to a bank and borrowed it and I would have been [really] rich today. But I'm OK, you know? Who's complaining?"

To play the pivotal role of Max Bialystock, Mel had one person in mind: Nathan Lane, who had excelled in a variety of Broadway shows over the last several years (including a revival of the musical *A Funny Thing Happened on the Way to the Forum*). One day in 1998 Lane was staying at the Ritz Hotel in Paris and decided to take a swim in the hotel pool. He recalled, "I got excited seeing the pool empty. And then up from the water pop the heads of Anne Bancroft and Mel Brooks. That was the first day he ever mentioned my playing Bialystock." Nathan was flattered by Mel's offer but was unconvinced that he could erase people's memories of Zero Mostel in the film original. Brooks remained tenacious in pursuing Lane to take on the key role.

On March 2, 2000, when Nathan was guest host on TV's *Late Show with David Letterman*, Brooks was a guest. During his segment, Mel whipped a piece of paper out of his pants, slapped it down the desk and said it was a contract for Lane to star in *The Producers*. Brooks demanded that the actor sign it on the spot. Lane said, "That's what I like about you. The soft sell." (Nathan didn't sign it because it wasn't a real contract. But the deal was already in the works.)

Matthew Broderick first won Brooks's attention after the actor did a Broadway revival of *How to Succeed in Business Without Really Trying* in the mid-1990s. Mel decided that he wanted Matthew to take on the Leo Bloom role in *The Producers*. After hearing the music and reading the script, Broderick said yes. Others to join the cast were Cady Huffman as the Swedish bombshell (Ulla), Brad Oscar as unhinged playwright Franz Liebkind, Gary Beach as bizarre stage director Roger De Bris, and Roger Bart as Carmen Ghia (Roger's prissy subordinate/lover).

After a sellout pre-Broadway engagement in Detroit, *The Producers* bowed on Broadway at the St. James Theater on April 19, 2001. Daniel Okrent (of *Entertainment Weekly*) cautioned, "If you're a Brooks fan who's been disappointed with his films recently (and not so recently; he hasn't made a good one in 20 years), you can rejoice in this cascade of bad taste, overripe satire, and inspired nuttiness. If you're not a Brooks fan, stay away. This show is too funny, over-the-top, and skillfully staged to waste on the likes of you." John Lahr (of *The New Yorker*) enthused, "What's first-rate about this particular seduction is not the lyrics or the music or the choreography but Brooks's antic imagination and the atmosphere of audacious liberty with which he whips up both the audience and his collaborators."

Michael Phillips (of the *Los Angeles Times*) was more cautious in his reaction to *The Producers*. He noted, "Brooks isn't above stealing from himself, not to mention anybody else. 'The King of Broadway' sounds a great deal like Brooks' 'Hope for the Best, Expect the Worst' from his 1970 film *The Twelve Chairs*. A lot of the *Producers* score glides in one ear and out the other ('I Wanna Be a Producer,' ''Til Him,' even Lane's climactic lament, 'Betrayed'). But arranger Glen Kelly and orchestrator Doug Besterman have done wonders in terms of fleshing out Brooks' efforts." Don Shewey (of *The Advocate*) alerted, "If you're the kind of person—like me—who has difficulty ignoring the fact that a straight audience is roaring at old-fashioned clichés of ditsy mincing queens, you may find *The Producers* hard to enjoy at times. Everybody else seems to love it."

Following the highly successful opening night, *The Producers* became *the* hottest show on Broadway—the biggest hit since 1975's *A Chorus Line*. Prices for the musical were raised to a $100 high (with scalpers selling prime seats at $400 to $500 a shot). In a typical week, the show was grossing $1.1 million. In less than six months, the show, which had cost $10.5 million to mount, made back its initial outlay.

Making Mel Brooks's miraculous comeback truly complete, *The Producers* won a series of awards, first from the Drama Desk, then at the Tony Awards in early June 2001. Out of 15 nominations, it claimed 12 Tonys, beating the previous record of 10 wins held by *Hello, Dolly!* A beaming Mel bounded onto the Radio City Music Hall stage that night to accept three personal awards: Best Book (with Thomas Meehan), Best Score, and Best Musical. Buoyed by the show's resounding success and his having proven all the doubters wrong about his ability to stage a show business resurgence, Brooks was at his most zany in accepting the trophies. At one point, he said, "I'm going to have to do the hardest thing I've ever done in my life—act humble." At another juncture in the limelight, Mel donned a Führer-like moustache and thanked Hitler "for being such a funny guy on stage." When Brooks called his fellow producers up on stage to join him in accepting the Best Musical prize, he said, "It would be foolish to try to thank them all." He then looked at the assemblage and said, "You should have worn signs." (Stroman, a two-time Tony winner that momentous night, said later of Brooks's chutzpah at the Tonys, "He's an extraordinary creature, really. No one else could have gotten away with what he did Sunday night." She also acknowledged his guidance on the musical, "He gave me some great advice. He said to me, 'Don't tap the bell—ring the bell!'")

During the course of his Tony Awards acceptance speeches, Brooks thanked, among others, Sidney Glazier, who had produced the film version of *The Producers* but had no participation in the profits of the Broadway show. By now, Glazier was in his mid-80s and in poor health. When his children called the retired producer and told him about Brooks's victory and his reference to Sidney, Glazier told his son, "The son of a bitch owes me money."

• • •

As the newly anointed king of Broadway, Mel was constantly in the limelight—and loved most every minute of it. When a PBS documentary was shot to capture the cast recording session of *The Producers*, Mel was the focal point of the footage. (Both the album and the documentary won Grammy Awards.) Brooks and Thomas Meehan coauthored 2001's *The Producers: The Book, Lyrics, and Story Behind the Biggest Hit on Broadway!* Later, Mel was on hand to help Susan Stroman pick replacements for Nathan Lane and Matthew Broderick when they departed the long-running Broadway version of *The Producers* (only to return later for a special encore run). It was Mel who got the lion's share of attention as various national touring companies of *The Producers* were launched and when he approved Jason Alexander (as Max Bialystock) and Martin Short (as Leo Bloom) for the musical's high-profile Los Angeles engagement in 2003. There was much ado about Richard Dreyfuss when he was hired to play Max Bialystock in the London production of the megahit. However, amid great controversy, Dreyfuss left the show before its West End bow and Nathan Lane flew to London to take over the demanding part until a replacement could be found.

Amid the avalanche of publicity concerning Brooks's Broadway success and his tremendous show business comeback, Mel's only sorrow was that neither his father (who had died back in 1929) nor his mother (who passed away in 1989) could share in his newfound acclaim. However, Brooks must have taken great comfort in knowing how proud they would have been of Melvin Kaminsky, who fought his way out of a Brooklyn ghetto to emerge the unsinkable monarch of comedy. As he told Thomas Meehan one day in Chicago during the tryout of *The Producers*, "This is the happiest I've been since I was 9 years old."

32

Carrying On

Don't grow up. Growing up will do you in. Getting old doesn't make you wise or smart. It just makes you old.

—Mel Brooks, 2004

In the wake of the hugely successful Broadway launch of *The Producers* in the spring of 2001, Mel Brooks found himself increasingly engulfed by supervisory chores on various U.S. and foreign productions of the acclaimed show. Over the coming years, versions of the hit musical were staged in Australia, Japan, Korea, Denmark, Italy, Israel, and elsewhere around the globe, including Las Vegas.

Certainly, Brooks thrived on all the newfound industry respect, public attention, and financial rewards generated by his fantastic comeback. However, eventually it reached a saturation point at which Brooks and Anne Bancroft felt the show essentially had taken control of their lives. (An amusing spin on this predicament of excessive success was played out in winter 2004 on the fourth season of the cable TV comedy *Curb Your Enthusiasm*. In this Larry David sitcom, Mel made several guest appearances as himself, and he was joined by Bancroft in the plot-twisting season finale that wrapped up a story arc about why Larry David had been cast to take over the demanding role of Max Bialystock on Broadway.)

The Brookses did their best to separate their daily existence from the swirling world of *The Producers*. When their married son, Max, who had been on the writing staff of TV's *Saturday Night Live* from 2001 to 2003, wrote a book parodying a survival guide (2003's *The Zombie Survival*

Guide: Complete Protection from the Living Dead), Mel used his celebrity status to help promote the tome. (Mel himself had been signed in early 2003 to write a book—an anecdotal memoir—but it had not yet reached fruition.) While Anne was seen in the cable TV version of Tennessee Williams's *The Roman Spring of Mrs. Stone* in 2003, Mel's one-act play, *Of Father and Sons*, was given a reading in New York City (but did not lead to a stage production). In addition, Mel took on the role of Wiley the Sheep in the PBS cartoon series *Jakers—The Adventures of Piggley Winks*, which debuted in September 2003. (Brooks accepted this TV series assignment as a project to amuse his young grandchild Samantha—the daughter of his son Edward.) Mel also lent his distinctive voice to the role of master inventor Bigweld in the expensively produced animated feature *Robots*, released in 2005.

Bancroft saw a showcase performance of Ann Randolph's one-woman show *Squeeze Box*, based on Randolph's experience working in a homeless shelter. Anne was so enchanted with the piece that, later, she backed an off-Broadway production of the property that was mounted in 2003. Having already provided a voice for the animated comedy/fantasy feature *Delgo* (set for a 2006 release), Bancroft was cast in late 2003 to play a character lead in the film *Spanglish*. However, she dropped out of this Adam Sandler vehicle due to poor health and was replaced by Cloris Leachman in the part of the star's mother-in-law.

• • •

Ever since *The Producers* became a smash hit in New York City, it was assumed that one day the stage show would be converted into a film musical. By mid-2004, that supposition had become a reality. The picture was to be made by Universal Pictures in conjunction with Brooksfilms and other backers. Nathan Lane and Matthew Broderick were hired to re-create their roles on screen, while Susan Stroman was greenlighted to make her film directing debut with this $45 million project.

Initially, the movie was to have been shot in Toronto, Canada. However, Brooks and the other decision makers were persuaded by tax incentives to shoot instead at the new Steiner Studios in Mel's hometown of Brooklyn. Nicole Kidman was announced to play the part of the high-voltage Ulla, but she dropped out and was replaced by Uma Thurman. TV/film comedian Will Ferrell was cast in the role of Franz Liebkind, while Gary Beach and Roger Bart repeated their roles as, respectively, Roger De Bris and Carmen Ghia.

It should have been a joyous time for Mel as filming on *The Producers* got under way at the Steiner Studios on February 28, 2005. The huge sets were ambitious and elaborate and the costumes flashy, and the screen adaptation had been done by Brooks and Thomas Meehan. (Mel wrote a new song, "There's Nothing Like a Show on Broadway," for the film edition.) However, as it was revealed later, Brooks was then undergoing tremendous personal stress. Anne Bancroft had been diagnosed with uterine cancer. Her condition had greatly deteriorated and she had been admitted to Mount Sinai Hospital. During this torturous period, Mel did his utmost to keep the tragic situation out of the media so he could deal privately with his wife's ordeal. As a result, Brooks was on the set of *The Producers* far less often than he had anticipated and was not available to the degree he had intended in order to help and guide Stroman through her directorial debut.

On June 6, 2005, Anne Bancroft, age 73, died at Mount Sinai Hospital. She was buried at the Kensico Cemetery in Valhalla, in Westchester County, New York. A few weeks later, on June 22, a tribute to Anne Bancroft was held at the Academy of Motion Picture Arts and Sciences in Beverly Hills. Carl Reiner hosted the event, at which a retrospective of film clips from Bancroft's movies and TV appearances was shown. At the start of the event, Brooks requested that no one come up to him to express their sympathy. He explained that he didn't need their tears; he had more than enough of his own. On June 27, 2005, Mel organized a private memorial for Anne at Manhattan's St. James Theater, where *The Producers* was still playing. Among the notables who spoke of their friendship with the luminous Bancroft were actors Matthew Broderick, Patty Duke, and Nathan Lane, and musician Paul Simon (who played a solo acoustic version of "Mrs. Robinson," the memorable song so closely associated with Anne's movie *The Graduate*). As at the prior service in Beverly Hills, Brooks instructed the attendees, "If any of you are grieving, keep it to yourself. I don't want to hear it."

• • •

In the months following Anne Bancroft's death, Mel remained much in seclusion, coping with his vast distress and anger at the loss of his wife of over 40 years. Because of his great grief, Brooks found it too difficult to participate much in the promotion of *The Producers* movie, which debuted on December 16, 2005. Unfortunately, the critical response to the movie was largely negative.

A. O. Scott (of the *New York Times*) labeled the 134-minute offering an "aggressively and pointlessly shiny, noisy spectacle." Scott asked, "How come the movie feels, in every sense, like a rip-off?" He answered his own question with, "No effort has been made to adjust the show to the scale of the movie screen. Mr. Lane rants and mugs with his characteristic energy and agility, but you wish he would modulate just the tiniest bit. Or failing that, that Mr. Broderick could dry off enough to function as an interesting foil, rather than as a flailing, hysterical ninny. . . . Ms. Stroman, meanwhile, does not have the filmmaking instincts to match her deft, emphatic choreography."

Kevin Crust (of the *Los Angeles Times*) observed of the PG-13–rated feature: "The original movie—a culture-clash time warp of New York theater nostalgia and '60s grooviness (remember Dick Shawn as L.S.D.?)—holds up because it's sharp and biting. The new film is more stolidly set in 1959, though as in the stage show, the Village People seem to have replaced hippies as the out-of-place pop cultural touchstone."

Mick LaSalle (of the *San Francisco Chronicle*) pointed out why the megasuccessful stage property did not translate well to the big screen: "Theater audiences are thrilled to see stars. If a star takes a pratfall, audiences are excited, because it's happening just for them and in real time. Theater audiences appreciate an effort. If something has the broad shape of comedy, they will often laugh, if only to acknowledge the energy and generosity being lavished on them. Yet all this translates into exactly nothing for a movie audience, which is why Lane and Broderick, who were reputedly great on stage (I never saw them), are barely good onscreen."

The costly, highly touted movie musical of *The Producers* generated a domestic gross of only about $20 million, and fared even worse abroad. It was a tremendous and awful anticlimax to the property's success on the Broadway stage, but Brooks was too stunned by his wife's untimely death to discuss publicly any reaction he might have had to the movie's whopping failure.

• • •

By early 2006, Brooks had begun to get on with the fabric of his life. Besides monitoring the assorted stage companies of *The Producers* that were playing—and scheduled to open—around the world, the tireless showman had several new projects in the works. Warner Bros. Pictures was preparing a big-screen version of Mel's old *Get Smart* TV series, with Steve Carell (the star of the movie *The 40 Year Old Virgin*) playing the lead. Meanwhile, MGM-TV had hired Brooks and Thomas Meehan to write a sequel to *Spaceballs* in the format of an animated series for the small screen. In addition, Mel and Thomas were collaborating on a stage musical adaptation of *Young Frankenstein*, hoping to strike the same jackpot as they had with *The Producers*. Of the "blood, sweat, and tears" expended on creating the new musical, Mel predicted—in typical Brooksian hype—that the new project was "going to be wonderful."

A DVD set of eight of Brooks's features (*The Twelve Chairs, Blazing Saddles, Young Frankenstein, Silent Movie, High Anxiety, History of the World: Part I, To Be or Not to Be,* and *Robin Hood: Men in Tights*) was released in the spring of 2006. By then, Mel had sufficiently regained his energy and humor to heavily promote the product. Shifting into high, wry huckster mode, he suggested of the DVD boxed set: "I think people should buy 20 of them. Buy 20 and save a lot of them for Christmas presents. Who knows how many of these they made?"

● ● ●

In retrospect, it has proved to be an amazingly bumpy, zigzagging, and colorful life's journey for Melvin Kaminsky, a poor Jewish boy from Brooklyn, to emerge as Mel Brooks, the world-famous show business personality (who, to boot, was married for decades to the glamorous, highly talented Anne Bancroft).

Brooks easily might have rested on his laurels gained as a comedy writer on the landmark 1950s TV programs *Your Show of Shows* and *Caesar's Hour.* Or after he made his sensational record album bow as the 2000 Year Old Man in 1960. Or after cocreating the classic TV sitcom *Get Smart* in the mid-1960s. Or, especially, following 1968's *The Producers,* his motion picture debut as a director and (Oscar-winning) scenarist. However, Mel was, and is, too full of creative energy and an overwhelming need for constant public recognition to allow himself to fade too long from public attention. This unquenchable thirst to entertain and be applauded by the world propelled him to turn out such milestone movie comedy fests as 1974's *Blazing Saddles* and *Young Frankenstein* (rated, respectively, numbers 6 and 13 on the American Film Institute's list of the 100 Funniest American Movies of All Time). Then, to satisfy his bent for filmmaking on serious topics, he formed Brooksfilms Ltd. in the late 1970s.

If mere survival for decades in the highly competitive entertainment industry—a forum increasingly monopolized by the young—isn't enough of an accomplishment on its own, Brooks enjoyed the comeback of comebacks when he spearheaded the creation of the Broadway musical version of *The Producers* in 2001.

According to Mel: "It's always been very important to me that I was not only funny, but that I was either the funniest person in the world, or one of the funnier people in the world. . . . I have never been really out of vogue because funny is funny. I will always be in vogue. I can always spot the insane of the bizarre in the commonplace. That's my job." As for Brooks's lifelong ambition to chisel his mark on the world, he has said, "You can win a conditional victory, I think [against death]. It all boils down to scratching your name in the bark of the tree. I was here. When you do that—whatever tree you carve it in—you're saying, 'Now, there's a record of me!' I won't be erased by death. Any man's greatness is a tribute to the nobility of mankind, so when we celebrate the genius of Tolstoy, we say, 'Look! One of our boys made it! Look what we're capable of!'"

Brooks's incessant need for a bit of immortality has pushed him to "try to give my work everything I've got, because when you're dead or you're out of business or you're in an old actors' home somewhere, if you've done a good job, your work will still be 16 years old and dancing and healthy and pirouetting and arabesquing all over the place and they'll say, 'That's who he is! He's not this decaying skeleton.'" (Another time, the vivaciously zany man said, "I believe when you die you rot. So you know what I want when I die? Fill me with formaldehyde, stick me under a kitchen table, eat over me and talk, and just let me listen.")

The celebrated laughmaker has emphasized repeatedly, "I never want to leave the Mel Brooks business, and that business is to make noises that make sense and that make people laugh. Enjoy! Revel! Live! Have yourselves one sweetheart of a good time. That's what my films are saying. That's what they're all about."

According to Mel, "I really get a kick out of making people feel good. There is no greater joy for me than to sit in the first row of a movie house showing one of my films and turn around. It's not so much the laughter; it's the glow of the faces in anticipation or just the silver light of the screen bathing over their faces. Success, money, they're all by-products. Fame, the enemy is a by-product. It's no good to be famous. It really doesn't pay. People watching you, they don't behave normally when you're around, and your God-given gifts of observation are out the window. Whatever anonymity I have I cling to."

As for the future of the film business, in which he has participated for over half a century, Brooks has acknowledged, "The home-entertainment technology scares me more than anything because I want an audience to laugh at my movies. I want people to sit in a dark theatre, let the silver screen bathe them with images and have them laugh as a group. It's thrilling to hear a lot of people laughing together. But with the direction of current technology, it seems we'll have tiny little groups at home, or sometimes even one skinny person watching a big fat Mel Brooks movie. You can't get a lot of laughs that way. I wasn't born to make one thin person laugh; I was born to make a lot of fat and skinny people sit in the dark and laugh together." (Once, when Mel Brooks was asked what he found to be the most difficult aspect about the filmmaking process, he amusingly responded, "Putting in the little holes. The sprocket holes are the hardest thing to make. Everything else is easy, but all night you have to sit with that little puncher and make the holes on the side of the film. You could faint from that work.")

•   •   •

Mel Brooks, the venerated elder statesman of show business, who refuses to abandon his career no matter how many ups and downs he experiences in the process, has never forgotten the best advice anyone ever gave him. "I asked a 97-year-old who was still the busy guy in the herring business, 'Mr. Horowitz, what's your secret?' He said, 'Follow your nature, boy. Follow your nature.'"

Mel Brooks's Film, Stage, and Television Credits

Feature Films*

New Faces

Twentieth Century-Fox, 1954, color, 98 minutes, no rating

Producers: Edward L. Alperson and Berman Swartz; director: Harry Horner; sketches: Melvin Brooks, John Cleveland, Luther Davis, Ronny Graham, and Paul Lynde, based on the Broadway revue *Leonard Sillman's New Faces of 1952*; camera: Lucien Ballard; editorial supervisor: Ace Herman

Selected cast: Ronny Graham, Eartha Kitt, Robert Clary, Alice Ghostley, June Carroll, and Paul Lynde (themselves)

The Producers

Embassy, 1968, color, 88 minutes, rated PG

Producer: Sidney Glazier; director/screenplay: Mel Brooks; original songs: Mel Brooks & John Morris; Norman Blagman; original music: John Morris; camera: Joseph Coffey; editor: Ralph Rosenblum

Selected cast: Zero Mostel (Max Bialystock); Gene Wilder (Leo Bloom), Kenneth Mars (Franz Liebkind), Christopher Hewett (Roger De Bris), Lee Meredith (Ulla), Andréas Voutsinas (Carmen Ghia), Dick Shawn (Lorenzo St. DuBois), and Mel Brooks (voice of Nazi soldier in "Springtime for Hitler")

---

*Mel Brooks's Brooksfilms Ltd. also produced the following films: *Fatso* (1980), *Loose Shoes* (1980), *The Elephant Man* (1980), *My Favorite Year* (1982), *Frances* (1982), *The Doctor and the Devils* (1985), *Solarbabies* (1986), *84 Charing Cross Road* (1987), and *The Vagrant* (1992), and Mel Brooks participated in such documentaries as *Sunset People* (1984) and *The Life and Times of Hank Greenberg* (1998).

Putney Swope

Cinema V, 1969, black and white/color, 84 minutes, rated R

Producers: Robert Downey Sr. and Ron Sullivan; director/screenplay: Robert Downey Sr.; original music: Charles Cuva; cinematographer: Gerald Cotts; editor: Bud S. Smith

Selected cast: Stanley Gottlieb (Nathan), Allen Garfield (Elias Jr.), Archie Russell (Joker), Ramon Gordon (Bissinger), Bert Lawrence (Hawker), Arnold Johnson (Putney Swope), David Kirk (Elias Sr.), Anthony Fargas (the Arab), Mel Brooks (Mr. Forget It), and Allan Arbus (Mr. Bad News)

The Twelve Chairs

UMC, 1970, color, 94 minutes, rated G

Producer: Michael Hertzberg; screenplay: Mel Brooks, based on the novel *The Twelve Chairs* by Ilya Ilf and Evgeny Petrov (Ilya Faynzilberg and Yevgeny Katayev) as translated by Elizabeth Hill and Doris Mudie as *Diamonds to Sit On*; original song: Mel Brooks; original music: John Morris; camera: Djordje Nikolic; editor: Alan Heim

Selected cast: Ron Moody (Ippolit Vorobyaninov), Frank Langella (Ostap Bender), Dom DeLuise (Father Fyodor), Andréas Voutsinas (Nikolai Sestrin), Diana Coupland (Madame Bruns), and Mel Brooks (Tikon)

Shinbone Alley

Fine Arts Films, 1971, color, 85 minutes, rated PG

Producers: Preston M. Fleet and John D. Wilson; director: John D. Wilson; screenplay: Joe Darion, based on the "archy and mehitabel" stories by Don Marquis and the Broadway musical (book by Joe Darion and Mel Brooks; lyrics by Joe Darion; music by George Kleinsinger); cinematographers: Ted C. Bemiller and Gene Borghi; editor: Warren Leighton

Selected cast (voices of): Eddie Bracken (archy), Carol Channing (mehitabel), John Carradine (Tyrone T. Tattersall), Alan Reed (Big Bill), Ken Sansom (Newspaperman Byron Kane), and Hal Smith (Spiders and Insects)

Blazing Saddles

Warner Bros., 1974, color, 93 minutes, rated R

Producer: Michael Hertzberg; director: Mel Brooks; screenplay: Mel Brooks & Norman Steinberg & Andrew Bergman & Richard Pryor & Alan Uger, based on the screen story by Andrew Bergman; original songs: Mel Brooks and John Morris; original music: John Morris; cinematographer: Joseph Biroc; editors: Danford Greene and John C. Howard

Selected cast: Cleavon Little (Sheriff Bart), Gene Wilder (Jim, the Waco Kid), Slim Pickens (Taggart), Alex Karras (Mongo), Mel Brooks (Governor William J. LePetomane/Indian chief/World War I aviator in bad men lineup/voice of German dancer/voice of moviegoer); Harvey Korman (Hedley Lamarr), Madeline Kahn (Lili Von Shtupp), and Dom DeLuise (Buddy Bizarre)

Young Frankenstein

Twentieth Century-Fox, 1974, black and white, 106 minutes, rated PG

Producer: Michael Gruskoff; director: Mel Brooks; screen story/screenplay: Mel Brooks & Gene Wilder, based on characters from the novel *Frankenstein, or the Modern Prometheus* by Mary Wollstonecraft Shelley; original music: John Morris; cinematographer: Gerald Hirschfeld; editor: John C. Howard

Selected cast: Gene Wilder (Dr. Frederick Frankenstein), Peter Boyle (the Monster), Marty Feldman (Igor), Madeline Kahn (Elizabeth), Cloris Leachman (Frau Blücher), Teri Garr (Inga), Kenneth Mars (Police Inspector Hans Wilhelm Friederich Kemp), Gene Hackman (the Blind Man), and Mel Brooks (voice of screeching cat/voice of werewolf)

Silent Movie

Twentieth Century-Fox, 1976, color, 87 minutes, rated PG

Producer: Michael Hertzberg; director: Mel Brooks; screenplay: Mel Brooks & Ron Clark & Rudy DeLuca & Barry Levinson; screen story: Ron Clark; original music: John Morris; cinematographer: Paul Lohmann; editors: Stanford C. Allen and John C. Howard

Selected cast: Mel Brooks (Mel Funn), Marty Feldman (Marty Eggs); Dom DeLuise (Dom Bell); Sid Caesar (Studio Chief); Harold Gould (Engulf); Ron Carey (Devour); Bernadette Peters (Vilma Kaplan); and Anne Bancroft, Liza Minnelli, Paul Newman, Marcel Marceau, and Burt Reynolds (guest stars)

High Anxiety

Twentieth Century-Fox, 1977, color, 94 minutes, rated PG

Producer/director: Mel Brooks; screenplay: Mel Brooks & Ron Clark & Rudy DeLuca & Barry Levinson; original songs: Mel Brooks; original music: John Morris; cinematographer: Paul Lohmann; editor: John C. Howard

Selected cast: Mel Brooks (Dr. Richard H. Thorndyke), Madeline Kahn (Victoria Brisbane), Cloris Leachman (Nurse Charlotte Diesel), Harvey Korman (Dr. Charles Montague), Ron Carey (Brophy), Howard Morris (Professor Lilloman), and Dick Van Patten (Dr. Philip Wentworth)

The Muppet Movie

Associated Film Distributors, 1979, color, 95 minutes, rated G

Producer: Jim Henson; director: James Frawley; screenplay: Jack Burns & Jerry Juhl; original songs: Paul Williams & Kenny Ascher; cinematographer: Isidore Mankofsky; editor: Christopher Greenbury

Selected cast: Jim Henson, Frank Oz, Jerry Nelson, Richard Hunt, and Dave Goelz (Muppet characters); Charles Durning (Doc Hopper); Austin Pendleton (Max); Mel Brooks (Professor Max Krassman); Dom DeLuise (Bernie the Agent); Madeline Kahn (El Sleezo Patron); Cloris Leachman (Lord's Secretary); Richard Pryor (Balloon Vendor); and Orson Welles (Lew Lord)

The Nude Bomb

Universal, 1980, color, 94 minutes, rated PG

Producer: Jennings Lang; director: Clive Donner; screenplay: Bill Dana, Leonard Stern, and Arne Sultan; based on characters created by Mel Brooks & Buck Henry; original song: Don Black and Lalo Schifrin; original music: Lalo Schifrin; cinematographer: Harry L. Wolf; editors: Walter Hannemann and Phil Tucker

Selected cast: Don Adams (Maxwell Smart), Sylvia Kristel (Agent 34), Rhonda Fleming (Edith Von Secondberg), Dana Elcar (Chief), Pamela Hensley (Agent 35), and Norman Lloyd (Carruthers)

History of the World: Part I
Twentieth Century-Fox, 1981, color, 92 minutes, rated R

Producer/director/screenplay: Mel Brooks; songs: Mel Brooks & Ronny Graham; original music: John Morris; cinematographer: Woody Omens; editor: John C. Howard

Selected cast: Mel Brooks (Moses/Comicus/Torquemada/Jacques/Louis XVI), Dom DeLuise (Emperor Caesar), Madeline Kahn (Empress Nympho), Harvey Korman (Count de Monet), Cloris Leachman (Madame DeFarge), Ron Carey (Swiftus), Gregory Hines (Josephus), Pamela Stephenson (Mademoiselle Rimbaud), Sid Caesar (Chief Caveman), Mary-Margaret Humes (Miriam), and Orson Welles (Narrator)

To Be or Not to Be
Twentieth Century-Fox, 1983, color, 107 minutes, rated PG

Producer: Mel Brooks; director: Alan Johnson; screenplay: Ronny Graham & Thomas Meehan, based on the 1942 screenplay by Edwin Justus Mayer and the screen story by Melchior Lengyel and Ernst Lubitsch; original songs: Mel Brooks & Ronny Graham; original music: John Morris; cinematographer: Gerald Hirschfeld; editor: Alan Balsam

Selected cast: Mel Brooks (Dr. Frederick Bronski), Anne Bancroft (Anna Bronski), Tim Matheson (Lieutenant Andre Sobinski), Charles Durning (Colonel Erhardt), Christopher Lloyd (Captain Schultz), José Ferrer (Professor Siletski), Ronny Graham (Sondheim), and Max Brooks (Rifka's Son)

Spaceballs
Metro-Goldwyn-Mayer, 1987, color, 96 minutes, rated PG

Producer/director: Mel Brooks; screenplay: Mel Brooks & Thomas Meehan & Ronny Graham; original song: Jeff Pescetto, Clyde Lieberman, & Mel Brooks; original music: John Morris; cinematographer: Nick McLean; editor: Conrad Buff IV

Selected cast: Mel Brooks (President Skroob/Yoghurt), Rick Moranis (Dark Helmet), Bill Pullman (Lone Starr), Daphne Zuniga (Princess Vespa), John Candy (Barfolemew ["Barf"]), George Wyner (Colonel Sandurz), Joan Rivers (voice of Dot Matrix), and Dick Van Patten (King Roland)

Look Who's Talking Too
TriStar, 1990, color, 81 minutes, rated PG-13

Producer: Jonathan D. Krane; director: Amy Heckerling; screenplay: Amy Heckerling & Neal Israel, based on characters created by Amy Heckerling; original music: David Kitay; cinematographer: Thomas Del Ruth; editor: Debra Chiate

Selected cast: John Travolta (James Ubriacco), Kirstie Alley (Mollie Ubriacco), Olympia Dukakis (Rosie), Bruce Willis (voice of Mikey), Roseanne Barr (voice of Julie), Damon Wayans (voice of Eddie), and Mel Brooks (voice of Mr. Toilet Man)

Life Stinks
Metro-Goldwyn-Mayer, 1991, color, 92 minutes, rated PG-13

Producer/director: Mel Brooks; screenplay/screen story: Mel Brooks & Ron Clark & Rudy DeLuca & Steve Haberman; original music: John Morris; cinematographer: Stephen B. Poster; editors: Michael Mulconery, David Rawlins, and Anthony Redman

Selected cast: Mel Brooks (Goddard "Pepto" Bolt), Lesley Ann Warren (Molly), Jeffrey Tambor (Vance Crasswell), Howard Morris (Sailor), Rudy DeLuca (J. Paul Getty), and Teddy Wilson (Fumes)

Robin Hood: Men in Tights
Twentieth Century-Fox, 1993, color, 104 minutes, rated PG-13

Producer/director: Mel Brooks; screenplay: Mel Brooks & Evan Chandler & J. David Shapiro; screen story: Evan Chandler and J. David Shapiro; original songs: Mel Brooks & Hummie Mann; original music: Hummie Mann; cinematographer: Michael D. O'Shea; editor: Stephen E. Rivkin

Selected cast: Cary Elwes (Robin Hood), Richard Lewis (Prince John), Roger Rees (Sheriff of Rottingham), Amy Yasbeck (Maid Marian), Dave Chappelle (Ahchoo), Isaac Hayes (Asneeze), Tracey Ullman (Latrine), Patrick Stewart (King

Richard), Dom DeLuise (Don Giovanni), Dick Van Patten (the Abbot), and Mel Brooks (Rabbi Tuckman)

The Silence of the Hams
October Films, 1994, color, 81 minutes, rated R

Producers: Julie Corman and Ezio Greggio; director/screenplay: Ezio Greggio; original music: Parmer Fuller; cinematographer: Jacques Haitkin; editors: Robert Barrere and Andy Horvitch

Selected cast: Ezio Greggio (Antonio Motel), Dom DeLuise (Dr. Animal Cannibal Pizza), Billy Zane (Jo Dee Foster), Joanna Pacula (Lily Wine), Charlene Tilton (Jane Wine), Martin Balsam (Detective Martin Balsam), and Mel Brooks (Checkout Guest)

The Little Rascals
Universal, 1994, color, 82 minutes, rated PG

Producers: Michael King and Bill Oakes; director: Penelope Spheeris; screenplay: Paul Guay & Stephen Mazur & Penelope Spheeris: screen story: Penelope Spheeris & Robert Wolterstorff & Mike Scott & Paul Guay & Stephen Mazur; original song: Leroy Shield; original music: William Ross; cinematographer: Richard Bowen; editors: Ross Albert and Peter Teschner

Selected cast: Travis Tedford (George "Spanky" McFarland), Kevin Jamal Woods (Matthew "Stymie" Beard), Jordan Warkol (Robert "Froggy" Lawford), Zachary Mabry (Patrick "Porky" Lee), Ross Elliot Bagley (William "Buckwheat" Thomas), Mel Brooks (Mr. Welling, the banker), Whoopi Goldberg (Buckwheat's Mom), and Reba McEntire (A. J. Ferguson)

Dracula: Dead and Loving It
Columbia, 1995, color, 88 minutes, rated PG-13

Producer/director: Mel Brooks; screenplay: Mel Brooks, Rudy DeLuca, and Steve Haberman; screen story: Rudy DeLuca & Steve Haberman; original music: Hummie Mann; cinematographer: Michael D. O'Shea; editor: Adam Weiss

Selected cast: Leslie Nielsen (Count Dracula), Peter MacNicol (R. M. Renfield), Steven Weber (Jonathan Harker), Amy Yasbeck (Mina Murray), Mel Brooks

(Dr. Abraham Van Helsing), Lysette Anthony (Lucy Westenra), Harvey Korman (Dr. Jack Seward), and Anne Bancroft (Madame Ouspenskaya, the gypsy woman)

The Prince of Egypt
DreamWorks, 1998, color, 99 minutes, rated PG

Producers: Penney Finkleman Cox and Sandra Rabins; directors: Brenda Chapman, Steve Hickner, and Simon Wells; screenplay: Phil LaZebnik; additional screenplay material: Nicholas Meyer; story: Ken Harsha and Anthony Leondis; additional story: Ronaldo Del Carmen, Carole Holliday, and Frank Tamura; original songs: Stephen Schwartz and Hans Zimmer; original music: Hans Zimmer; editor: Nick Fletcher

Selected voices: Val Kilmer (Moses/God), Ralph Fiennes (Rameses), Michelle Pfeiffer (Tzipporah), Sandra Bullock (Miriam), Jeff Goldblum (Aaron), Danny Glover (Jethro), Patrick Stewart (Pharaoh Seti I), Steve Martin (Hotep), Martin Short (Huy), and Mel Brooks (additional voice)

Screw Loose
Italian, 1999, color, 85 minutes, rated R

Producers: Ezio Greggio and Whitney R. Hunter; director: Ezio Greggio; screenplay: Rudy DeLuca & Steve Haberman; original music: Silvio Amato and Umberto Smaila; cinematographer: Luca Robecchi; editor: Gib Jaffe

Selected cast: Ezio Greggio (Bernardo Puccini), Mel Brooks (Jake Gordon), Julie Condra (Dr. Barbara Collier), Gianfranco Barra (Guido Puccini), Randi Ingerman (Sofia), and John Karlsen (Dr. Caputo)

Sex, lögner & videovåld
Swedish, 2000, color, 94 minutes, no rating [made in 1992]

Producers: Mikael Beckman, Anders Ek, Johan Holm, Richard Holm, and Henrik Wadling; director: Richard Holm; screenplay: Johan Holm & Richard Holm; original music: Christer Plånborg

Selected cast: Mikael Beckman (Micke), Johan Holm (Franz), Zara Zetterqvist (Little Sis), Camilla Henemark (Camilla), Micke Dubois (Hot Dog Vendor), Mel Brooks (Stressed Old Man), and Brandon Lee (Man in Line at Nightclub)

Robots

Twentieth Century-Fox, 2005, color, 91 minutes, rated PG

Producers, Jerry Davis, John C. Donkin, and William Joyce; director: Chris Wedge; codirector: Carlos Saldanha; screenplay: David Lindsay-Abaire and Lowell Ganz & Babaloo Mandel; screen story: Ron Mita & Jim McClain & David Lindsay-Abaire; original song: Adam Schlesinger; original music: Ian Ball and John Powell; editor: John Carnochan

Selected cast (voices of): Paula Abdul (Watch), Halle Berry (Cappy), Lucille Bliss (Pigeon Lady), Terry Bradshaw (Broken Arm Bot), Jim Broadbent (Madame Gasket), Mel Brooks (Bigweld), Amanda Bynes (Piper), and Drew Carey (Crank)

The Producers

Universal, 2005, color, 134 minutes, rated PG-13

Producers: Mel Brooks and Jonathan Sanger; director/choreographer: Susan Stroman; screenplay: Mel Brooks & Thomas Meehan, based on the 1968 screenplay by Mel Brooks and the 2001 stage play (book by Mel Brooks & Thomas Meehan; songs by Brooks); original song: Mel Brooks; cinematographers: John Bailey and Charles Minsky; editor: Steven Weisberg

Selected cast: Nathan Lane (Max Bialystock), Matthew Broderick (Leo Bloom), Uma Thurman (Ulla), Will Ferrell (Franz Liebkind), Gary Beach (Roger De Bris), Roger Bart (Carmen Ghia), and Mel Brooks (voice of Nazi soldier in "Springtime for Hitler"/Hilda the cat/Tom the cat)

Broadway Shows*

Leonard Sillman's New Faces of 1952

Opened May 16, 1952, Royale Theater, 365 performances

Sketches: Ronny Graham and Melvin Brooks

Selected cast: Robert Clary, June Carroll, Alice Ghostley, Eartha Kitt, Ronny Graham, Paul Lynde, and Rosemary O'Reilly

Shinbone Alley

Opened April 13, 1957, Broadway Theater, 49 performances

Book: Joe Darion and Mel Brooks, based on the "archy and mehitabel" stories by Don Marquis

Selected cast: Eddie Bracken, Jacques d'Amboise, Allegra Kent, Eartha Kitt, and Erik Rhodes

All American

Opened March 19, 1962, Winter Garden Theater, 80 performances

Book: Mel Brooks, based on the novel *Professor Fodorski* by Robert Lewis Taylor

Selected cast: Ray Bolger, Anita Gillette, Eileen Herlie, Ron Husmann, and Fritz Weaver

The Producers

Opened April 19, 2001, St. James Theater, still running

Book: Mel Brooks & Thomas Meehan; songs: Mel Brooks, based on the screenplay and songs from the 1968 film *The Producers* by Mel Brooks

Selected cast: Matthew Broderick, Nathan Lane, Roger Bart, Gary Beach, Cady Huffman, and Brad Oscar

---

* Mel Brooks also served as script consultant on the following Broadway shows: *Nowhere to Go But Up* (1962), *Kelly* (1965), and *The Best Laid Plans* (1966).

Television Series

Admiral Broadway Revue
NBC and Dumont, 1949

Uncredited joke/sketch consultant: Mel Brooks

Selected cast: Sid Caesar, Imogene Coca, Mary McCarty, and Marge & Gower Champion

Your Show of Shows
NBC, 1950–1954

Writing team member: Mel Brooks

Selected cast: Sid Caesar, Imogene Coca, Howard Morris, and Carl Reiner

The Imogene Coca Show
NBC, 1954–1955

Writing team member: Mel Brooks

Selected cast: Imogene Coca, David Burns, Hal March, and Bibi Osterwald

Caesar's Hour
NBC, 1955–1957

Writing team member: Mel Brooks

Selected cast: Sid Caesar, Nanette Fabray, Howard Morris, Carl Reiner, and Janet Blair

The Polly Bergen Show
NBC, 1957

Producer/writer: Mel Brooks

Selected cast: Polly Bergen, Peter Gennaro Dancers, Bill Bergen, and the Luther Henderson Jr. Orchestra

Sid Caesar Invites You
ABC, 1958

Writing team member: Mel Brooks

Selected cast: Sid Caesar, Imogene Coca, Carl Reiner, and Paul Reed

Get Smart
NBC and later CBS, 1965–1970

Cocreator/occasional scripter: Mel Brooks

Selected cast: Don Adams, Barbara Feldon, Edward Platt, Dick Gautier, and Bernie Kopell

The Electric Company
PBS, 1973–1977

Role of Blond-Haired Cartoon Man: Mel Brooks

When Things Were Rotten
ABC, 1975

Cocreator/coproducer/occasional scripter: Mel Brooks

Selected cast: Richard Gautier, Dick Van Patten, Bernie Kopell, Richard Dimitri, Henry Polic II, and Misty Rowe

The Nutt House
NBC, 1989

Coproducer/writer: Mel Brooks

Selected cast: Harvey Korman, Cloris Leachman, Mark Blankfield, Brian McNamara, Molly Hagan, Gregory Itzin, and Ronny Graham

Get Smart

Fox, 1995

Cocreator of original 1965–1970 series: Mel Brooks

Selected cast: Don Adams, Barbara Feldon, Andy Dick, Elaine Hendrix, and Heather Morgan

Jakers! The Adventures of Piggley Winks

PBS, 2003–present

Voice of Wiley the Sheep: Mel Brooks

Bibliography

Books

Adams, Joey, and Henry Tobias. *The Borscht Belt*. New York: Bentley, 1966.

Adler, Bill, and Jeffrey Feinman. *Mel Brooks: The Irreverent Funnyman*. New York: Playboy, 1976.

Baxter, John. *Woody Allen: A Biography*. New York: Carroll and Graf, 1999.

Bedell, Sally. *Up the Tube: Prime-Time TV in the Silverman Years*. New York: Viking, 1981.

Bloom, Ken. *Broadway: An Encyclopedia*. New York: Routledge, 2003.

Blumberg, Esterita "Cissie." *Remember the Catskills: Tales by a Recovering Hotel-keeper*. Fleischmanns, N.Y.: Purple Mountain, 1996.

Brooks, Max. *The Zombie Survival Guide: Complete Protection from the Living Dead*. New York: Three Rivers, 2003.

Brooks, Mel, Ron Clark, Rudy DeLuca, and Barry Levinson. *Silent Movie* (a screenplay). New York: Ballantine, 1976.

Brooks, Mel, and Tom Meehan. *The Producers: The Book, Lyrics, and Story Behind the Biggest Hit in Broadway History! How We Did It*. New York: Roundtable, 2001.

Brooks, Mel, and Carl Reiner. *The 2000 Year Old Man: The collected recorded wisdom of the venerable sage in one fully illustrated volume*. New York: Warner Books, 1981.

———. *The 2000 Year Old Man Goes to School*. New York: HarperCollins, 2005.

———. *The 2000 Year Old Man in the Year 2000: The Book*. New York: Harper Entertainment, 1997.

Brooks, Tim, and Earle Marsh. *The Complete Directory to Prime Time Network and Cable TV Shows: 1946–Present* (8th ed.). New York: Ballantine, 2003.

Brown, Jared. *Zero Mostel: A Biography*. New York: Atheneum, 1989.

Bryer, Jackson R., and Richard A. Davison (eds.). *The Art of the American Musical: Conversation with the Creators*. New Brunswick, N.J.: Rutgers University Press, 2005.

Caesar, Sid, with Bill Davidson. *Where Have I Been? An Autobiography*. New York: Signet, 1983.

Caesar, Sid, with Eddy Friedfeld. *Caesar's Hours: My Life in Comedy, with Love and Laughter*. New York: Public Affairs, 2003.

Castleman, Harry, and Walter J. Podrazik. *Watching TV: Four Decades of American Television*. New York: McGraw-Hill, 1982.

Crick, Robert Alan. *The Big Screen Comedies of Mel Brooks*. Jefferson, N.C.: McFarland, 2002.

Davis, Lee. *Scandals and Follies: The Rise and Fall of the Great Broadway Revue*. New York: Limelight, 2000.

Denman, Jeffrey. *A Year with* The Producers: *One Actor's Exhausting (But Worth It) Journey from* Cats *to Mel Brooks' Mega-Hit*. New York: Routledge, 2002.

Dresser, David, and Lester D. Friedman. *American-Jewish Filmmakers: Traditions and Trends*. Urbana: University of Illinois Press, 1993.

Epstein, Lawrence J. *The Haunted Smile: The Story of Jewish Comedians in America*. New York: PublicAffairs, 2001.

Erens, Patricia. *The Jew in American Cinema*. Bloomington: Indiana University Press, 1984.

Fisher, James. *Eddie Cantor: A Bio-Bibliography*. Westport, Conn.: Greenwood, 1997.

Fox, Julian. *Woody: Movies from Manhattan*. Woodstock, N.Y.: Overlook, 1996.

Friedman, Lester D. *The Jewish Image in American Film: 70 Years of Hollywood's Vision of Jewish Characters and Themes*. Secaucus, N.J.: Citadel, 1987.

Frommer, Myrna Katz, and Harvey Frommer. *It Happened in the Catskills: An Oral History in the Words of Busboys, Bellhops, Guests, Proprietors, Comedians, Agents, and Others Who Lived It*. New York: Harcourt Brace Jovanovich, 1991.

Gabler, Neal, Frank Rich, and Joyce Antler. *Television's Changing Image of American Jews*. New York: The American Jewish Committee, 2000.

Garr, Teri, with Henriette Mantel. *Speedbumps: Flooring It Through Hollywood*. New York: Hudson Street, 2005.

Gelbart, Larry. *Laughing Matters: On Writing M*A*S*H, Tootsie, Oh, God!, and a Few Other Funny Things*. New York: Random House, 1998.

Goldberg, Lee. *Unsold Television Pilots, Vol. 1: 1955 through 1988*. Jefferson, N.C.: McFarland, 1990.

Goldman, Albert, from the journalism of Lawrence Schiller. *Ladies and Gentlemen: Lenny Bruce!* New York: Ballantine, 1974.

Green, Joey. *The Get Smart Handbook*. New York: Collier, 1993.

Gregory, Mollie. *Women Who Run the Show*. New York: St. Martin's, 2002.

Grossinger, Tania. *Growing Up at Grossinger's*. New York: David McKay, 1975.

Heller, Joseph, and Speed Vogel. *No Laughing Matter*. New York: Plume, 1995.

Holtzman, William. *Seesaw: A Dual Biography of Anne Bancroft and Mel Brooks*. Garden City, N.Y.: Doubleday, 1979.

Kanfer, Stefan. *A Summer World: The Attempt to Build a Jewish Eden in the Catskills, from the Days of the Ghetto to the Rise and Decline of the Borscht Belt*. New York: Farrar, Straus and Giroux, 1992.

Kent, Nicolas. *Naked Hollywood: Money and Power in the Movies Today*. New York: St. Martin's, 1991.

Kisseloff, Jeff. *The Box: An Oral History of Television, 1920–1961*. New York: Viking, 1995.

Krutnik, Frank. *Inventing Jerry Lewis*. Washington, D.C.: Smithsonian Institution Press, 2000.

Levy, Shawn. *King of Comedy: The Life and Art of Jerry Lewis*. New York: St. Martin's, 1997.

Lloyd, Norman. *Stages: Of Life in Theatre, Film and Television* (revised edition). New York: Limelight, 1993.

Logan, Joshua. *Josh: My Up and Down, In and Out Life*. New York: Delacorte, 1976.

———. *Movie Stars, Real People, and Me*. New York: Delacorte, 1978.

Lyman, Darryl. *Great Jews in the Performing Arts*. Middle Village, N.Y.: Jonathan David, 1999.

———. *Great Jews on Stage and Screen*. Middle Village, N.Y.: Jonathan David, 1987.

———. *The Jewish Comedy Catalog*. Middle Village, N.Y.: Jonathan David, 1989.

Malarcher, Jay. *The Classically American Comedy of Larry Gelbart*. Lanham, Md.: Scarecrow, 2003.

Manbeck, John B. (consulting ed.). *The Neighborhoods of Brooklyn*, 2nd ed. New Haven, Conn.: Yale University Press, 2004.

Manchel, Frank. *The Box-Office Clowns: Bob Hope, Jerry Lewis, Mel Brooks, and Woody Allen*. New York: Franklin Watts, 1979.

Mason, Marsha. *Journey: A Personal Odyssey*. New York: Simon & Schuster, 2000.

Mazursky, Paul. *Show Me the Magic: My Adventures in Life and Hollywood*. New York: Simon & Schuster, 1999.

McCrohan, Donna. *The Life and Times of Maxwell Smart*. New York: St. Martin's, 1988.

Meade, Marion. *The Unruly Life of Woody Allen*. London: Weidenfeld & Nicholson, 2000.

Mostel, Kate, and Madeline Gilford, with Jack Gilford and Zero Mostel. *170 Years of Show Business*. New York: Random House, 1978.

Nachman, Gerald. *Seriously Funny: The Rebel Comedians of the 1950s and 1960s*. New York: Pantheon, 2003.

Parish, James Robert, and William T. Leonard, with Gregory W. Mank and Charles Hoyt. *The Funsters*. New Rochelle, N.Y.: Arlington House, 1979.

Parish, James Robert, and Vincent Terrace. *The Complete Actors' Television Credits, 1948–1988: Vol. 1: Actors*, 2nd ed. Metuchen, N.J.: Scarecrow, 1989.

———. *The Complete Actors' Television Credits, 1948–1988: Vol. 2: Actresses*, 2nd ed. Metuchen, N.J.: Scarecrow, 1995.

Phil Brown (ed.). *In the Catskills: A Century of the Jewish Experience in "The Mountains."* New York: Columbia University Press, 2002.

Pilpel, Robert H. *High Anxiety* (a novelization). New York: Ace, 1977.

Pomerantz, Joel. *Jennie and the Story of Grossinger's: The Warm, Inspiring Story of the Poor Immigrant Girl Who Built a Hotel-Castle in the Catskills and Became One of the World's Most Renowned Hostesses.* New York: Grosset & Dunlap, 1970.

Radner, Gilda. *It's Always Something.* New York: Avon, 1990.

Reiner, Carl. *Continue Laughing.* New York: HarperCollins, 1995.

———. *My Anecdotal Life: A Memoir.* New York: St. Martin's, 2003.

Richman, Irwin. *Borscht Belt Bungalows: Memories of Catskill Summers.* Philadelphia: Temple University Press, 1998.

Robbins, Michael W., and Wendy Palitz. *Brooklyn: A State of Mind: 125 Original Stories from America's Most Colorful City.* New York: Workman, 2001.

Rosenblum, Ralph, and Robert Karen. *When the Shooting Stops . . . the Cutting Begins: A Film Editor's Story.* New York: Viking, 1979.

Sainer, Arthur. *Zero Dances: A Biography of Zero Mostel.* New York: Limelight, 1997.

Samberg, Joel. *Reel Jewish: A Century of Jewish Movies—Comedy, Tragedy, Musicals, Dramas.* Middle Village, N.Y.: Jonathan David, 2000.

Sennett, Ted. *Your Show of Shows* (revised edition). New York: Applause, 2002.

Shipman, David. *The Great Movie Stars: The International Years* (revised edition). New York: Hill and Wang, 1980.

Sikov, Ed. *Mr. Strangelove: A Biography of Peter Sellers.* New York: Hyperion, 2002.

Simon, Neil. *The Play Goes On: A Memoir.* New York: Touchstone, 2002.

———. *Rewrites: A Memoir.* New York: Simon & Schuster, 1996.

Sinyard, Neil. *The Films of Mel Brooks.* New York: Bison Books, 1987.

Smith, Ronald L. *Johnny Carson: An Unauthorized Biography.* New York: St. Martin's, 1987.

Smurthwaite, Nick, and Paul Gelder. *Mel Brooks and the Spoof Movie.* New York: Proteus, 1983.

Snyder-Grenier, Ellen M. *Brooklyn! An Illustrated History.* Philadelphia: Temple University Press, 2004.

Spalding, Henry D. (compiler and ed.). *Encyclopedia of Jewish Humor: From Biblical Times to the Modern Age.* Middle Village, N.Y.: Jonathan David, 1969.

Spignesi, Stephen J. *The Woody Allen Companion*. Kansas City, Mo.: Andrews and McMeel, 1992.

Squire, Jason E. (ed.). *The Movie Business Book: The Behind-the-Scenes Story of Global Movie Financing, Marketing, Revenue Streams, Technology and More*, 3rd ed. New York: Simon & Schuster, 2004.

Suskin, Steven. *Opening Night on Broadway: A Critical Quotebook of the Golden Era of the Musical Theatre*, Oklahoma! *(1943) to* Fiddler on the Roof *(1964)*. New York: Schirmer, 1990.

Terrace, Vincent. *Experimental Television, Test Films, Pilots and Trial Series, 1925 through 1995: Seven Decades of Small Screen Almosts*. Jefferson, N.C.: McFarland, 1997.

———. *Television Characters: 1,485 Profiles from 1947 to 2004*. Jefferson. N.C.: McFarland, 2005.

———. *Television Specials: 3,201 Entertainment Spectaculars, 1939–1993*. Jefferson, N.C.: McFarland, 1995.

Weissman, Ginny, and Coyne Steven Sanders. *The Dick Van Dyke Show* (revised edition). New York: St. Martin's, 1993.

Wilde, Larry. *The Great Comedians*. Secaucus, N.J.: Citadel, 1973.

Wilder, Gene. *Kiss Me Like a Stranger: My Search for Love and Art*. New York: St. Martin's, 2005.

Wilk, Max. *Every Day's a Matinee: Memoirs Scribbled on a Dressing Room Door*. New York: Norton, 1975.

———. *The Golden Age of Television: Notes from the Survivors*. New York: Moyer Bell, 1989.

Yacowar, Maurice. *Method in Madness: The Comic Art of Mel Brooks*. New York: St. Martin's, 1981.

Young, Jordan. *The Laugh Crafters: Comedy Writing in Radio and TV's Golden Age*. Beverly Hills, Calif.: Past Times, 1999.

Publications

Among those utilized were: *American Film, Backstage West, Billboard, Biography, Boxoffice, Cable Guide*, the *Chicago Sun-Times*, the *Chicago Tribune, Cinefex, Classic Film Collector, Classic Image, Cult Movies, Current Biography, Daily Variety*, the *Detroit Free Press, Drama-Logue, Ebony, Empire, Entertainment Today, Entertainment Weekly, Family Weekly, Film Comment, Film Threat, Filmfax, Films in Review, Films of the Golden Age, Flightime, Forward, Globe, Hollywood Citizen News*, the *Hollywood Reporter, InStyle, Interview, Jewish Exponent, Jewish Journal, Jet, L.A. Weekly*, the *London Daily Telegraph*, the *London Evening Standard*, the *London Guardian*, the *London Sunday Telegraph*, the *London Times, Los Angeles*, the *Los Angeles Daily News*, the *Los Angeles Herald*

Examiner, the *Los Angeles Times*, *Monthly Film Bulletin*, *Movie Collectors World*, *Movieline*, the *National Enquirer*, the *New Jersey Record*, *New York*, the *New York Daily News*, the *New York Observer*, the *New York Post*, the *New York Times*, *The New Yorker*, *Newsweek*, *Parade*, *People*, *Playboy*, *Premiere*, *Rocky Mountain News*, *Rolling Stone*, the *St. Louis Post-Dispatch*, the *San Francisco Chronicle*, *Saturday Review*, *Sight & Sound*, *Star*, *Time*, *Time Out London*, *Total Film*, *Travel & Leisure*, *TV Guide*, *US Weekly*, *USA Today*, *Valley Vantage*, *Vanity Fair*, the *Village Voice*, *Virginian Pilot*, *Vogue*, the *Wall Street Journal*, and the *Washington Post*

Web Sites

Associated Press
www.ap.org

BBC News
news.bbc.co.uk

Box Office Mojo
www.boxofficemojo.com

Catskills Institute
www.brown.edu/Research/
    Catskills_Institute

Contactmusic.com
www.contactmusic.com

E! Online
www.eonline.com

Find a Grave
www.findagrave.com

Get Smart Webpage
www.wouldyoubelieve.com/
    episodes.html

Highbeam Research
www.highbeam.com

The Hollywood Reporter
www.hollywoodreporter.com

Internet Broadway Database
www.ibdb.com

Internet Movie Database
www.pro.imdb.com

Larry King Live
www.cnn.com/CNN/Programs/
    larry.king.live

Mel Brooks at Topix.net
www.topix.net/who/mel-brooks

Movieweb
www.movieweb.com

National Public Radio (NPR)
www.npr.org

Playbill
www.playbill.com

Public Broadcasting System (PBS)
www.pbs.org

People Online
www.people.aol.com

The Sid Caesar Collection
www.sidcaesar.com

The Smoking Gun
www.thesmokinggun.com

StarPlus
www.starplus.com

Tiscali Film & TV
www.tiscali.co.uk/entertainment/
   film/biographies

Variety.com
www.variety.com

Yahoo News
news.yahoo.com

Other Sources

Press books of Mel Brooks's feature films, liner notes of Mel Brooks's Broadway shows and comedy albums, and commentary tracks of DVDs of Mel Brooks's feature films and television work.

Index

About the Author

James Robert Parish, a former entertainment reporter, publicist, and book series editor, is the author of many biographies and reference books about the entertainment industry, including *The Hollywood Book of Break-ups*; *Fiasco: A History of Hollywood's Iconic Flops*; *Katharine Hepburn: The Untold Story*; *The Hollywood Book of Scandals*; *Whitney Houston*; *The Hollywood Book of Love*; *Hollywood Divas*; *Hollywood Bad Boys*; *The Encyclopedia of Ethnic Groups in Hollywood*; *Jet Li*; *The Hollywood Book of Death*; *Gus Van Sant*; *Jason Biggs*; *Whoopi Goldberg*; *Rosie O'Donnell's Story*; *The Unofficial "Murder, She Wrote" Casebook*; *Let's Talk! America's Favorite TV Talk Show Hosts*; *Gays and Lesbians in Mainstream Cinema*; *The Great Cop Pictures*; *Ghosts and Angels in Hollywood Films*; *Prison Pictures from Hollywood*; *The Hollywood Reliables*; *The RKO Gals*; and *Hollywood's Great Love Teams*.

Mr. Parish is a frequent on-camera interviewee on cable and network TV for documentaries on the performing arts both in the United States and in the United Kingdom. He resides in Studio City, California. Visit his Web site, www.jamesrobertparish.com.